THE RULING CLASS

THE RULING CLASS

INSIDE THE IMPERIAL CONGRESS

ERIC FELTEN

FROM THE HERITAGE FOUNDATION'S
U.S. CONGRESS ASSESSMENT PROJECT
DAVID M. MASON, DIRECTOR

REGNERY GATEWAY
Washington, D.C.

126861

Library of Congress Cataloging-In-Publication Data

Felten, Eric.
    The ruling class: inside the imperial congress / Eric Felten.
        p.   cm.
    "Produced under The Heritage Foundation's U.S. Congress Assessment Project."
    Includes bibliographical references and index.
    ISBN 0-89526-506-0 Cl.; 0-89526-732-2 Pa.
        1. United States. Congress. 2. Legislators — United States.
3. Separation of powers — United States. I. Heritage Foundation
(Washington, D.C.). U.S. Congress Assessment Project. II. Title.
JK1061.F45   1992
328.73'073 — dc20   92-36247
                                                         CIP

Published in the United States by
Regnery Gateway
1130 17th Street, NW
Washington, DC 20036

Distributed to the trade by
National Book Network
4720-A Boston Way
Lanham, MD 20706

Printed on acid free paper
Manufactured in the United States of America

97 96 95 94 93   10 9 8 7 6 5 4 3 2 1

ACKNOWLEDGEMENTS

This book would not have been written if Dr. Edwin J. Feulner, Jr., President of the Heritage Foundation, and Phil Truluck, Executive Vice President, had not unequivocally supported the idea that an effective program to reform Congress could best grow out of a journalistic investigation into how Capitol Hill actually works. I am grateful for their commitment to me and my work as a Congressional Studies Fellow at Heritage. Thanks also go to the Foundation's Kate O'Beirne and David Mason, who helped to shape the book from beginning to end. William McGurn, now an editor of the *Far Eastern Economic Review*, provided editing that was gentle, but much needed. Andy Seamans was a speedy and capable copy editor and indexer.

The staff of Heritage's U.S. Congress Assessment Project assisted me with invaluable research. Rob Schmults, in particular, toiled with such diligent speed and accuracy, that I was forced to work harder in order to keep up. Much help also came from Mike Rowan, Nathaniel Moffat, Susan Shumaker, and Steve Schwalm. Additional research came from journalists Alan Randolph, who helped with the chapter on staff, and Martin Morse Wooster, who helped with the chapter on spending. David Brock was generous with research from his own book projects and with his time.

Encouragement and advice came from a number of mentors and friends. Morris Fiorina, John Fund, Harvey Mansfield, and Judith Shklar all read early drafts and suggested important changes. Faryar Shirzad, Joe Lehnen, Diana West, John Podhoretz, Ian Brzezinski, Nancy Woodward, Philip Chalk, and Mark Pastin through lively debate and crucial moral support helped more than they know. Friends who work on Capitol Hill provided good inside dirt, but for obvious reasons can't be mentioned here by name. My sincere thanks go to them all for their efforts. Any errors in fact or judgment that remain, however, are strictly mine.

Most of all, I want to thank my parents, Lester and Barbara Felten, Jr., and my grandparents, Relve and Gretchen Barr, Lester Felten, Sr., and the late Anne Felten, not only for the love and encouragement that got me through this project, but also for all that came before. And finally, I am grateful to Laura Whitehouse for her unswerving patience and support.

Eric Felten
Washington, D.C.
September, 1992

TABLE OF CONTENTS

PREFACE

The new 103rd Congress has an historic opportunity to help restore confidence in American government. However, it can do so only by restoring confidence in the United States Congress.

That confidence has been shaken to its foundations in recent years, not only by a succession of highly publicized congressional scandals, but by the inability of Congress—on a continuing basis —to do its job.

In the eyes of some critics, Congress's law-making responsibilities now rank far below its other perceived priorities: constituent service, bringing pork home to the state, and appearing on television in the company of Hollywood personalities. The result: a preoccupation with the politically popular fads and myths which engage various celebrities and special interests, while the important business of Washington — establishing spending limits and budget priorities, for example—goes begging.

For years, Congress apparently assumed it could shirk its responsibilities and the voters would be none the wiser. The 1992 elections —beginning in primary season—indicate the free ride is over.

The Heritage Foundation has produced this book because we believe a strong and effective Congress is necessary to the proper functioning of our constitutional democracy. The separation of powers is also critical to that system. The Constitution invests

Congress with important powers that it gives no one else. For this reason, Congress has been the principal focus of The Heritage Foundation's research since our founding, in 1973.

At one time, we thought Congress took its responsibilities seriously, and that reasoned arguments—backed by thoroughgoing data and analysis — would help dictate the direction of public policy. With but a few exceptions, federal lawmakers have done their best to prove us wrong. This truth has now caught up with the Congress.

As recently as the early seventies, conservatives and liberals alike considered Congress an engine of innovation and change. We conservatives, especially, frequently didn't like the direction in which Congress attempted to lead us, but it usually didn't shy from its duties. While the "solutions" often involved major commitments of money to untested programs, nobody would have accused the 93rd Congress—which confronted Richard Nixon—of being shy. For better or worse, the Congress at the time was seen as part of the solution, not part of the problem.

Today, however, there seems no more staunch defender of the status quo than Congress. Even legislation that has the apparent support of a majority in both Houses of Congress—such as urban "enterprise zones" — is allowed to stagnate for years because Congress doesn't have the courage to cross swords with entrenched interest groups. The nation is the poorer for this — as is Congress itself.

The Heritage Foundation started examining Congress as an institution some five years ago, long before it was politically in vogue. *The Imperial Congress*, which we published jointly with California's Claremont Institute in 1988, provided an historical look at the role of Congress and how the contemporary House and Senate had strayed from their constitutional mandate. Subtitled "Crisis in the Separation of Powers," the book argued that Congress had created the current government gridlock: presenting the executive branch with broad mandates, and then second-guessing the executive on the implementation of those mandates. This effort to micromanage the executive was evident throughout the government, from the regulatory agencies to the Pentagon and State Department. *The Imperial Congress* used the analogy of 535 Secretaries of State, each — through the committee hearing process, press releases, subpoena power, and even direct contact with foreign officials (and dissidents)—attempting to establish U.S. foreign policy. Today, we not only have 535 Secretaries of State on Capitol Hill, we also have 535 Secretaries of Defense, Health, Housing, Interior, Labor, Transportation, and just about everything else, and we have thousands of would-be chiefs-of-staff among congressional aides.

The most obvious and needful remedy—and the one we recommended in 1988—was a vigorous reassertion by the President of his own rights and responsibilities against the encroachments of Congress. We subsequently established the U.S. Congress Assessment Project, now headed by David Mason — who has broad experience in both the executive and legislative branches of government—to continue and expand this much-needed look at Congress the institution. It was under Mason's guidance that the concept for this book, and the Heritage reform program, were developed.

Since 1988, we have examined the congressional budget process, Congress's own spending and staffing practices, its ethical standards, how campaigns are financed, and the procedures for considering legislation. The authors of these studies have suggested a variety of remedies, ranging from specific changes in congressional rules to term limitations and constitutional amendments. One conclusion they unanimously have reached: Vigorous executive action in opposing congressional excesses, while essential, is not enough. Congress itself will have to change—its rules and procedures, as well as its incentives and assumptions.

Eric Felten joined Heritage as a Congressional Studies Fellow to expand on this work. His explanation of why and how the Imperial Congress must be reformed is comprehensive and detailed, while remaining incisive and understandable.

It is not our intention merely to push the pendulum of government power back toward the executive branch. Conservatives always have been wary of too much power congregated in the hands of a single individual or institution; that's the genius of our system of government. The competition for power between the legislature and executive was designed to limit the government's reach, not to expand it. In fact, re-establishment of a clear separation of powers may serve more to limit the executive than the legislature.

Still, presidential action is necessary, and in this—despite disappointments in many other areas—George Bush stood firm. Presidential Counsel Boyden Gray, and Attorneys General Richard Thornburgh and William Barr, led a concerted effort to identify encroachments upon legitimate executive powers and to fight them. The President could and should have gone further, but at least he moved in the right direction. Attorney General Barr's successful opposition to congressional abuse of the independent counsel law and the President's determination in the face of the congressional challenge on the use of force to oust Iraq from Kuwait were the high water marks. Congressional dithering and hand-wringing before the Gulf War, and its fault-finding afterwards, stand in sharp contrast to the President's sense of purpose and duty.

And here lies the point of *The Ruling Class*: It is not the executive branch, or even the government at large, that suffers most from Congress's departure from its constitutional role—it is the Congress itself that's most harmed. This book explores, more than any other previous work with which we are familiar, institutional solutions to Congress's institutional problems. Far from engaging in Congress bashing, our intent is to help Congress.

While they may gain temporary comfort, U.S. voters should not place too much hope in the powerful anti-incumbent tide that swept Congress's huge new Class of 1992 into Washington. New faces alone do not change anything, any more than Ronald Reagan's 1980 landslide victory rolled back big government. If the congressional class of 1992 is serious about change, however, *The Ruling Class* provides them with the necessary road map and compass, much as our 1980 volume *Mandate for Leadership* provided the new Reagan administration with guidance.

Whether Congress has the will to change things, only history can tell us. If it has that will, *The Ruling Class* will show the way.

Edwin J. Feulner, Jr., Ph.D.
President
The Heritage Foundation

INTRODUCTION

E veryone agrees that Congress needs to be reformed, but there is too little agreement about what is wrong in the first place: gridlock, deficits, pork, avoiding important issues, and self-aggrandizement are some of the frequent complaints. The expected revolution in the 1992 congressional elections was both more and less than many had hoped precisely because of the broad agreement that Congress isn't working, coupled with the lack of consensus about why. Term limits passed overwhelmingly in the fourteen states where it was voted on, yet 93 percent of the congressional incumbents on the November ballot were reelected, and most incumbents who lost had serious ethics or redistricting problems.

The Ruling Class solves the riddle of why voters hate Congress, but love (or at least reelect) their Congressman by examining in detail what Congress does, what it doesn't do, and how it operates. The root problem is that the United States Congress is a legislature that has stopped legislating. This curiosity explains why Congress doesn't work, and why individual Congressmen escape blame.

Legislation requires votes, which produce accountability. If the results are bad, or not what the public desires, voters can throw the bums out. But today Congress exercises most of its power through methods other than legislation and spends most of its time on non-legislative pursuits. The legislation that remains, and the legislative process, is twisted into a convoluted and intentionally confusing mess. *The Ruling Class* sketches out these problems in illuminating detail through telling anecdotes joined to structural analysis. The first three chapters show how Congress willfully frustrates accountability while riding a publicity bandwagon and handing off the real decisions to bureaucrats. But Congress doesn't really want to give up control, so the middle chapters examine how Congress manages the government through staff, investigations, and spending in order to claim credit for popular decisions while avoiding blame for problems. This approach even encroaches into our foreign policy, as discussed in Chapter Seven. While it is easy to see, with such a rigged system, how incumbents manage to secure reelection, Chapter Eight reveals the crowning touch in campaigns: constituent service. While recommendations are integrated throughout the book, the final chapter pulls together a comprehensive program for institutional reform of Congress.

Author Eric Felten's approach combines that of investigative journalist and political analyst: uncovering the real and often outrageous story of how Congress operates and then analyzing the structural and political incentives that transform well-intentioned representatives into self-serving porkmongers. Avoiding partisanship and technocratic jargon, the book is written from the perspective of a public-minded and well-informed citizen. Republicans as well as Democrats come in for some much-needed criticism. Felten avoids, however, the temptation to engage in emotionally satisfying but politically futile Congress bashing. In fact, the recommendations are not intended either to enervate Congress or to turn over sweeping powers to an Imperial Presidency, but rather to strengthen Congress by restoring the vigorous but limited legislative role intended in the Constitution.

New faces and even term limits will not alone solve the problems in Congress. Clearly, the entrenched powers will fight to remain in control. Just days after the 1992 congressional elections House Speaker Tom Foley and other Democratic leaders flew around the country meeting with newly elected House Democrats. This unprecedented effort acknowledges the progress that reformers have made while also serving as a reminder of the challenges remaining. *The*

Ruling Class zeroes in on the structural and institutional changes necessary to rejuvenate the legislative powers of Congress and to restore the political accountability that goes with it. In so doing, the book is a hopeful one. Rather than whining about the pettiness of yesterday, *The Ruling Class* maps out possibilities for tomorrow. Its advice, if heeded, would restore to Congress the degree of dignity and public approval that ought to attend the nation's highest deliberative body. And if our representatives need encouragement about heeding this advice, this book will contribute to an American public more aware of how Congress operates and, consequently, less easily misled by those who would continue to manipulate Congress and the public.

David M. Mason
Director,
U.S. Congress Assessment Project

THE
RULING
CLASS

PROLOGUE

In the early hours of Wednesday, November 27, 1991, a string of lawmakers took to the floor of the House of Representatives to declare their support for the Intermodal Surface Transportation Efficiency Act of 1991. Rep. Rosa DeLauro was among them. In the *Congressional Record* is a long speech by the Connecticut Democrat extolling the virtues of what was commonly known as the Highway Bill.

But Rep. DeLauro never did deliver that speech. As a routine matter it was given to the typesetters at the *Congressional Record*, where the text was inserted as though she had spoken at length. So far so good. But somehow the pages of her speech on the Highway Bill became mixed up with the pages of a speech on the Crime Bill she had wanted inserted elsewhere in the *Record*. The result was that DeLauro's text jumps from a discussion of all the new jobs that would be created by building roads to comments on the number of criminals who would be thwarted by a tough gun-control law. She concludes her defense of the Highway Bill by imploring her colleagues to "vote for the Omnibus Crime Control Act."

DeLauro's mixed-up speech is a perfect example of today's Congress: a non-speech that was (not) delivered as part of a non-debate about a bill that no Member had actually read. Indeed, the non-debate on the Highway Bill raced on that Wednesday morning

3

well before staff aides had even finished writing the bill. Members voted overwhelmingly for the measure without ever seeing it. A hefty thousand pages of small print, the bill was dumped onto a table in the House chamber just one hour before the final vote. This is how Congress spends $151 billion.

Rep. Christopher Cox looked on, astonished, as the bill sped toward passage. The California Republican sits on the Public Works and Transportation Committee, which drafted the initial House version of the Highway Bill. As a committee member he had hoped to have an intimate knowledge of the bill's details. But not even committee members had the opportunity to read the bill's text. In fact, several months earlier the committee chairman had made the committee vote on the original measure on the same day the several-hundred-page document was passed out. After the committee approved the unread bill, it was sent for the first time to the House floor where only a half dozen amendments were allowed. By the time the measure reached the House-Senate conference committee, the final stage before a bill gets its last up-down vote in each house and is sent to the President, no one but the conference participants knew what the bill would look like. In a conference, leaders from the House and Senate committees that initiated a bill work out the differences between their bodies' respective versions. Because the Senate version of the Highway Bill was wildly different from that approved by the House, everything was up for grabs in the meetings.

And grab they did. Members may not have been given a chance to see the bill after the conferees were done with it, but they didn't care. Each Member knew there would be some road, bridge, tunnel, sidewalk, bus, or subway earmarked for his home district. Conferees bought their colleagues off with the promise that each legislator would get his own little slice of pork, something to tout when the next election rolled around.

On the afternoon of November 26, the next to last day before Thanksgiving (when Congress planned to close up shop for the year), the leaders of the conference announced they had reached an agreement. They then handed out a two-page outline of the thousand-page bill. Staff aides were still busy writing up the compromise text. Although Cox tried to get the conference staff to show him the measure, they told him he would have to wait. Around 2:00 a.m. on the 27th, the bill was taken up by the House Rules Committee, which sets the ground rules for debate on legislation before it is sent to the floor, specifying what amendments can be considered and in what order.

In the case of the Highway Bill, however, there was not much point in specifying amendments because the Rules Committee itself did not have a copy of the measure, which was still being drawn up. Without having seen the bill, the Rules Committee waived the House requirement that no measure be taken up until three days after it has been printed in the *Congressional Record*. They then sent the bill to the floor.

At 4:00 a.m. debate began—though no one had yet seen the text. Not until nearly 5:00 a.m., halfway through the debate, was one copy of the document plunked down on the Speaker's table on the House floor. There it sat, more than one-thousand pages, until 6:00 a.m., when the vote was taken. The approval was overwhelming, 372 Members voted for the bill and only 47 opposed. Not a single Member, Cox realized, had read it.

This is all too typical of how today's Congress legislates, with empty votes on bills known only to unelected staff aides, all crammed into the last hours before vacation. Legislation has become the stepchild of Capitol Hill. Cumbersome and difficult, legislating requires coalitions and compromises. More often than not, this translates into a package held together with pork paste. How much easier it is for lawmakers to act without having to legislate. Just call a bureaucrat and demand a favor for a constituent; write a regulator and insist that a federal rule be changed; hold a hearing and drum up some press; fly to the Third World and exercise a little personal diplomacy. Congress was created to make laws; yet the modern Congress has all but abandoned the practice of legislating, choosing instead to exercise power more directly and with less accountability.

Welcome to the Ruling Class, whose members, by rejecting legislative means have shielded themselves from the scrutiny of the voters. They have become the barons in an Imperial Congress where the protection and expansion of personal fiefdoms outweighs the needs of the nation. Deceit, calumny, and character assassination are commonplace as our representatives strive to augment their power. Washington has been poisoned with their machinations and our political system sickened as well.

The how and why of the Imperial Congress follows. Also the how and why of dismantling this empire. Why? Because in a government of, by, and for the people, we bear the ultimate responsibility for the decisions and actions of those whom we have charged to legislate on our behalf. Among free citizens in the world's greatest democracy, there is no room for an imperial class. Our task is to remind Members of Congress — through the ballot box where necessary, through reform where possible — that they are our representatives, *not* our rulers.

1

SLEIGHT OF HAND

It has been said here many times tonight that we want to make the Senate the same as everyone else, that we want to treat Senators the same as everyone else, that we want to have the Senate treated the same as the private sector.

Mr. President, not a single Senator believes that. Not a single Senator wants that.

Senate Democratic Leader George Mitchell explaining why the Senate should not be covered by a major civil rights bill.

House Democrats would love to send Rep. Newt Gingrich back to his life as a journeyman college professor. The Georgia Republican is fond of feisty tactics and fiery rhetoric, and represents one of the few real threats to the Democrats' domination of the House of Representatives. Yet in the fall of 1990, when the Democrats had their chance to get rid of Gingrich once and for all, they gave him a pass. Gingrich had voted for a congressional pay raise, a fact that his opponent, Democrat David Worley made the centerpiece of his campaign. Polls showed Worley nearing a major upset. But then his own party's congressional campaign committee cut off his supply of campaign cash. Despite the setback, Worley lost by only 974 votes. Why did the Democrats starve out Worley and give

up the chance to knock off their nemesis? Because they had promised to: The same pay raise that nearly cost Gingrich his seat ended
up saving it for him.

So universal is the need to cover up a pay grab, that it is one of
the few issues that can bind Congress together in a display of
bipartisan unity. When a cleverly crafted salary boost for Representatives teetered on the verge of collapse in 1990, Democratic and
Republican leaders signed a "non-aggression pact." Everyone
agreed that it just wouldn't be sporting to mention either the pay
raise or the way it was achieved when elections rolled around.
Lawmakers agreed that neither party's congressional campaign
committee would give any money to challengers who made the pay
raise a campaign issue. So committed to the pay raise deal were
Democrats that they let slip their opportunity to defeat Gingrich.
When Worley questioned the pay raise, his party disowned him. If
collusion on this scale were practiced by makers of paper clips,
rather than makers of law, they would be in jail.

A few lawmakers are so secure in their seats that they can openly
defend a congressional pay raise: Sen. Robert Byrd was un-
apologetic in his boosterism for a recent Senatorial salary increase.
That is not to say the argument he offered to the world's greatest
deliberative body was coherent—the West Virginia Democrat gives
money to his grandchildren who are college science students;
America needs scientists to compete with Japan; therefore, said
Byrd, a congressional pay raise would help keep the U.S. competitive.

As silly as Byrd's arguments for a pay raise were, at least he was
up front about voting for it. The public hates it when lawmakers
vote to hike their own pay. But legislators, usually slavish followers
of opinion polls, are not about to be chastened by public opinion
when it comes to an issue so dear to their hearts. But how do
Members of Congress get away with voting for things the public
despises? They use camouflage.

For the most part, lawmakers need not resort to such extraordinary means as the non-aggression pact to protect pet legislation:
Usually, technical language and obscure legalisms will do the trick.

How else does one explain this provision in the 1992 legislative appropriations bill:

> The rate of pay for the offices referred to under section 703 (a) (2) (B) of the Ethics Reform Act of 1989 (5 U.S.C. 5318 note) shall be the rate of pay that would be payable for each such office if the provisions of section 703 (a) (2) (B) and 1101 (a) (1) (A) of such act (5 U.S.C. 5318 note and 5305) had not been enacted.

Translation: Senators get a $23,200-a-year raise.

Unfortunately for the taxpayers, arcane wording is not the only trick up Congress' sleeve. Through a variety of procedural sleights of hand, gimmicks and fleece-over-the-eyes stunts, Members of Congress labor to mislead their constituents, avoid taking embarrassing stands, and, above all, evade accountability. Votes, alas, require lawmakers to take stands. And so Congressmen have found innumerable ways to get around votes. Perhaps the most insidious trick, and one most frequently used by lawmakers, is to let conference committees — the groups assigned to work out differences between House and Senate versions of a bill—do the dirty work for them. And so it is with the conference committees that we will begin.

The 1990 Chapman Amendment to the Americans with Disabilities Act (ADA) is a case in point. The amendment would have allowed restaurants to move cooks and waiters with AIDS into jobs where they wouldn't handle food. Although both Houses of Congress supported the amendment, it somehow never made it into the final bill. This incensed Rep. William Dannemeyer. "The Chapman Amendment was adopted on the floor of the House after a big debate," the California Republican told the House. "The Senate... instructed its conferees to adopt the same language, and...when the conferees got together on this measure, they totally ignored it."

Rep. Hamilton Fish, one of the conferees being accused of ignoring the will of the House and Senate, leaped to his feet to defend himself and his conference committee colleagues who had put together the final ADA package. "The simple fact is that there were some 81 or 82 issues between the Senate and the House; 79 of these were resolved by the staffs prior to the Members meeting in conference, so there were only two or three issues to be considered, and one of them was the Chapman Amendment, and it was the burden of the time spent," said the New York Republican. "The conferees had considered in some detail the question of the Chapman Amendment."

Fish was right; the conferees had not ignored the Chapman Amendment. What they did was draw a careful bead on the measure and pull the trigger. According to any civics text (not to mention House and Senate rules), conference committees are supposed to address the differences between the two houses over a piece of legislation in order to work out a compromise. But in this case, and in many like it, conferees ignore how Congress voted and rewrite the bill as they want. In killing the Chapman Amendment the conferees were not seeking a compromise, they were overriding the stated will of both houses.

"This is typical of the arrogance of the problem," complained Rep. Tom DeLay, a Texas Republican. "As they have done so many times before, the conferees decided that the will of Congress and the will of the American people are less important than their own subjective decision about right and wrong, good or bad."

But why, if the will of the Congress had been trampled by the conferees, did both houses vote to adopt the conferees' version of the bill? Perhaps for the same reason both houses voted to adopt a conference report in 1989 that included millions of dollars for congressional mass mailings, though both houses had gone on record opposing such mailings. And maybe for the same reason the Senate and House approved a conference bill in 1991 that allowed National Endowment for the Arts funding for excrementitious artworks, again against the stated preference of both the House and Senate.

Could it be that conferees are simply doing what Congress wants them to do? That our representatives are teases, saying no when they mean yes and yes when they mean no?

"Your man told my man you were just going to roll us."

The short answer is yes. For all the partisan wrangling, fiery denunciations, and plain old bickering, both sides of the aisle in Congress have much more in common with each other than with the public they ostensibly represent. While some conference meetings are contentious, the mood at the House-Senate conference on the 1991 Crime Bill was casual and jovial, which might have come as something of a surprise, given that at least one of the Senators had been pulled away from the stadium skybox where he was watching the football season's big grudge match, the Washington Redskins against the Dallas Cowboys.

Sen. Orrin Hatch showed up in a turtleneck and ski sweater, without the over-starched and tight-collared shirt that is the Utah Republican's trademark. Democratic Rep. Jack Brooks of Texas, the chairman of the House Judiciary Committee, after being harangued by one of the committee's most vocal Republican members, Henry Hyde of Illinois, for emasculating the bill and stifling the Republican minority, made up with his colleague by offering him a cigar. Beaming appreciatively, Rep. Hyde slid the stogie in his pocket.

As the conference-ending gavel went down—with the Democrats in possession of a final draft of the bill that frustrated Republican druthers at every turn — the ranking Republican on the Senate Judiciary Committee, South Carolina Sen. Strom Thurmond joked with the committee's chairman, Joseph Biden, a Delaware Democrat. "Joe," said Thurmond, "your man told my man you were just going to roll us on this bill, and, by God, you did!" They all laughed.

Why all the good humor by Republicans? They had indeed been rolled. Not only had the Democratic majority on the conference rewritten the crime bill to their own liking, the Members leading the conference committee didn't even bother to show the others on the committee exactly what they were voting on.

As with most conferences, the real details of the compromise on the omnibus crime legislation had been worked out in advance through meetings between House and Senate majority staff. The voluminous legislative language containing those details was not given to the conferees, however, even though they were to vote on

the various issues over the next two hours. Instead, a three-page
outline was handed to them at the beginning of the meeting, listing
the compromise proposals. A few of the outlined proposals were
straightforward. But most were ambiguous, such as number two,
dealing with "Death Penalty Offenses":

> The House and Senate bills both contain over 50 federal
> capital offenses.
> HOUSE PROPOSAL: House recedes, with modifications.

"What modifications?" asked Kathryn Hazeem, a lawyer on
Hyde's staff representing the Republican minority. The majority
staff knew exactly what modifications they had in mind, but they
didn't feel it important to tell the minority what those specifics
were.

Most vague and subjective was the provision on terrorism:

> Both bills provides [sic] for additional penalties and
> funding to combat terrorism.
> HOUSE PROPOSAL: Adopt best features of both bills.

No doubt, favoring the "best features" of any bill is a noble
sentiment. Again, however, a minority conferee might wonder
whether the majority's definition of "best" jibed with his own. Not
that it really mattered. Thurmond and the other Republicans knew
that the parts of both houses' bills most friendly to criminal defen-
dants would be pieced together in a "compromise" package. The
Democrats, after all, had the votes. An interesting conference battle
might have shaped up if the Senate conferees had been interested
in pushing for the Senate version of the bill, which was much
tougher than that of the House. But the Senate conferees clearly
were not prepared to fight for their draft: Of the eight Senate
conferees, only three — Biden, Thurmond, and Democrat Dennis
DeConcini of Arizona — had actually voted for the bill they were
supposedly defending.

It didn't matter to the Republicans that they were losing every
point in conference, because there was no way the bill was actually
going to become law. The only issue was who would be left holding
the political bag. Even in the unlikely event that the Democrats had
managed to put together the 60 votes in the Senate needed to invoke

cloture (they did not), and thus end the inevitable Republican filibuster, the bill lacked the support needed to override what certainly would have been a Presidential veto (the conference report was approved in the House by a bare 205-203 margin).

Because President Bush had been hammering the Democrats for months as "soft on crime" for not presenting him with a crime bill, the quick conference at the end of the legislative session was needed by the Democrats to say they had finally given birth to legislation on crime. Democrats were able to protect themselves against the soft-on-crime charge; and Republicans covered themselves politically as well, by killing the measure with a filibuster, sustained on a procedural vote. In the end, nothing of substance happened, yet each side could point to all the votes it had won.

Finding free votes such as these has become Congress' most avid pastime. Harvard government professor Morris Fiorina explains this phenomenon in his *Congress, Keystone of the Washington Establishment*. Over the last 30 years, legislators have discovered that, by concentrating on constituent service (everything from intervening for a voter in his dispute with the IRS to helping out a constituent's child in a homework assignment), they can build enough good will and loyalty to put themselves out of electoral striking distance of any challenger. As we will see in examining the sources of incumbents' electoral strength (Chapter Eight), add the hallowed pork barrel to constituent service and you get a reelection rate near 100 percent.

Voting is one of the few activities that ever threatens to wrench this nifty reelection machine: Whereas constituent service makes almost everyone happy, a vote on even a mildly divisive issue is sure to annoy a number of voters. "As long as the incumbent can elude a personal morality rap and refrain from casting outlandish votes, he is naturally preferred over a newcomer," notes Fiorina.[1] So real and meaningful votes are what Members of Congress most try to avoid.

Nowhere is congressional vote-avoidance more obvious than when Congress and the voters both feel strongly about an issue and yet come down on different sides. Take the question of lawmakers' mass mailings. Most Members of Congress are devoted to the frank, which allows them to mass-mail "newsletters" as well as respond to constituent inquiries, all without the inconvenience of paying for stamps. Voters rightly think of this as another boondoggle that should be abolished. On the surface, it looks as though there's no real way out: It's one or the other. Except in Congress, that is. They found the perfect solution. Lawmakers rigged the voting mechanism so that Members could pretend to do the popular thing while reversing themselves when no one was looking. That is, they voted against the frank and took the mail out the back door.

This little dance began in early September 1989, when Sen. Pete Wilson, a California Republican, saw an opportunity to rid voters' mailboxes of congressional junk mail (and at the same time do a little pre-season grandstanding in his bid for the California governor's chair). Senators were wrapping up their debate on the 1990 legislative appropriations bill (which funds their mail and other congressional expenses) when Wilson offered an amendment cutting Congress' postage budget from $134.7 million to $35 million, of which only $4 million could be used in 1990. The measure called for Congress to pay the $31 million Post Office tab Members had run up when they (as is customary) mailed more than the 1989 budget allowed. Unsolicited mass mailings were ruled out altogether.

Wilson's measure might have scored fewer votes had he not wired it to the hot-button issue of the year: drugs. Democrats had been making fun of the Republican drug strategy, caricaturing it as a combination of fruitless self-improvement hype ("Just Say No") and dangerous police-state tactics. Treatment for addicts, they were saying, was the way to win the war on drugs. So Wilson offered an amendment that not only cut funding for franking, but spent the savings on drug treatment *for pregnant women*. Senators had to choose, publicly, between personal privilege and crack babies. Of course, babies won, 83-8.

House Members got a chance to choose as well, with a September 25 motion telling House conferees to agree to the Wilson Amendment. This is known as a "motion to instruct," which is non-binding. Because conferees can choose to ignore them, such motions represent one of the best sources of free votes: Lawmakers can go on record supporting Policy X knowing that, with a wink and a nod, the conferees will ignore their instructions. So without too much concern the House voted by a solid 245-137 margin to acquiesce to the Senate position slashing franking funds. A scant three hours later, conferees cut a deal to restore the mass mailings.

A few legislators complained. "I thought our votes were supposed to mean something around here," complained Lynn Martin, at the time a Republican Representative from Illinois. Even some of the conferees objected, sore that they were being stuck with the dirty work: When the conference report came to a vote in the House, Rep. David Obey, a Wisconsin Democrat, argued that it should be supported by all those who came to him days earlier saying "Look, I didn't want to vote for that amendment. I hope you guys turn it around in conference." Three days after the House had voted to end mass mailings, the body overwhelmingly approved a conference-reported bill which included $84 million for just such mail. In a 274-137 vote, over 100 Representatives who had opposed the mailings supported the bill as a whole.

The flip-flop on the frank is by no means unusual. Legislators occasionally get heat from the media when they vote for a final version of a bill missing key provisions they voted to adopt just days before. But usually they can explain their support for the final bill in terms of all the non-controversial, advantageous items it includes. This indeed was the defense for the notorious "Corn for Porn" deal made in the 1992 Interior Appropriations bill conference: Rep. Norman Dicks, a Washington Democrat, argued, "To defeat this entire bill which funds our parks, wildlife, endangered species, American Indians, health care for American Indians... is an outrage." Colleague Joe Skeen made the point even more explicitly. "This is a bill for every American in every community," the New Mexico Republican argued, "because there is something in this bill for every Member of this body, be it a park, a trail, national forest, energy project, or visitor center." Then he added the clincher. "This bill embodies all that is truly America."

Well, at least all that is truly congressional. The conference deal managed simultaneously to delete two controversial provisions— restrictions on National Endowment for the Arts (NEA) funding of the sexual and scatological, and increased grazing fees for ranchers using federal lands — while providing political cover for all involved. It was a swap, mused Rep. William Dannemeyer, of corn for porn.

Sen. Jesse Helms, a frequent critic of NEA funding, had hit political paydirt when he pointed out that the agency was underwriting Robert Mapplethorpe's homo-erotic photography (including the artist's now-famous self portrait with bullwhip) and the work of Andres Serrano, who used his grant to photograph a crucifix drowned in urine. Democrats were in a jam. Those with the most liberal constituencies could publicly oppose Helms and ballyhoo their commitment to the First Amendment. But most had difficulty explaining to middle-of-the road voters why tax dollars are spent on displays that are, at best, insulting. Under pressure from constituents, Congress passed a measure banning the agency from funding obscene art for one year.

But it didn't end there. Helms continued to push for tougher measures to chastise the NEA. At one point he tried to kill the agency altogether. Fighting the proposals was a source of continual embarrassment to Democrats, who simply could not convince most voters that they should be paying to be offended. Lawmakers might have acquiesced to their constituents' wishes. Instead, they came up with a way to make it *look* as though they had. The first attempt was a totally unenforceable ban on money for the obscene. When that didn't do the trick, the locked doors of a closed conference committee once again gave Congress the cover to do exactly the opposite of what they had told the public they were up to.

The face-saver was a measure drawn up by Rep. Sidney Yates, an Illinois Democrat, allowing the NEA to demand its money back from any artist who was convicted of obscenity. A clever move, says Helms' legislative assistant John Mashburn. "The Yates language says that any work that beats a criminal obscenity rap is OK," Mashburn says. "But the Supreme Court has held that if something has any artistic merit it can't be criminally obscene. If a work is done with NEA funding, the grantee can point to that as proof of 'artistic merit.' So no court will ever find anything done with NEA money, by definition, to be obscene."

To eliminate the Catch-22, Helms offered an amendment to the 1992 Interior Appropriation (through which the NEA is funded) prohibiting any of the agency's money from being used to "promote, disseminate or produce materials that depict or describe, in a patently offensive way, sexual or excretory activities or organs." Pretty clearly, bullwhips protruding from rectums would be out. Whether or not the majority of Senators thought the Yates language was sufficient, and Helms' excessive, Senators fell into line to pass Helms' amendment by a 68-28 margin. The House likewise went on record with overwhelming support for Helms: Representatives voted by more than 2-to-1 to instruct conferees to agree to the Helms Amendment.

But the chair of the House conference, Sidney Yates, was not about to be bound by what is, of course, a non-binding vote. A mere four hours after the 286-135 vote in the House, Yates struck a deal with Western-state Representatives: He would drop a House provision requiring ranchers to pay a higher price to graze their cattle on federal land if they would support him in killing the Helms Amendment.

The conference, which was closed not only to the public but to non-conference lawmakers and their staff (Sen. Robert Byrd stopped the proceedings when a Helms staff member entered the room to deliver a message), was marked by frequent arguments between Yates and Republican Sen. Don Nickles of Oklahoma over the Helms Amendment. One thing that was never mentioned in their debates, which often went on for 20 to 30 minutes, was the fact that both houses had approved the measure, that there was no disagreement between the two bodies for the conferees to sort out. So irrelevant were the recorded floor votes that they didn't even come up in discussion, let alone decide the issue.

The conference report was challenged, but it was not defeated. With the votes of Western conservatives to back it up, the Interior appropriation conference was a done deal. This made the recorded votes taken on the floor of the Senate and House a sham, though only political insiders would know it. The conscientious taxpayer, eager to assess his lawmaker's record on the issue, is told his Representative or Senator voted against obscene art. How is he to know that the vote was cast in full confidence that it would be meaningless?

Nor does one have to be a fan of Helms' campaign against the NEA to think badly of the legislative bait-and-switch. Where, for example, were the principled defenders of the First Amendment? Rather than taking the lead and arguing for their beliefs, those who disagreed with Helms voted for his measure solely to give themselves cover with their constituents. It's Capitol Hill's version of Three-Card Monte: We put our tax money down and try to follow the shuffling of legislation as closely as we can; but when we turn a bill over, we find that what we thought was there is not.

Leaving key provisions out is not the only conference trick. Just as often, Members sneak special-interest provisions in. These shenanigans are all the easier because, as with the 1991 Crime Bill conference, most of the time even the majority of conferees don't know exactly what is in the final bill. Still, conference reports are rarely defeated. Voting against a report angers the Members who run the conference, and thus control who will get crucial goodies, like grants and other pork for the home district, in the next conference. Yates, for his part, let it be known what would happen to projects favored by Members who voted against the report if it was sent back to conference. On the House floor, he warned that the Helms Amendment and grazing fees would not be the only things to be reconsidered. "All issues would be up for negotiations," he said. "Every single issue that is in the conference report, including all those that we have agreed upon in connection with land acquisitions and every other kind of agreement, would be up for discussion." The message was out: Those who defected would be punished. The ability to back up this kind of threat is precisely what gives conference chairmen so much power, and allows them to ignore the recorded will of the Congress with impunity.

This kind of trickery helps Congress maintain one of its most blatant double standards: Members are exempt from most of the laws, rules, and regulations they inflict on the rest of us. The Americans with Disabilities Act (ADA), for instance, might have applied to Congress had it not been for another creative use of conference committees, which allowed Congress to claim it was covered while escaping effective enforcement. Most civil rights legislation was fought out over familiar ground in the 1980s, Democrats pushing for the expansion of regulation protecting newly coined group rights, and Republicans responding that the cost to business (especially small business) far outweighed any benefits the regulations would confer. In this case, however, President George Bush had already promised in his acceptance speech at the 1988 Republican National Convention to "do whatever it takes to make sure the disabled are included in the mainstream." The then-Vice President confirmed his commitment to a disabilities rights bill in his second televised debate with Democrat Michael Dukakis. Unlike his campaign pledge of "No new taxes," when the ADA was reported to the Senate floor at the end of August 1989, Bush honored his promise to support it.

With the backing of both the White House and Democrats on the Hill, the ADA raced through the Senate. About the only sticking point was an amendment by Sen. Orrin Hatch giving tax credits to small businesses for their compliance costs. (The ADA requires businesses to alter facilities to accommodate handicapped employees and customers.) The Utah Republican's amendment earned a simple majority but was rejected when it failed to get the 60 votes needed to override the budget act (the credit would have cost the government, and therefore added to the deficit). The debate, however, exposed how little Senators knew about the legislation they were adopting. Sen. Lloyd Bentsen argued against the amendment on the grounds that no one knew how much it would cost small business to build all those ramps and install all those elevators, and therefore no one knew how much it would cost the Treasury to reimburse them: "We have no estimate of how much the amendment will cost the federal government," the Texas Democrat said. "Before we ask the taxpayers of America to provide that relief, we should know what the cost will be."

There it would have stood, save for an inconvenient amendment by Sen. Charles Grassley. The Iowa Republican had long been pursuing a concern that traces itself back to James Madison in Federalist No. 57. There, Madison had warned that Congress could be kept from passing oppressive measures only if "they can make no law which will not have its full operation on themselves and their friends, as well as on the great mass of the society." Madison stressed that by living under the same laws as the governed, legislators would have a "communion of interests and sympathy of sentiments... without which every government degenerates into tyranny." Grassley pointed out, as he had done on several previous pieces of legislation, that Congress had exempted itself from the most important and far-reaching pieces of modern legislation: the Civil Rights Act of 1964, the Freedom of Information Act of 1966, the Age Discrimination Act of 1967, the Occupational Safety and Health Act of 1970, the Equal Employment Opportunity Act of 1972, Title 9 of the Higher Education Act of 1972, the Rehabilitation Act of 1973, the Privacy Act of 1974, the Age Discrimination Act Amendments of 1975, the Ethics in Government Act of 1978, and the Civil Rights Restoration Act of 1988.

In some areas, such as racial and sexual discrimination, Congress tries to govern itself with House and Senate rules that are shadows of the real laws. But in other areas Congress is completely exempt; just try to file a Freedom of Information Act request to get information on Senate staffers' handling of the Clarence Thomas-Anita Hill imbroglio. And where the chambers' own rules do apply, enforcement is notoriously slipshod, biased, and, above all, lax. The wrists of the Keating Five were slapped, not by the federal judiciary but by the Senate Ethics Committee, using, not the Ethics in Government Act but the rules of the Senate. Not quite the stuff to strike fear into the hearts of wayward legislators.

The amendment Grassley offered went straight to the point. It said simply that the ADA would apply to the Senate. Offered late in the evening, at about a quarter to 10 o'clock, there were few present on the Senate floor to object. Sen. Wendell Ford emitted the stock congressional response to Grassley's amendments: allowing the executive branch to bring charges against a Member of Congress for employment discrimination would be an unconstitutional violation of the separation of powers. The Kentucky Democrat suggested it would be better to smuggle an expurgated version of the Grassley Amendment into the legislation through the conference report, if Grassley would only withdraw it for the time being. "I think we ought to at least have some discussion with the proponents of the amendment to be sure that there is some agreement that we work it out in conference," said Ford, "and we do not leave it to the executive branch to take over the legislative branch."

Notwithstanding Ford's complaints, Grassley's amendment passed on a voice vote of the few Senators actually on the floor at that hour. Grassley's success on the floor was due in large part to the support of Sen. Tom Harkin, Chairman of the Disability Policy Subcommittee and prime sponsor of the ADA. The Iowa Democrat was for the amendment for somewhat different reasons than Grassley. It was not that Grassley was against a disabilities bill, but rather that he wanted lawmakers to think carefully about the burdens they were imposing on the private sector. By making Congress subject to the same burdens, Grassley hoped to make those costs salient. Harkin, on the other hand, whose brother is deaf, was thoroughly committed to imposing the toughest rules everywhere, even on Capitol Hill. Grassley proposed the amendment because he had doubts about the ADA; Harkin supported Grassley's amendment because he believed wholeheartedly in the disabilities bill.

Yet Harkin still gave his colleagues a wink. Even though they were voting to cover Congress just like any business, large or small, they needn't worry, the measure wouldn't look that way once the conference committee was done with it, he said. Vote for Grassley's amendment "to make sure that Congress is covered," Harkin urged, and in conference he would work it out so that "it is Congress, the legislative branch, that enforces the provisions of the act."

Sam Gerdano, at the time senior counsel to Grassley, says the Senator and he were besieged by lawmakers worried they might be sued for discrimination under the bill. "ADA was a perfect bill," says Gerdano. "Everybody was for it, and nobody had read it. Not even most of its sponsors." To find out whether, or how, or for how much, they could be sued, Senators would actually have to find out what was in the bill they were all so busy lauding. When lawmakers asked Grassley or Gerdano what congressional coverage would mean to them, the two would answer mischievously that it would mean for the Senate "exactly what it means to everyone else." Little help to those who haven't figured out the broad implications of the legislation. That's the point, of course.

But those worries did not translate into any second thoughts about the bill, because of Harkin's assurance that the Grassley Amendment would be eviscerated in conference. And so might Senators' worries have vanished if only the conference committee had done what it was expected to do—what Harkin had advertised it would do. But there was a snag.

The House had dealt with congressional coverage in the traditional fashion, leaving the chamber to police itself. But the House remained purposefully silent on the question of how the Senate would be covered. According to Bobby Silverstein, chief counsel to Harkin's Disability Policy Subcommittee, House conferees made it clear that the Senate negotiators could do whatever they liked with the Grassley Amendment and its Senate coverage. Since it did not affect the House, the reasoning went, it was not their problem.

The conference delivered on part of Harkin's promise. The court of first resort for those with complaints against a Senator was to be the Senate's own disciplinary review board. But the kicker was that those not satisfied with the Senate's justice could appeal to federal court—which is not what Senators had in mind when they thought the Grassley Amendment would be killed. It seems the Senators feared citizen juries as much as they feared the executive branch. Panicked cries resounded throughout the Senate, which sat on the conference report. Two weeks later, it was finally sent back to conferees, this time with explicit instructions not to allow appeals beyond the Senate.

Conference reports are almost never rejected. Then again, conferees can usually be counted on to do the disagreeable work out of earshot. But by putting in the appeal to a federal court, the conferees made it necessary for those who wanted to kill off the Grassley Amendment to do it themselves, out in the open. Not to say that the action they took was straightforward and transparent. The Grassley Amendment had been simple and potent; the enforcement procedures with which it was replaced are neither—page after page of intricate procedural flapdoodle leading... nowhere. But the most important priority was preserved: Congress protected its own interests, Senators would not face trial by jury, and even the astute voter would be none the wiser.

Parliament of Tricksters

While the messy work can usually be handled in closed conference sessions, sometimes even conference reports and legislative mumbo-jumbo are not enough. That is when procedural gimmicks come into play. Parliamentary trickery is more difficult in the Senate, where Members are relatively free to attach amendments to legislation, thus forcing some accountability. In the House, by contrast, inconvenient issues are all too often simply swept under the parliamentary rug. Increasingly, the procedures under which legislation is considered in the House are crafted to protect Members from embarrassing or politically sensitive votes. Sometimes the rules give everyone cover, but more often than not they shield Members of the Democratic majority by limiting the number and type of amendments Republicans can bring up.

So open to strategic manipulation are the procedures by which an issue is voted on that game theorists—academics who study strategy and conflict—have developed complex theories of voting tactics. Thomas Schelling, one of the fathers of game theory, devotes half of his chapter, "What is Game Theory," in *Choice and Consequence* to voting strategy. The opportunities to game even a simple set of votes are so vast that with two players (or voters) considering a sequence of three related votes the theorist needs a 42X42 matrix, with a staggering 1,764 cells, to illustrate all the possible choices. Any real congressional voting situation, with hundreds of players considering dozens of related measures, swamps the capability of theorists to map and plot the strategies.

The overwhelming complexity of such legislative strategy may seem daunting, at least from the point of view of game theory. But, says one House staffer, "Legislators who know how to use parliamentary maneuvers are like pool sharks: They may not understand the physics but they know the angles."

Something as simple as the order in which a string of amendments is considered can make a difference in voting. And often, lawmakers

will vote against their preferences in one area because it will set up
the situation so that they might win on a larger question. "Someone
who dislikes public housing may vote in favor of a civil rights
amendment he despises," Shelling writes, "knowing that only with
the amendment can the [public housing] bill itself be killed on a
subsequent ballot."[2]

Drafting amendments so as to pose difficult choices for the
opposition is not particularly·objectionable. There's no way to take
strategy out of the voting game, any more than one could take
strategy out of baseball. The problem is not that legislators fight out
their differences strategically but that the rules of the game are
skewed. The Democratic majority in the House is like a baseball
team that always plays at home and changes the ground rules for
each game. If an opposing team is known for using squeeze plays,
then bunts are ruled out. If the visitors are a bunch of heavy hitters,
then shots over the wall are called ground-rule singles. The House
Rules Committee draws up a fresh set of ground rules for nearly
every piece of important or controversial legislation considered on
the floor. It's no wonder the Republican bats are so often silent.

In the late 1950s the House Rules Committee was controlled by
a coalition of Republicans and conservative Southern Democrats
who frustrated civil rights efforts by keeping much of the
movement's legislation from coming to the floor. In 1961 that hold
was loosened when a majority of Members joined Speaker Sam
Rayburn to expand the size of the committee, putting a number of
new, and more liberal, Members on it. Still unhappy with the way
the old guard on the Rules Committee was using so-called closed
rules to keep liberal initiatives from being voted on, Democrats
changed their rules in 1973 to make instructions from the Democratic Caucus binding on Democratic members of the committee.
This new partisan grip on the Rules Committee was tightened in
1975 when the Democratic Caucus gave the Speaker the power to
appoint (with their consent) all the Democratic members of the
committee. As congressional scholar Walter Oleszek puts it, "Today,
the [rules] committee functions as an arm of the majority leadership."[3]

The Rules Committee now cleans up for the majority leadership after all the small-d democratic, open-government reforms of the early 1970s. Liberals had been frustrated in the House by the committee system, which, because of its premium on seniority, allowed sclerotic conservative Democrats (like those on the Rules Committee) to control legislation. Floor amendments were often the only end run around committee chairmen open to liberals. But amendments were hard to get and, more often than not, unsuccessful. Wresting control of the Rules Committee made it easier to get amendments on the docket, but most still lost, largely because they were not subject to recorded votes.

In other words, the problem earlier was largely the same, although the cast was different. Most real House business is conducted in the Committee of the Whole, where, until 1970, no roll call votes were allowed on amendments. Instead, the most formal votes on amendments were so-called teller votes: House Members formed two lines, one for yes and one for no. The number of Representatives for and against a measure was recorded, but how individual Members voted was not.

Of course, there was *some* accountability. Although the public couldn't tell how particular lawmakers voted, committee chairmen could. These chairman took note of those who had voted against them. Not surprisingly, the committee chairmen's position usually won. Members, after all, had more incentive to vote with the committee chairmen (who could punish them for disloyalty) than for the progressive measures then popular with voters. Liberals blamed the teller voting system for a whole string of losses on crucial votes that they believed would have gone their way had the votes been subject to public scrutiny.[4]

Tip O'Neill, the Massachusetts Democrat who later became Speaker of the House, proposed an amendment to the Legislative Reorganization Act of 1970 to allow individual Member's votes to be recorded on teller votes. "The secrecy of the Committee of the Whole has allowed too many Members to duck issues, to avoid the perils of controversial votes," said then-Representative O'Neill. "But that is not in the spirit of this Nation, nor of this Congress." He went on to cite votes that he was sure would have gone the other way if legislators had to vote on the record. "The ABM, the SST, the invasion of Cambodia, were all dealt with in the Committee of the Whole, in non-recorded teller votes."[5]

O'Neill did not expect recorded votes to be demanded often, and then only on questions of vital importance. And, of course, he and the liberals who pushed the measure through expected to win most of the votes. It didn't turn out that way. During the 1971-72 sessions of Congress in which O'Neill's rule was first put in force, there were 193 recorded votes in the Committee of the Whole. Six years later the 95th Congress saw 505 such votes.[6] By the late 1970s the explosion of recorded votes was no longer working to the liberals' advantage. The reason? With the committee reforms of 1974, younger and more liberal Democrats controlled more committees and the legislation that came out of those committees. They didn't need amendments, therefore, and the pesky things were now stocking the arsenal of the Republicans. On top of it all, the Republicans' amendments often won.

With committee deals falling apart on the floor (wedged open by politically sensitive amendments) and Republicans using high-profile votes on divisive issues to embarrass Democrats during election season, the same Democrats who had fought to bring the process under the klieg lights of public debate now turned to the Rules Committee to save them from the democratic monster they had created. The Democratic Caucus had taken over the Rules Committee to stop the use of closed rules. Once in control of the committee, however, they found that a variety of closed and semi-closed rules could be used to frustrate the Republicans' agenda, and they quickly proved they had no qualms about doing so.

The growth of these restrictive rules has been astounding. In the 95th Congress (1977-78) only 15 percent of the rules restricted what amendments could be offered; by 1991, the first year of the 102nd Congress, 61 percent of rules limited amendments and debate. Democrats insist that the restrictive rules are used to bring order to an institution made chaotic by democratic reforms. But Republicans complain that the rules are almost exclusively partisan.

The 1990 Crime Bill is a case in point. Perhaps its most contentious provision, approved by the House Judiciary Committee, was

Title XIII, a "reform" of the procedure for death penalty appeals (a reform from the perspective of those opposed to capital punishment). This provision would have made it even easier for death-row inmates to put off their executions with never-ending strings of last-second appeals, known as habeas corpus petitions. The big floor showdown on the bill was to be a Republican assault on Title XIII in the form of an amendment by Rep. Henry Hyde imposing a sharp limit on number of appeals capital convicts might file.

The Rules Committee held a hearing to consider the more than 100 amendments (including Hyde's) that Representatives wanted to offer to the Crime Bill. Finally, they came up with a rule allowing 45 of those amendments to be considered and voted on. Hyde's was not among them. The most important and politically contentious vote on the whole bill simply vanished, and the only way to get the amendment back was to defeat the rule that had been proposed.

Such a tricky gambit usually works because defeating a rule is almost impossible. Not only do Members have to vote against the Rules Committee (which has the power to put amendments by disloyal lawmakers down the memory hole), the votes on rules are procedural votes. This makes it difficult to hold an opponent's feet to the fire because what he is voting for is not the substance of a proposal but merely a resolution to consider a bill. Absent public pressure the only heat Members feel comes from the House leaders, who twist arms until they get the votes needed for the rule that they tailor-made for some specific purpose. Thus, in most years only one or two rules will be defeated.

The majority, then, thought they had the perfect way to kill the Hyde Amendment. Although these Democrats believe they are right about the evils of the death penalty, they know they have difficulty persuading their constituents of their position. So, instead of following popular will by voting in favor of the death penalty or following principle and trying to convince constituents that the vote was right, House procedure is used to throw the measure out quietly and undemocratically.

That's not what they told the folks back home, though. They excluded certain amendments simply because there wasn't enough time to get to them all, they said. Rep. Jack Brooks was typical.

"Naturally, not all of the Members who wished to offer amendments to H.R. 5269 could be accommodated in the rule that is before us today," he said, sounding like an essay-contest judge consoling the third-graders who lost. "If each of these [over 100 amendments] had been made in order, it is highly unlikely that we could have had enough time to complete this important piece of legislation in these final days of the session." Brooks saved the real whopper for last: "The amendments that the Committee on Rules has made in order under this rule strike a careful balance between the constraints of time and the important effort to ensure that the bill will reflect the will of the House."

This kind of partisan maneuver, bathed in saccharine apologies about the "constraints of time," occurs on almost every important piece of legislation that comes before the House. And Republicans almost always roll over. Sure they complain, and then compile statistics about how the Democrats have tightened the rules stranglehold over the years. But such complaints are a weak response compared with what Republicans were able to achieve on the Crime Bill rule.

This time the Democrats, perhaps drunk with procedural confidence, overplayed their hand. The most important measure offered to the bill had disappeared entirely. They might have gotten away with it had they used a more clever rule allowing a vote on Hyde's amendment, but in a way that the vote had no effect. A King-of-the-Hill rule would have done nicely. Under this procedure, a string of votes is taken on an issue, and the last version to get a majority is the one adopted. The earlier votes are then utterly meaningless, but they provide opportunities for lawmakers to posture. Republicans rarely complain about the King-of-the-Hill procedure either, because they too are interested in posing. "We know we're going to lose," says one minority staffer, "so the only thing left is for us to try to look good." Not surprisingly, King-of-the-Hill rules are increasingly invoked these days: They represent free votes for everyone.

But, because the Democrats had shut the Republicans out completely on the Crime Bill, the GOP mounted a full-scale assault on the proposed rule. Hyde and the Republican leadership declared that the vote on the rule *was* the vote on the Hyde Amendment, and then mobilized support. Letters from a bipartisan chorus of state attorneys-general were presented demanding the Hyde Amendment be heard and voted on. Republicans stripped away the procedure and revealed the vote as one of crucial substance. The restrictive rule was defeated. Hyde's amendment was allowed under a revised rule, and was adopted.

Needless to say, Hyde's amendment was dropped out of the bill by the conference committee.

Nonetheless, the battle over the Hyde Amendment showed that the minority can occasionally win when they fight hard enough, however skewed the rules. Most restrictive rules receive little more than token opposition, a situation which leaves some of the blame for House legislative misdirection on the minority. Democrats use the rules to win and look good doing so. But Republicans all too often acquiesce as long as they're given the chance to look good too. Posing is a bipartisan sport.

When Republicans do choose to play pit bull, however, the majority can resort to more drastic procedural baffles, such as passing bills with no votes at all. The ultimate in stealth legislation is House Rule XLIX. Congress' inability to control spending has been an embarrassment to lawmakers, particularly Democrats. Nowhere has that embarrassment been more keenly felt than in the need to raise the federal debt ceiling. Each year, sometimes more than once a year, Congress has to vote to hike the debt limit as the federal deficit grows. Republicans had made much of the votes, refusing to vote to increase debt and castigating those Democrats who did. Many Democrats, desperate to look fiscally responsible, defected on the votes, endangering the majority's ability to keep the financing flowing. The Democrats needed a solution. But instead of cutting spending, they came up with the perfect out, Rule XLIX.

Now a standing rule of the House, XLIX raises the debt ceiling automatically. When Congress adopts its annual budget resolution, which almost always increases the deficit more than is allowed by the statutory limit on borrowing, the House no longer has to go on record as voting for the debt limit to go up. Instead, "the vote by which the conference report on the concurrent resolution on the budget was agreed to in the House... shall be deemed to have been a vote in favor" of raising the debt ceiling. In other words, Congress now has turned to voting without voting. How can a Representative be held accountable for votes he's only *deemed* to have made?

No more than he can be held accountable for votes that never come to pass, another nifty trick that can be arranged in the House. Often Members sign up as cosponsors of bills which they do not really favor. They can point out the cosponsorship to voters all the while knowing that the relevant committee chairman will bottle up the measure so that it will never get voted upon. When this happens, Members may sign what is known as a discharge petition. If a majority of lawmakers sign the petition, the bill is kicked out of the committee and comes up for a vote. So an easy way to tell if a legislator favors a stalled bill is to see if he has signed the discharge petition. Unfortunately, the names on the petition are kept strictly confidential—for Representatives' eyes only until all 218 required signatures are gathered. The signatures are so secret that Members who leak them are to be punished.

Can there be any reason for this secrecy other than to protect lawmakers from the scrutiny of their constituents? Since the late '80s, more than half the Members of the House listed themselves as supporters of a bill to amend the Constitution to require a balanced federal budget. Yet there were never enough signatures on the discharge petition to bring the measure up for a vote until the spring of 1992. Clearly someone was lying.

What is to be done?

Even the most diligent citizen is likely to be confused by Congress' legislative sleight of hand. Lawmakers defend practices such as House Rule XLIX by saying they are necessary to protect the public from demagogues, and ultimately from itself. But as we have already witnessed, and will continue to see, Congress makes the wisest decisions when it is most clearly accountable to the public. Insulating Congress from public pressure leads to its doing not the right thing but the self-interested thing. Even in those few cases in which public opinion is grossly misguided, true leaders do not look for ways to sneak things past the citizenry, but rather engage voters in the debate and seek to persuade them. The arrogance of our legislators is well displayed by their assumption, when confronted with public opinion at odds with their own, that the public is wrong.

Given the congressional penchant for trickery, prospects for reform may appear bleak. But it is within our power to force Congress to change, to demand accountability. The Senate's last sneaky pay raise, for example, proved to be too much. State legislatures dusted off a proposed constitutional amendment that had languished for two centuries, short of the votes to make it part of the Constitution. The so-called Madison Amendment requires that an election intervene before any congressional pay raise can take effect. Following large pay raises in 1989 and 1991, twelve states ratified the amendment, providing the necessary additional votes to add it to the constitution.

Adding a 27th constitutional amendment represents a structural change. Unlike House or Senate rules, it cannot be bent, ignored or overridden on a whim. Taking the trickery out of Congress will require other structural changes. One of the most useful would be a line-item veto. Often thought of as a budget tool, the item veto might well be more useful against the kind of stealth legislation that Congress frequently hides in large "must-pass" bills. The item veto would also allow the President to eliminate pork-barrel spending projects. The problem with pork is not just the cost but the fact that the goodies give senior Congressmen the power to demand and enforce secret deals. Eliminate pork and you take away the power of key lawmakers to punish upstart Members. Free from the fear of retribution, more lawmakers will be willing to oppose legislative chicanery.

This is not to say that changes in House and Senate rules would not help. In the House in particular the rules should be reformed to produce a more open and accountable legislative process. For instance, discharge petitions should be completely open to the public. We may not want our representatives to vote with every change in public opinion, but we do want them to take up measures that have broad public support. Discharge petitions allow that to happen, and they should be made easier to achieve. There is no reason why two-fifths or a third of the House should not be able to force consideration of a measure if they feel strongly, rather than the majority now required to wrest a bill from an uncooperative committee.

Another key to accountability is to eliminate votes that are "deemed" to have happened without anyone's having to go on record. Rule XLIX, for instance, should be abolished. Far from leading to more responsible spending, taking the debt-ceiling vote away from the so-called demagogues meant only that one of the few hindrances to deficit spending has been removed. The debt, not uncoincidentally, has burgeoned. The House Rules Committee has made a common practice of deeming votes through self-executing rules. That is, when the rule for considering a bill is adopted, certain amendments are deemed to have been agreed to and are thus added to the bill. Nothing is gained by these self-executing rules except the ability to avoid the accountability that comes with voting.

The most serious obstacle to the open consideration of important amendments are the closed rules so frequently employed by the partisan House Rules Committee. The argument that special rules are necessary to bring efficiency to a chaotic House floor is not without some merit. But that by no means justifies the all-too-common practice of excluding amendments that are politically inconvenient or, even worse, those that might win. One way to satisfy the interests of efficiency while protecting minority rights might be to use, when some limitation on amendments is needed, a standard rule that allows each party to offer a set number of amendments of its choice. Or perhaps Congress should allow a vote on any amendment that has the support of a significant number of Representatives. Such reforms would make the more elaborate closed rules drafted by the Rules Committee largely unnecessary. If special rules are still needed for particularly complex measures, they should require a three-fifths or two-thirds majority to ensure that such procedures are used only in extraordinary circumstances.

Quelling the abuse of conference committees is a more difficult proposition. One simple step would be to make instructions to conferees binding. But the House and Senate might then fall into intractable battles, each practicing legislative brinkmanship to put certain issues outside the realm of compromise. But such is not the case when the instruction is for one house's conferees to accept the other house's version of a measure. With a binding instruction to yield to the other house, the disagreement vanishes. Thus, there is no reason that instructions to yield should not be binding. Another remedy would be to require a recorded vote when conferees have ignored an instruction. At least then flip-flopping legislators would have to go on the record clearly.

In the end, however, procedural changes can help only a little to reform conference committee abuses. Both House and Senate rules already say conferees may neither take out a provision about which there was no disagreement or put in provisions that were previously not in either bill. Yet conferees regularly do both. The only cops available to enforce these breach-honored rules are the lawmakers themselves. What good are elaborate new rules restricting conferees as long as lawmakers are eager to ignore them when politically expedient?

So it falls on us to demand the kinds of structural changes needed to insure accountability. Congress doesn't like it when voters resurrect ancient constitutional amendments, or demand new ones, but as long as legislators play fast and loose with the public, it is what they deserve, and what we should give them.

2

THE BULLIES' PULPIT

We merely take testimony.

> Rep. Tom Lantos explaining that it did not
> matter that Members of Congress were duped
> on national TV.

Remember the Great Alar Scare of 1989?

That February, CBS' *60 Minutes* charged that Alar—a growth-regulating chemical used widely on apples—was causing an epidemic of cancer deaths, with children being at particular risk. "The most potent cancer-causing agent in our food supply," intoned correspondent Ed Bradley, "is a substance sprayed on apples to keep them on the trees longer and make them look better."

In the public panic that ensued, apples, apple juice, applesauce, and apple pies were pulled from store shelves and school lunch-counters. Parents threw out anything apple-related. The wholesale price of Red Delicious apples plummeted.

There was nothing to the scare, of course. Alar is perfectly safe. But the scare was not without its price: Apple growers estimate they lost somewhere between $60 million and $140 million.[1]

Nor was the scare innocent. The Alar panic occurred because of a publicity stunt staged by Congress and a special-interest group to get media attention. The *60 Minutes* broadcast had been arranged by David Fenton, whose firm, Fenton Communications, was being paid more than $180,000 a year to promote the anti-Alar campaign of the Natural Resources Defense Council (NRDC). The network had been given exclusive use of a new NRDC report on the dangers of Alar and other agricultural chemicals. The report was called "Intolerable Risk: Pesticides in Our Children's Food," and CBS played it to the hilt.

Now, one scare story on TV is a good start, but anti-Alar hysteria would never have taken off without teamwork: the combined efforts of federal regulatory agencies, interest groups, and Congress are needed to yield such bountiful press coverage. In the case of Alar, Fenton had also arranged that one week after *60 Minutes* gave credence to the NRDC charges, actress Meryl Streep would announce the formation of a citizen's group called "Mothers and Others for Pesticide Limits."

Within a month of the *60 Minutes* story the Senate Subcommittee on Children, Family, Drugs and Alcoholism, chaired by Connecticut Democrat Christopher Dodd, had arranged a hearing. The hearing had every publicity ingredient: child victims, a press in full gallop, and, best of all, an honest-to-goodness movie star, Meryl Streep. It didn't even matter that they couldn't produce any actual children who had become sick because of Alar. It was enough to talk solemnly about the thousands "at risk."

The hearing provided for such juicy publicity that it attracted Senators who were not members of Dodd's subcommittee. Connecticut Democratic Sen. Joseph Lieberman, for example, put in a guest appearance to ask Streep a few fawning questions. Rep. Gerry Sikorski went one better — the Minnesota Democrat appeared before the Senators as a witness: "I'm not a scientist or researcher, a medical doctor or oncologist, a biologist or horticulturist. I am a father—a concerned, scared, and more than a little angry father." It was an encore performance for Sikorski, who had already railed against Alar on the *60 Minutes* broadcast. Now he added a cute sound-bite: Alar-treated apples were the sort a wicked stepmother would give to Snow White.

Even Sen. Brock Adams, a Democrat from the apple-growing state of Washington, went along with the hype, arguing that the problem was with the chemical's manufacturer rather than with the apple farmers: "Uniroyal... would do us all a great public service if they suspended production of the chemical until the controversy on the product safety is resolved," said Adams. "That allows the processors and those who are using apple products to avoid boycotts."

The lone sour note came from Sen. Steve Symms, a third-generation apple-grower. The Idaho Republican suggested that the environmentalists' report was absurd. And he was right. The NRDC's risk estimates had been produced by exaggerating the results of a study that had itself been discredited. The previous report, the Toth study, had been rejected in 1985 by an EPA Scientific Advisory Panel as a grounds for banning Alar: The mice in the study had been fed such extraordinarily high levels of the chemical that they were dying from the sheer toxicity of the dose. The NRDC combined the Toth figures with high estimates of the amount of apples actually consumed by children, and came up with the alarming conclusion that as many as 910 children per million would get cancer from the agricultural use of Alar. By comparison, a study by the California Department of Food and Agriculture found that Alar use had a probable lifetime cancer risk of only 3.5 per trillion.[2]

With most such hypes, a few lawmakers will break ranks and try to do some debunking. But the Alar case is instructive, because such skepticism usually owes itself (as with Symms) to a personal or constituent reason rather than any general commitment to sound science. In those cases in which a constituent's ox is gored—such as apple growers in Washington state — a lawmaker does not necessarily have to struggle to burst the hype. Like Brock Adams, all one has to do is redirect the fire toward someone else's constituents; in this case, pointing the finger not at the apple growers who used Alar but the chemical manufacturers who produced it. Or, in best huckster fashion, a lawmaker can play along with the hysteria, reap the publicity benefits, and overcome constituent concerns with ... more publicity.

Look at how Sen. Tom Harkin handled an exchange with Meryl Streep. "There are those who think that this is hysteria—you have addressed that, that it is not hysteria, that it is based upon facts," the Iowa Democrat said, after commending the actress for being present. Clearly the farm-state Senator was not about to assail the contention that agricultural chemicals pose huge dangers to children. But how could he pacify his farmer constituents, who rely on such chemicals for their livelihood?

> **Sen. Harkin:** Let me just ask you a very personal question. I have been contacted by the Iowa Farm Bureau. They are in town today. Would you be willing to meet with some farm families and talk to them?

> **Sen. Dodd:** She has got a plane to catch at 1:30 p.m.

> **Sen. Harkin:** Not today, but I mean at any time.

> **Ms. Streep:** Yes, I would love to, as a matter of fact, yes.

> **Sen. Harkin:** Would you come out and meet with some farm families?

> **Ms. Streep:** Yes, absolutely.

Streep never actually went to Iowa with Harkin to meet with farm families, but just getting her to say she would was good enough for some TV clips.

The Alar hearing did not result in legislation. But it didn't have to. The flip-side of all the good publicity for the Senators and the NRDC was bad publicity for apple-growers and for Uniroyal. Under pressure from the public, farmers, and Congress, the chemical company withdrew Alar from the market. Thus lawmakers were able to speak out on behalf of victims without having to follow through with actual legislation (which might have required looking at the NRDC's claims more carefully), and they could claim credit for getting Alar off the market.

Though probably one of the more notorious, Alar is by no means the only innocent scalp taken by Congress and special-interest groups in their collaborative efforts to produce publicity. Again and again the groups and legislators work together to build media hypes and keep themselves in the spotlight. The special-interest groups provide the scripts, and the lawmakers provide the stage. Alar was the Tony Award winner in this Broadway on the Potomac. Hearings concocted by the Environmental Defense Fund (EDF) and willing Senators proclaiming lead poisoning as the next environmental epidemic were a similar show: Using figures provided to him by the EDF, Sen. Harry Reid claimed that three-to-four million American children suffer from lead poisoning. In opening the session of his Subcommittee on Toxic Substances, Environmental Oversight, Research and Development, in 1989 the Nevada Democrat quickly brought the crisis close to home: "In Las Vegas, where my son and daughter-in-law live, 28.6 percent of the children between the ages of six months and five years have dangerously high levels of lead in their blood," he charged. "In Reno, Nevada, 22.6 percent of preschool children have dangerously high levels of lead in their blood." However bad it might be in Nevada, he added, it was even worse elsewhere—51.7 percent of preschoolers in Washington, 74.7 percent in New York City, 58.2 percent in Los Angeles, 47 percent in Atlanta, and 62 percent in Chicago have dangerously high levels of lead in their blood.

The statistics are indeed frightening, as they are no doubt meant to be, not least because lead poisoning in children has been linked to permanent neurological damage. Part of what makes the figures so frightening is their very specificity, something of a puzzle, inasmuch as there have been no nationwide surveys of amounts of lead in children's blood. Upon examination, the flap over lead poisoning had less to do with dispassionate science than with highly charged politics in which Congress and special-interest groups cooperate in pursuit of ever more publicity.

"... a genuine basis in fact... "

Three days before Sen. Reid opened his hearings the EDF, a Washington-based litigation and advocacy group, held a press conference to herald its new report, "The Legacy of Lead: America's Continuing Epidemic of Childhood Lead Poisoning." The timing of the release was no accident. The EDF had worked closely with Sen. Reid's subcommittee for months to arrange the Senate hearings, providing the staff with advance copies of the report, and helping line up the witnesses giving testimony. Thus the

EDF report served two purposes: Its release would create interest in the hearings, and, in return, the report would be used as a source —*the* source—in the hearings.

The EDF report listed the number and percent of children in major cities across the country who have enough lead in their systems to impair their intelligence. The figures were astounding, with 490,997 children in New York City, 221,654 children in Philadelphia, and 380,905 in Los Angeles suffering from lead poisoning. Boston, though it has a lead-paint abatement program, still had one of the highest levels of lead poisoning in the nation—69.4 percent, or 122,862 children.

What made these figures so irresistible is that they were tailor-made to maximize local television and newspaper publicity. In every town, the media could give an exact number of afflicted children in the area, complete with their percentage of the city's childhood population, taken out to compelling tenths of a point. And Senators could claim to be standing on science. Sen. Lieberman said the lead poisoning of American children was "right at the top of the hazards that are facing us." It was unclear, however, whether the Senator considered lead poisoning a greater or lesser hazard than Alar, which, it will be remembered, Lieberman had also helped to hype. He went on to add that the EDF report and the work of Dr. Herbert Needleman, on which the report was based, gave the subcommittee "a genuine basis in fact—not fiction—to be concerned."

But did it? What the hearings didn't tell you was how the EDF had arrived at such specific figures. Nor was it explained how an epidemic of such proportions (brain damage in three of four children in New York City!) could go unnoticed.

Lead in the blood is measured in terms of micrograms per deciliter ($\mu g/dL$). Moderate or high levels of lead in the blood—40 $\mu g/dL$ and up—causes various types of irreparable damage to the brain and the nervous system; levels higher than 70 $\mu g/dL$ can bring on convulsions and even death. Levels of lead down to 25 $\mu g/dL$ have been shown to cause mental impairment. But the EDF defined lead poisoning as 10 $\mu g/dL$, an amount so low that it is nearly half the amount of lead an average person had in his blood just 10 years ago. To put this in perspective, since 1980, largely because of lower lead-content in gasoline and food cans, average blood lead-levels have dropped from 18 µg/dL to just 6 µg/dL. Under the EDF definition, nearly everyone in the United States 10 years ago was brain-damaged.

The brain damage being alleged is based on the claim that the IQ scores of children with blood lead over 10 µg/dL are on average one or two points lower than those of children with very low lead-levels. The evidence for these IQ disparities comes almost exclusively from the work of Needleman and Dr. David Bellinger, who, together, formed the Alliance to End Childhood Lead Poisoning. Well before the hearings started, the work of both men had been challenged as seriously flawed, and potentially fraudulent, for leaving out data that contradicted their thesis. Since then, Needleman's studies have come under even more scrutiny, becoming the focus of a formal investigation initiated by the National Institutes of Health's Office of Scientific Integrity.

Yet Needleman, who testified early in the hearing, was not challenged by the Senators. The closest he came to criticism was a softball question by Sen. Reid meant to defuse questions about the doctor's research. Ellen Silbergeld, senior toxicologist with the Environmental Defense Fund, also found the Senate panel easy going, even though the EDF report she was explaining was palpably absurd.

The EDF had taken an estimate of the prevalence of children with elevated blood lead from an Agency for Toxic Substances and Disease Registry (ATSDR) report and break down that estimate city by city. Never mind that the ATSDR report was itself a guesstimate projected from 15-year-old surveys; never mind, too, that the ATSDR report strictly warned that no breakdown for geographic areas smaller than the nation as a whole could be made from the data. The EDF even added another vague assumption: that cities with older houses have more lead paint and thus a higher incidence of lead poisoning. This, in turn, was used to weight its division of the ATSDR numbers into city-by-city figures.

But Ellen Silbergeld had gone even further, taking each number out to the final decimal place as though the estimates were scientific and exact. Some newspapers fell for it. Most embarrassing, perhaps, was *USA Today*, which published the city-by-city tables verbatim. A few did not, though. A North Dakota paper questioned whether the EDF numbers for children suffering lead poisoning in that state were accurate, and pointed out that the group had used an "unscientific formula and unsubstantiated data." Reid did ask Silbergeld about that article, but, as with his question to Needleman, it was offered simply as an opportunity for her to dispel any doubts about the report. There were no serious follow-ups or attempts to get at the truth.

Representatives of the lead industry, on the other hand, were not extended quite the same courtesies. When Jerome Cole of the industry-sponsored International Lead Zinc Research Organization detailed the problems with Needleman's studies, Sen. Reid switched to hardball. "I have a conviction that we have a problem with lead," the Senator stated. "It would seem to me that the lead industry would be best served by trying to work something out rather than trying to be like the tobacco companies have done for years, saying that there is not a problem with tobacco." To make sure his point was not lost on the lead industry, he repeated his confidence in the dangers of lead and the advantages for the industry in cooperating, not once but twice, finishing the admonishment with: "We have enough knowledge to know that lead is a problem. There may be some further studies necessary, but I think it would be in the best interest of the lead industry that you cooperate with us."

In short, the Reid/Lieberman hearing was the environmental equivalent of a show trial. It was not about gathering information; the subcommittee had the information it wanted before the opening gavel had sounded. Industry was invited, of course (a veneer of even-handedness is important to a hearing's credibility). But those who questioned the position the subcommittee had already adopted were publicly threatened with reprisals.

To be sure, skepticism about industry research is always warranted. But this was a case of hostility, not skepticism. It was also a case of double standards. The environmentalists' research, which was at best slipshod, and perhaps purposefully misleading, was met with not even a sliver of doubt.

"We merely take testimony."

If not to get at the truth, then what are hearings for? Such shows are one of Congress' most versatile, not to mention dangerous, weapons. For one thing, they help manufacture a written record that lawmakers can use to justify their actions. Or they can help Members of Congress play catch-up when they've been left behind on a high-profile issue. Hearings in October 1990 on Iraqi military atrocities exemplified both these purposes.

As hostilities between the U.S.-led allies and Iraqi strongman Saddam Hussein continued to escalate, Democrats in Congress had been dragging their feet. But when it became clear that the White House was going to take military action, and—more importantly —that the public supported such a move, the lawmakers rushed to jump on the bandwagon. The Congressional Human Rights Caucus used its hearings to cover the change of heart.

The centerpiece of the caucus hearings, chaired by California Democrat Tom Lantos, was testimony by "Nayirah." Nayirah was a 15-year-old Kuwaiti girl who broke into tears as she told of seeing Iraqi soldiers steal maternity-ward incubators, leaving infants to die on the hospital floor. This tale of shocking cruelty became a refrain in the speeches of lawmakers seeking to justify their support for action in the Persian Gulf. But, though Iraqis committed thousands of brutal crimes against Kuwaitis, stealing occupied incubators does not seem to have been among them.

Nayirah's real name was kept a secret, ostensibly to protect her family from retribution by Iraq. As it turned out, her family was already as high profile a target as it was likely to be: Nayirah's father was the Kuwaiti ambassador to the United States, Saud Nasir al-Sabah. Rep. Lantos kept that fact under wraps, along with information that her appearance had been arranged by Kuwait's public-relations firm, Hill and Knowlton. Had Nayirah's real identity been known, it might have led some lawmakers to be more skeptical toward her story (for the same reasons one ought to be skeptical of industry research, or any other self-interested information). Instead, Nayirah's testimony was repeated widely and uncritically on Capitol Hill for months.

Not until after the war were reporters able to investigate Nayirah's claims by asking Kuwaiti doctors and nurses about the theft of incubators. No evidence could be found to confirm the girl's account. When it finally got out that Nayirah was the ambassador's daughter, Lantos was asked why he and his fellow House Members had so unskeptically accepted her story. "Whether every single claimed human rights violation took place exactly the way the claim was made is utterly secondary," he responded. "We merely take testimony." Even under false pretenses, it appears.

Hearings have still other functions. For one, they can be used to embarrass administration officials with whom lawmakers disagree — a sort of bullies' pulpit. Congress has expanded its power over the last 20 years, not through more far-reaching legislation, but through informal means, such as phone calls to federal regulators demanding that agency rules be written this way or that. The bullies' pulpit is crucial to this back-channel way of doing business. Much of Congress' informal power comes from its ability to punish foes by making them look foolish (or worse) on national television. That power is sometimes used to pressure officials to toe the congressional line, and sometimes simply as retribution for past clashes with Capitol Hill. Hearings can also function as a convenient tool in partisan electoral politics. Republican Fife Symington without warning became the target of a Senate Judiciary subcommittee hearing, where Ohio Democrat Howard Metzenbaum accused him of being an S&L crook weeks before a squeaker of a runoff election with Democrat Terry Goddard for the Arizona governorship.

The accusation was hurled during a February 7, 1991, hearing to which Symington had not been invited. There Metzenbaum railed against the Republican candidate, saying he had violated federal conflict-of-interest regulations and was "knee deep in ... slimy business practices." But the ploy backfired, thanks to quick thinking by Republican Arlen Specter of Pennsylvania, also a member of the Metzenbaum subcommittee. Sen. Specter had the hearing extended into the afternoon so Symington, who happened to be in Washington for a fundraiser, could come to Capitol Hill to defend himself.

When Symington arrived he came out swinging. "I resent this attempt to denigrate my achievements," he said. "If this is what you can expect from seeking public office, I suggest that it is just not worth it." With the slightest veil, he accused Metzenbaum of using the hearing to influence the outcome of the Arizona gubernatorial election. "I am certain that the distinguished Senator from Ohio has no partisan interest in the outcome of that contest. I hope not."

Clearly unprepared for the afternoon confrontation, Metzenbaum tried to backpedal. "Now with respect to my own conduct, let me say to you that I have made no allegations against you. I have made no allegations against you."

Symington read from the morning transcript the allegations Metzenbaum had made against him.

Flustered, Metzenbaum was reduced to swearing that he did not even know the name of Symington's opponent in the governor's race.

Fife Symington had discovered what Clarence Thomas would learn just eight months later, during the hearings on his Supreme Court nomination: The old saw about bullies being cowards applies on Capitol Hill. Members of Congress love to rant from the exalted heights of their hearing-room podiums, all righteous rage and indignation. But the rage is hardly ever genuine. Instead it is a trope, a bluster learned by bullies who are accustomed to victims who cower. Let a victim strike back, however, and the bullies discard their rage like routed soldiers tossing away their weapons.

The attack on Symington was just a mugging, and easily thwarted —he simply resisted, holding firm with the mere suggestion that the Senator was engaged in dirty tricks. If Metzenbaum had been engaged in anything other than a political hit, he might have stood his ground. But legislators are fundamentally unserious about the charges they bring—however serious the consequences may be. The Resolution Trust Corporation, charged with recovering losses in the nationwide S&L bailout, recently made similar charges against Symington. Though the Arizona governor has defended himself far more vigorously against the RTC than he did against

Metzenbaum, RTC officials have not abandoned their efforts the way the Senator did.

The charges against Clarence Thomas were another matter altogether. When the Senate Judiciary Committee descended on Judge Thomas with 11th-hour charges of sexual impropriety, the attack was far better organized, and a far more serious threat to his career. Thomas resisted with the force needed. He didn't try simply to deflect the blows, he went nuclear, calling the proceedings "a high-tech lynching for an uppity black."

What? Senators accustomed to the casual destruction of others' reputations now found themselves being likened to Klansmen. On national television! Prime time! Judge Thomas had dressed them in sheets and, terrified, they scattered. So complete was the rout that later in the hearings Metzenbaum was buffaloed by even John Doggett, a transparent braggart who was one of the least-compelling witnesses in the entire debacle.

Nevertheless, the hard truth is that bravado often represents the only protection a witness has. At "investigative" hearings such as the one Metzenbaum used to fling charges at then-candidate Symington, the accused have little in the way of rights or procedural safeguards. The American Bar Association has called for Congress to adopt minimal standards for its hearings, rights that would be just a fraction of those accorded in judicial or administrative settings, but lawmakers have ignored the ABA's recommendations.

Witnesses subpoenaed by congressional committees, for example, frequently are not allowed to have lawyers present when they testify. And when they do have attorneys, private conversations with their attorneys are often prohibited: Congress, unlike the courts or the executive, does not respect the lawyer-client privilege of confidentiality. Rep. John Dingell, the Michigan Democrat who has built a personal empire by turning his House Energy and Commerce Subcommittee on Oversight and Investigations into a Star Chamber, maintains that the lawyer-client privilege doesn't apply to those being investigated by Congress.[3] The need for such rights is emphasized by the fact that witnesses have been investigated and faced with criminal allegations based on statements made at congressional hearings.

The Orange Juice Police

Conversely, hearings provide political cover for bureaucrats who want to go against administration policy. Indeed, this is one of the main ways lawmakers cement their relationship with the permanent staff of the federal bureaucracy. Members of Congress have the power to reward as well as punish, and, in best Skinnerian fashion, bureaucrats learn to press the buttons that produce rewards. Hearings can provide a prized award for bureaucrats: public praise. Just as lawmakers can humiliate witnesses who are uncooperative, they can heap kudos on those who get with the congressional program. By contrast the President—the bureaucrats' ostensible boss—has no equivalent power of public praise and punishment. Is it any wonder the agencies more often than not side with their congressional masters?

Take the Food and Drug Administration (FDA), which under the new and aggressive leadership of David Kessler is the exemplar of an executive agency that knows where its bread is buttered. In practice, this means following the lead of two key congressional powers, California Democrat Henry Waxman and Michigan Democrat John Dingell. For its fealty the agency in the summer of 1991 was rewarded in the best Capital Beltway fashion. Not only were Kessler and his key deputies praised in a July House hearing on amendments to the Food, Drug, and Cosmetic Act, with all the joviality enjoyed by friends of the Hill, they were offered increased funding, increased authority, and increased enforcement powers: a federal regulator's Christmas list.

This payoff followed a decision by Kessler to flex the FDA's muscles after the regulatory lull of the Reagan years. A few months before the July hearings the agency staged a raid, seizing a warehouse loaded with orange juice labeled as "fresh" though it was made from concentrate. To seize the "mislabeled" juice, however, the agency had to obtain a warrant and enlist the aid of federal marshals. At worst, the juice was misrepresented: Although the cartons had the words "fresh choice" on them, the label also noted that the juice was reconstituted. The juice was not seized to protect consumers from any health hazard. In fact, the feds donated the contraband to a homeless shelter. It was seized to make an example of the company, to show that the FDA was not to be trifled with, that its regulatory demands were henceforth to be obeyed immediately.

The administration responded to the action with mild concern, wondering whether the seizure might have been an overreaction. The response from the agency overseers on Capitol Hill was quite the opposite: The FDA had been hindered by the requirement that it get a warrant and use marshals, according to Rep. Waxman, who in early June had introduced a bill that would give FDA agents their own subpoena and police powers. If Waxman's bill became law, the orange juice police would even carry guns.

Before the juice bust, the Bush administration had planned to acquiesce in the new police powers for the FDA. Kessler had even been given the go-ahead to testify favorably on the Waxman bill at the July hearings. But the juice bust was so chilling an example that the business community appealed to the White House, pleading that the FDA's power not be expanded. Kessler's bosses agreed and instructed him that he was not to say anything in support of the Waxman bill.

So Kessler showed up at the hearing flanked by four FDA bureaucrats. After one of the briefest opening statements ever heard on the Hill, Kessler signaled he was ready for questions. Rep. Waxman asked if the agency needed new enforcement authority. Kessler, a presidential appointee, turned to one of the career bureaucrats, who obligingly answered, yes. The administrator avoided endorsing Waxman's bill by having his staffers—who were more than happy to argue for an expansion of their powers—do it for him. The ruse was so transparent that the crowd in the hearing room kept laughing when the staffers answered questions. The joke was on the President, not to mention the tax-paying consumer.

Whether on apples, Kuwait, lead, or orange juice, congressional hearings are rarely about gathering information or getting at the truth. The meetings allow legislators to justify their actions, pressure the White House, bully those who have crossed them and, conversely, coddle and encourage their allies. Above all, hearings are about publicity.

Electronic Boilerplate

In our media age, one of the greatest advantages an incumbent has is the ability to get himself on television. As Congress has increasingly tooled up as a reelection machine, lawmakers have become ever more sophisticated media hounds. Twenty years ago, only one in eight Members of the House had full-time press secretaries. Today, well over half do: The number of House flacks has gone from 54 in 1970 to more than 280 in 1992. And that's not counting press people on committee staffs or in the offices of the leadership. Nor are these press secretaries' jobs as limited as they once were. They do not simply send out press releases and set up interviews for reporters. Sometimes they pretend to be journalists themselves.

Each Wednesday afternoon a crowd of legislators can be found on the lawn in front of the east side of the Capitol. Camera crews from both parties' congressional campaign committees roll video tape while Members are interviewed... by their own press secretaries. The interviews are edited down to usable sound bites and beamed back to home district TV stations, where, more often than not, the electronic boilerplate is presented as if it were the product of a news team.[4]

These Wednesday afternoon interviews are but one example of one of the least known, but most useful, perks of congressional office: subsidized media production. Not only do taxpayers foot the bill for franked mail that serves as little more than government advertisements for incumbents, they pay for House and Senate television studios. The Senate media center is tucked inside a tunnel that used to be part of the Capitol Hill subway, with two television studios, two radio studios, two control rooms, and two television editing rooms. Studio time is heavily subsidized. Although most electronic boilerplate for home district radio and television stations is produced at the studios run by the campaign committees (paid for with private donations), the Senate Recording and Photographic Studios still have over 60 employees with combined salaries of over $2 million. Operating costs for the studios are over $300,000. The House TV operation includes 20 production people, 10 cameramen, two TV studios, and four radio studios.

The reason these operations are so important is that the all-important "media hit" is critical for reelection. Lawmakers don't look for hits on the networks, because only the most accomplished congressional news hounds achieve coverage by the national media; network congressional coverage is usually limited to the party leaders and those lawmakers who are in the news because they are running for President.[5]

In their own districts, however, Members of Congress are celebrities. Most of that celebrity is maintained through the local media. Incumbents have several times the visibility of challengers, thanks largely to their more frequent and consistent appearances in the press and on radio and TV. The annual National Election Study, among other things, asks constituents whether they had seen or heard of their congressional candidates in any of a variety of ways. Half of the respondents had read about the incumbent in the newspaper; only one in five had seen mention of the challenger. A fourth of the voters had heard the incumbent on the radio; less than one in 10 had heard the challenger. More than half had seen the incumbent on television; less than a fifth had seen the challenger.

This incumbent visibility is created, in no small part, through the barrage of video and audio "feeds," as the electronic boilerplate is known. Local television and radio stations eagerly snap up the material. They do so partly because most are in small markets with budgets too limited to afford their own coverage of Washington. They also like the information supplied from Congress because, unlike network coverage, it is customized for their audiences. The feeds may not be objective, unbiased journalism, but for local stations trying to fill air time, it is better than the nothing they would have without it. So vital to reelection have these video feeds become that Hedrick Smith calls them the first of his "Five Pillars of Incumbency."[6]

Not that Members of Congress ignore newspapers. Many congressional offices put out what are called "slicks," press releases produced to look exactly like an op-ed column in a newspaper. Slicks come complete with photos, headlines, and text, all ready to be pasted right into a newspaper column. Most larger metropolitan newspapers look down on this prepackaged copy, but many smaller

dailies or local weeklies (where lawmakers can get that all-important hometown coverage) are happy to have their congressional
coverage provided to them free.

Hearings add a "news" angle to such coverage. "The value of a
hearing as a propaganda channel is that it is an event," wrote
congressional scholar David Truman in 1971. "It is news. Especially when the participants are prominent or the testimony involves
startling revelations or sharp conflicts, the event is likely to receive
generous coverage in the media. At some points in the development
of a measure, in fact, the primary purpose of hearings lies in their
propaganda value."[7]

If hearings implied an opening of the government to the citizens,
the attendant evils of congressional grandstanding would be easier
to abide. As with pay raises, conference committees, and tricky
rules however, lawmakers go to great lengths to muddy the media
waters when it comes to substantive and controversial issues. Real
legislation tends to have losers as well as winners, and taking a
public stand on such issues means angering the losers. Better to seek
publicity on issues without much of a down side, or at least those
in which the losers can be portrayed so unsympathetically that they
will get no support. This is where victims come in handy.

Sen. Harry Reid's lead hearings, for example, had a surplus of
victims: four million schoolchildren, according to the Senator's
opening statement. Victims make compelling news; just look at
Geraldo, *Oprah*, or *Donahue*. Members of Congress know this
better than anyone, and they do their best to oblige by cramming
their hearings full of victims. True enough, their stories are frequently compelling, but only rarely do they have any relevance to
serious public policy. In fact, the very hunt for victims and the
publicity they provide almost guarantees that consideration of real
policy issues is excluded. Thus do Members of Congress buy into
an endless succession of environmental, consumer, and public-
health scams.

It's not always easy to find victims, even with the vast staffs
Members of Congress have, and here is where the public-interest
lobbies play their part. These groups are comprised of a variety of
interests, from environmental groups and Ralph Nader-affiliated

consumer organizations to civil-rights and public-health organizations. These groups also depend on publicity, and appearing at congressional hearings, in addition to conferring legitimacy on their work, represents a rich source of exposure. These ad hoc relationships are at the heart of a new power structure on Capitol Hill, a structure so dependent on cheap showmanship that we might call it the Barnumocracy.

Iron Triangles, Issue Networks, and Barnumocracy

Victims were out in force at a March 26, 1990, House hearing on the diet industry. Rep. Ron Wyden, an Oregon Democrat, was ringmaster. His Small Business Subcommittee on Regulation, Business Opportunities, and Energy had convened the hearings to discuss whether the diet industry was putting the nation at risk. The answer must have been yes, given the complaints of the opening panel. Loretta Pameijer testified that her daughter's dieting had put the girl in the hospital: Her gallbladder had to be removed a few months after she had gone on the Doctor's Quick Weight Loss Center program. Sherri Steinberg blamed her attack of gallstones on Nutri/System. In the course of the hearings the company was also blamed for the heart attack and consequent brain damage of Carol Householder's husband. He had been losing weight eating Nutri/System food and collapsed while jogging.

Certainly these are tragic stories, and it's impossible not to sympathize with the women, particularly Mrs. Householder, whose husband's brain was irreparably damaged. But that sympathy all too easily displaces the questions of how and why the injuries really happened. For example, it was not clear whether Mr. Householder suffered his heart attack because of his diet or because he was exercising too strenuously. Similarly, were the gallbladder difficulties suffered by the two women in the hearing the result of a loss in weight or the fact that these women had previously been overweight? (There is a higher incidence of gallstones among the obese as well as among those losing weight.) The women could not answer those questions (that is, if they had been asked them). In fact, they could offer no medical evidence that the diets had been at fault.

That didn't matter. It didn't matter, because answers never do in hearings. The network news picked up the story, complete with the suggestion that the health of all dieters was seriously at risk. The hearing got so much publicity that Nutri/System had to hold press conferences to defend itself and take out advertisements in major national newspapers detailing the safety of their diet program. The company had not been invited to the hearing; according to a spokesman for Rep. Wyden, D. Ann Murphy, the event was put together on such short notice that Nutri/System would not have had time to prepare its testimony. It would have been unfair to the company, she said, to have them appear.

No legislation was passed as a result of the hearing, but in Wyden's office the diet event is considered a paradigm of congressional success. It is also a paradigm of the Barnumocracy. Rep. Wyden's staff did not go out searching for people who had been stricken by faulty diets. Instead, his staff was approached by lawyers representing plaintiffs in lawsuits against the diet industry. The lawyers provided the script and the cast and helped whip up publicity for the congressional show. In return, public pressure to settle built up on the objects of their lawsuits.

The media are crucial to the success of these efforts. And, although the press has a reputation for cynicism and street smarts, reporters are not all that hard to manipulate for a cheap headline. Take the road show put on jointly by Rep. Charles Schumer, a New York Democrat, and Allstate Insurance. At hearings in his New York district, and then on Capitol Hill, Schumer staged the dismantling of an automobile. Allstate supplied the cars, the mechanics to disassemble them, and the statistics on the value of the cannibalized parts. The lawmaker supplied the hearings (on legislation to thwart auto theft) and enjoyed the publicity. The New York stunt was quite the media success, prompting coverage in the *New York Post*, the *Daily News*, and on all the local television stations. The Washington exhibition succeeded as well with stories in the *Washington Post* and on *ABC Nightly News*.

The *Washington Post* article was typical of the kind of coverage generated by the stunt, and of the ease with which journalists are taken in by exaggerated claims. "Over the next 10 minutes, off came

wheel covers ($1,489.18), the four doors ($13,257.80), the front
assembly ($7,288.62), and the seats ($4,895.19)," the *Post* reported.
"When it was all over, and all the parts were removed, the 1990
Cadillac Brougham d'Elegance was worth far more in pieces than
it was whole—$35,740 compared with a book value of $20,800."[8]

The reporter never thought to ask, why, if 10 minutes' effort could
turn a $20,800 car into $35,740 worth of parts, there isn't a booming
legal business in buying Cadillacs and taking them apart. Or, why
is the "street" value of hubcaps one thousand four hundred eighty-
nine dollars *and eighteen cents*? Are we to believe there is a
hoodlums' parts catalogue in which the items are priced out to the
penny? If the press cannot dredge up some skepticism when the
publicity factor is this transparent, or when the exaggerations are
this farfetched, it is no wonder the Barnumocracy functions so
smoothly.

It is not difficult to see why Allstate did its part in the car stunt.
After all, insurers hate getting stuck with the bill for replacing
stripped or stolen cars. It is less obvious, initially, why the public-
interest lobbies play their part in the hyping of health scares and the
like. It is argued that the Nader groups, such as Public Citizen, are
funded to some extent by trial lawyers, and thus are motivated to
aid litigators who profit from the lawsuits the scares promote. That
may be the case. Although Public Citizen and its many affiliates
deny that they accept money from lawyers' groups, they are
strangely coy about actually listing who their contributors are. But
the more plausible explanation is twofold. First, the groups enjoy,
and need, publicity themselves. Second, their visibility and public
relations skills make them invaluable congressional allies, a service
for which they are well and variously rewarded by Congress.

This ad hoc cooperation between lawmakers and special interests,
made possible by a media eager to sell stories of misery and distress,
is the Barnumocracy. Scholars like David Truman recognized that
hearings could be used as propaganda but thought the publicity
would be used primarily to advance legislation. Little could one
have predicted that the "legislative process" would be corrupted to
the point where legislation frequently is irrelevant. It's the show

that matters. And it's all built on the assumption that we are the suckers P.T. Barnum took us for.

The Barnumocracy evolved out of what used to be the dominant paradigm of the Washington power structure (as political scientists like to call such things), the "iron triangle." Under the rule of iron triangles, bonds would develop among powerful congressional committees, the federal bureaucrats those committees would oversee, and the special constituent interests that were the "clients" of both the lawmakers and the bureaucrats. The special interests, who made up one corner in these triangles, were generally big business interests who tapped into federal largess through their relationships with Congress and the federal agencies. Together the legislators, bureaucrats, and their clients would control a plot of policy turf. These "subgovernments," as they have also been known, would lock out other parties, including the President and his staff, and would toil away in their own interest largely out of sight of the general public.

In the areas of public works, defense, and agriculture, iron triangles were once bolted in place. The phenomenon was first identified by Arthur Maas in 1951, with his description of the politics of the Army Corps of Engineers.[9] Students in the Maas school soon began to find subgovernments everywhere. Another example was the cozy relationship among the defense committees on Capitol Hill, the Pentagon, and arms manufacturers. Those in Congress with defense contractors in their districts would gravitate toward the defense committees, where they were in a position to serve their most important constituents. Similarly, lawmakers from farm states seek positions on agricultural committees, where they can do the most for *their* client constituencies. Rep. Jamie Whitten, the Mississippi Democrat known as the "Permanent Secretary of Agriculture" for his control of federal farm programs, long ran an iron triangle made up of his subcommittee on agriculture appropriations, farm interests, and the Department of Agriculture. The nation's policy on pesticides for decades was driven by Rep. Whitten's desire to provide his farm clients with as many, and as potent, pest killers as possible.[10]

Though Whitten still directs much of the agricultural pork that Congress so copiously slathers on farmers, he no longer has the control he once enjoyed over pesticides. The cozy triangles of the 1950s and 1960s are no longer made of iron. The strength of the triangles was forged by the congressional committee and seniority systems. Committees had much more authority, and they could run policy in their particular jurisdictions largely unmolested. Since committee control was largely based on seniority, committee chairmen typically were those who had been in Congress for decades, building the relationships with the federal bureaucracy essential to the iron triangle.

The reforms of the early 1970s, however, both dismantled the seniority system and displaced the focused power of committees. No longer were committees controlled by a conservative southern gerontocracy; no longer did a few lawmakers have almost exclusive jurisdiction over their pieces of policy turf. In 1971 Democrats decreed that House Members could chair only one subcommittee apiece: almost overnight, more than half of all Democratic Representatives led a committee or subcommittee.[11] This diffusion of power in the House was complicated by the creation of ever more federal agencies, many with overlapping jurisdictions. Rep. Whitten, for example, no longer runs pesticide policy, partly because the U.S. Department of Agriculture, where he has the most influence, has lost the main say in pesticide regulation to the Environmental Protection Agency (created in 1970), and partly through the proliferation of committees and subcommittees claiming at least some jurisdiction over chemicals (at least eight by last count).

Of course, the end of the iron triangle was by no means the demise of cozy relationships between Members of Congress, special interests, and federal bureaucrats. If anything, those relationships have become more promiscuous. Iron triangles were stable and monogamous. In many case members of the triangles stayed together for life, excluding the influence and scrutiny of others. In sharp contrast, policy affairs today are much more fluid, with bedfellows coming and going with each particular issue. This new fluidity was recognized in the late 1970s by Hugh Heclo, who wrote:

> Based largely on early studies of agriculture, water, and public works policies, the iron triangle concept is not so much wrong as it is disastrously incomplete... the conventional view is especially inappropriate for understanding changes in politics and administration during recent years .... Looking for closed triangles of control, we tend to miss the fairly open networks of people that increasingly impinge upon government.[12]

The most prominent newcomers in these "issue networks" have become known as "public lobbies," environmentalists, consumerists, and other advocates of increased social regulation. Born partly in reaction to the political clout enjoyed by business groups in the old cozy triangles, and partly out of the New Left tumult of the late 1960s and early 1970s, the public lobbies have achieved a clout and permanence in Washington that could not have been imagined in the decade before their emergence. For one, groups devoted to broad common interests tend to fall apart rather quickly. Usually the only way to keep members involved in such organizations (labor unions are a classic example) has been to make membership and participation mandatory.[13]

Yet, not only have these public lobbies survived, they have prospered and multiplied. They have survived because, though masquerading as grassroots organizations, the bulk of their funds have come from foundations, government contracts, and a few wealthy contributors.[14] They have thrived because they have become the linchpins in the new Washington establishment. Their stock in trade is the hyping of hazards, from autos unsafe at any speed to environmental toxins unsafe at any dose. Such hyperbole is the coin of Congress' new Barnumocracy, and the public lobbies are the mint.

A study of interest groups on Capitol Hill asked lobbyists from both the private sector and the public lobbies whether the congressional reforms of the early 1970s, which fractured power in the House of Representatives, had made their jobs harder or easier. Overwhelmingly, business, association, and corporate lobbyists

said the diffusion of power had made their lives much harder.
Public-interest lobbyists, on the other hand, overwhelmingly
praised the reforms for having made their jobs much easier.[15]

Why the difference? It's not hard to see why lobbying on behalf
of business became tougher. When a few powerful chairmen ran the
show, business representatives knew where to go to peddle their
influence. When those few congressional leaders were on board, the
deal was done. Now there are hundreds of lawmakers who consider
themselves "policy entrepreneurs," which is to say, each has his pet
issues and is looking for ways to sell them. Instead of fixing deals
with a committee or two, business lobbyists must now build legislative coalitions. The unpredictable world of policy entrepreneurial-
ism makes building such coalitions almost impossible.

The public lobbies are not as interested in building broad legislative coalitions. When the lobbies do pursue big legislative pack-
ages, such as environmentalists' drive for the new Clean Air Act,
compromise is achieved by leaving the law vague and contradictory, the details to be filled in by regulators under pressure from the
lobbies and legislators. But primarily, the public lobbies' success
lies more in helping Congress' entrepreneurs publicize particular
issues. The lobbies provide the hypes, victims, and hysteria essential for political publicity. Congressional policy entrepreneurs become the clients for those services. Consequently, the diffusion of
power in the House helps the public-interest lobbies because it
creates more and more Representatives who are looking for just the
kind of publicity they can provide.

Nor should we overlook the financial interests involved. Though
most public lobbies can survive on the money they receive from
foundations and a few rich donors, to flourish they need the contributions of a wider public. To get the attention of that public they
manufacture hypes, scares that are legitimized by being played on
the congressional stage. Fundraising letters and annual reports are
full of references to these efforts. The Environmental Defense Fund
(EDF), for example, touts its role in prompting the Senate lead
hearings: "EDF's influential *Legacy of Lead* report increased the
national resolve to combat lead poisoning. Legislation based on

EDF proposals has been introduced in Congress to provide a $1 billion annual trust fund to help control lead hazards."[16]

There are also more direct financial interests involved. Most of the environmental and consumerist laws that have been passed since 1970 have included what are known as citizen-suit provisions. Laws like the Clean Water Act allow individuals or groups to act as "private attorneys general." That is, they may bring lawsuits against violators of the law, even if they have not personally been injured by the violation. Under most citizen-suit provisions the groups have their attorneys' fees paid, even if they lose the suit. Thus, by helping to shape federal environmental laws, environmentalists got their friends in Congress to write in mechanisms that fund the groups' litigation efforts.

Even more money is to be had through citizen suits, though. If a citizen-brought Clean Water Act violation is decided in court, any fines assessed go to the U.S. Treasury. But few cases ever go to trial. Most are settled out of court, with settlement monies (often millions of dollars) donated to environmental or other charitable groups. Businesses are happy to settle out of court because charitable donations are tax-deductible and are (the semblance of) exemplary corporate citizenship. Federal fines are neither. Citizen groups are happy to settle, because it means money for them and their friends rather than for the federal government. The Nader-affiliated Public Interest Research Groups (PIRGs) in various states have been the most aggressive at bringing and settling Clean Water cases, though more mainstream organizations (e.g., the Sierra Club) have settled their share of such cases as well.[17]

Sometimes public lobbies seek aid directly from Congress. Consider the Violence Against Women Act of 1991. Hearings on the bill, as usual, featured victims. In this case the victims were followed by activists, such as Mary Koss, a professor at the University of Arizona, who grossly exaggerated the number of victims of sexual violence. One would think that one in 10, or one in 100 women, so victimized would be enough to elicit concern and spur action. But one in three makes for better slogans, and so statistics were, as is custom, subordinated to sloganeering.

The bill proposed would stiffen penalties for sex crimes by, among other things, making rape punishable as a gender-based "hate crime" under federal civil rights laws. More interestingly, it would dole out hundreds of millions of dollars in grants to states, localities, and groups. The public lobbies that helped Sen. Joseph Biden's staff draft the legislation would get a cut of those grants. The draft bill virtually ensured that only favored groups would be eligible for grants to run "technical assistance centers" — that is, programs that train social workers to deal with cases of domestic violence. To receive funds, groups must demonstrate "a minimum of three-years experience with issues of domestic violence... include on its advisory boards representatives from domestic violence programs who are geographically and culturally diverse; and... demonstrate strong support from domestic violence advocates for their designation as the special-issue resource center."[18]

These kinds of grants provide the public lobbies with a bedrock of funding that, together with large contributions from foundations and wealthy donors, is crucial to groups that would otherwise rely on the vagaries of grass-roots organizing. More importantly, the grants put the lobbies in quasi-governmental positions, in this case training local officials. The lobbies' propaganda efforts are thus not only subsidized by Congress, they are legitimized.

How do we drop the curtain on Capitol Hill's stage shows? To begin with, we might cultivate a habit of disbelief when it comes to congressional hearings, treating them as we would pitches for patent medicines. We might demand that our representatives actually prove their points and defend their positions. We should be particularly suspicious of any hearing that is not clearly tied to legislation. Hearings allow Members to posture and grandstand. Voting — though it can also allow for posing — at least usually requires lawmakers to get serious about an issue. Clearly defined votes produce legislative accountability. The cheap showmanship of the Barnumocracy cannot withstand the scrutiny that real accountability brings.

Making Congress play by the same rules it imposes on everyone else would also help to tame the hype monster. If lawmakers could be prosecuted for misleading Congress—the charge so often hurled at executive branch officials who have confronted the legislature—they might think twice about manufacturing publicity stunts. The House of Representatives might begin by bringing ethics charges against Rep. Tom Lantos for the Nayirah hoax.

How willing would lawmakers be to work closely and deceptively with public-interest lobbyists and plaintiffs' lawyers if lists and details of their contacts with the groups could be demanded through Freedom of Information Act (FOIA) requests? Applying the FOIA to Congress not only might make it easier to burst phony scares, the potential embarrassment for legislators might discourage them from playing along with the hypesters in the first place. Congress keeps putting on its big shows, all the while telling us to pay no attention to that man behind the curtain. We should not only confront the men behind the curtains, we should ask our representatives why they have hung the draperies in the first place.

3

LEGISLATING BACKWARDS

*We create the government that screws you, and then
you're supposed to thank us for protecting you from it.*

—Former Rep. Vin Weber (R-Minn.)

I f Congress spends most of its time trying to evade difficult
choices and participating in overly dramatic but largely fruitless
hearings, then how do the laws get made? Someone else does it, of
course, and that someone is usually a bureaucrat.

A major element of congressional sleight of hand is to write
hopelessly vague and contradictory laws, which delegate broad
legislative authority to the federal bureaucracy. The agencies, then,
have to make the rules and regulations, the legal specifics that step
on people's toes. This process of legislating without actually passing laws allows Congress to avoid accountability for the laws that
are made. But this doesn't mean that lawmakers actually leave the
rulemaking process to the bureaucrats. Legislators want to have
their say, and have given special interests their say as well. To make
sure that their friends in the public lobbies get the regulations they
desire, Congress has devised a number of ways for lobbyists to
intervene in rulemaking, of which the most recent invention is the
so-called "regulation negotiation" or "reg neg."

In the Spring of 1992 the Environmental Protection Agency (EPA) held a reg neg in Washington to work out regulations for coke ovens under the new Clean Air Act Amendments. A meeting room in the Quality Inn Capitol Hill was all set up, with a large, square table for the negotiators from the EPA, public-interest lobbies, business groups, and trade unions. In the back was a refreshment table loaded with glasses, bowls of ice, and six-ounce bottles of Coke, Diet Coke, and mineral water. Several rows of chairs were set up for observers. But there was little to observe. In fact, the room was nearly empty. The idea of a reg-neg is that all the parties interested in a given regulation get together and hash out a deal with the respective federal agency. In exchange for having a hand in shaping the rule, the interests promise not to challenge the regulation in court. But the interests gathered at the Quality Inn were not actually at the table negotiating with one another and the EPA. The government officials had the room to themselves, standing around like brides left at the altar. The interest groups were upstairs in one of the hotel's suites, reserved and paid for by the EPA, working out their own compromise, which they would later present, as a fait accompli, to the EPA.

Professors of administrative law defend these developments, claiming that because all interests are represented the regulations being written can't help but be fair. But they are wrong, for several reasons. To begin with, it is a mistake to think that businesses are always anti-regulation. Many firms thrive on the fact that bureaucratic red tape strangles their rivals. Big companies in particular have an incentive to push for greater regulation: Large corporations have legal departments to navigate the demands of regulators; their upstart competitors most often do not.

No wonder, then, that regulation negotiations usually produce rules much tougher than those made through the normal adversarial regulatory process. The types of businesses that have representatives to lobby at the Quality Inn are those big enough to benefit from costly regulations. Marriott Hotels, for example, eagerly, and successfully, pushed for tough standards during a regulation negotiation under the Americans with Disabilities Act. The hotel chain has been building its lodgings to be handicapped-friendly for more than

10 years. Making compliance with such architectural standards federal law was a boon to the company: It would not have to change a thing, whereas the firm's competitors now would have to spend millions to meet the new rules. The "fair" reg-neg procedure was used by Marriott's lobbyists (who admit they got most of what they wanted in the negotiations) to gain a competitive edge over other firms.[1]

But the biggest problem with the idea that reg-neg is a fair alternative to real legislation is the assumption that democracy can be replaced by special-interest haggling. So comfortable has Congress become in doing the bidding of the new special interests that it now sees no problem with simply handing over to them the task of legislating, as though Congress now recognizes itself as merely the middleman. The legislative process intended to tame the influence of factions has been abandoned. In the Barnumocracy, factions rule.

The scramble to shape and clarify the Clean Air Act Amendments after they had been signed into law in 1990 was played out first in reg negs by the Quality Inn lobbyists. Among the most controversial negotiations was that regarding so-called clean fuels. The clean-fuels provisions held within them the key to a growth industry: the reaping of huge government subsidies for the businesses lucky— or clever—enough to be making the new fuels required by the law. Congress wanted to hand out these subsidies to powerful constituents but ran into trouble because the White House was backing fuels different than their own favorites. Instead, Congress relied on the EPA to accomplish, through regulation, what they had been unable to achieve through legislation. This is not to say that Congress just left it to the agency: When the EPA suggested it might implement the administration position, legislators quickly intervened in the rulemaking process.

The politics of this fight also highlights how little a bill like the Clean Air Act Amendments has to do with, say, clean air. President Bush had made clean fuels a cornerstone of his clean-air proposal, based on the idea that pollution could be reduced by using fuels that produced fewer toxins in exhaust, or caused less smog. President Bush's proposal was meant to be fuel-neutral, that is, to encourage cleaner fuels, whatever they were made from. But some of the details in the President's plan did favor methanol, which can be made from either natural gas or coal. This did not sit well with certain lawmakers, specifically those from key farm states. The reason? At least one "clean fuel"—ethanol—is made from corn. Not uncoincidentally, it is also produced by one of the most powerful lobbies on Capitol Hill, the Archer Daniels Midland Company (ADM).[2]

To favor ethanol, farm-state lawmakers did not have to write "buy ethanol" into the bill. Different fuels produce different types of emissions. Allowing certain emissions and disallowing others can thus determine which fuels are crowned "clean." Ethanol has a high oxygen content, which reduces carbon monoxide in auto exhaust; methanol does not have a high oxygen content, but it is less volatile than ethanol, which evaporates quickly and thus contributes to urban smog. If the bill required high oxygen content in fuel, then ethanol wins. But if there is a limit on the smog-causing vapors that evaporate from gas tanks, ethanol loses. In a crunch between farm and oil and gas constituencies, Congress punted: The bill required that fuels used in the smoggiest cities have a high oxygen content, but allowed the EPA to waive that requirement if it interfered with other efforts at cleaning the air.[3]

The upshot was that the question of which fuels would be required under the Clean Air Act was handed to the EPA. This in turn meant bringing in the Quality Inn lobbyists. By passing the tough political decision off to the EPA the lawmakers avoided angering constituents and evaded any blame. But just because they evaded blame doesn't mean they did not seize credit for helping constituents in their regulatory battles.

By late July 1991, the clean fuels reg neg, organized by the EPA, had ground to a contentious halt. Representatives of smog-prone cities and environmental groups, concerned about ethanol's tendency to evaporate, had joined forces to tip the new regulations in favor of methanol. The Renewable Fuels Association (representing ADM and other ethanol producers) was threatening to walk out on the negotiation. Just then friendly lawmakers stepped in to solve the problem. On July 31, 1991, 27 lawmakers signed a letter to EPA

Administrator William K. Reilly expressing their concern that the regulations proposed by the negotiators were not consistent with their "legislative intent": "The final rule should more clearly reflect the intent of the Congress on this issue," they said.[4]

Signed by farm-state powers from both sides of the aisle—Senate Minority Leader Robert Dole, a Kansas Republican, and Sen. Thomas Daschle, a South Dakota Democrat—the letter was obviously a constituent-driven end-run around the negotiated rulemaking procedure. Just as surely, there was no clear legislative intent: When legislators want to be clear and precise they know how to be so, and they write their intent into the law. When they cannot reach a compromise, or do not want to do so in public, they fudge the matter, as they did on clean fuels. One way to fudge is by writing vague or incomprehensible provisions into the bill. Another way, the method chosen here, is to write specific, but contradictory, provisions. Even though the particulars are inconsistent, partisans can then point to the specific provision that favors them and claim it represents the true legislative intent.

All this was known by the participants of the clean fuels reg neg. But it didn't matter: The letter was initially successful, leading the EPA to circulate tentative ethanol-friendly regulations by the middle of August 1991. Farm-state lawmakers had been unable to get pro-ethanol provisions written unambiguously into the Clean Air Act. But what they were unable to achieve legislatively, they attempted do by pressuring federal bureaucrats. The EPA proposal didn't stick, however, so the controversy dragged on for another year until President Bush bowed to farm state pressure and issued an ethanol waiver in the fall of 1992. With this kind of delegation of power, there are no messy votes to take, just phone calls made quietly to relevant bureaucrats, or, when push comes to shove, a letter or a hearing calling for agency adherence to legislative intent.

This habit of delegating legislative powers is the key to understanding how the federal government has grown so large. Even a casual glance at the U.S. Constitution rules out the idea that the Founding Fathers had in mind a mammoth national government with millions of employees directing the details of the lives of hundreds of millions of citizens. The divisions of power in the

Constitution were designed not only to guard against tyranny. More fundamentally, the separation of powers made governing difficult. It required that government action be taken through an unwieldy and tortuous legislative process. As long as that process was followed, the capabilities of the federal government were constricted. These procedural constraints narrowed the scope of federal power.

Today these pesky procedural constraints have been discarded. The courts bear some share of the blame for the blurring of Constitutional boundaries. But the bulk of the blame rests on the shoulders of Congress: In its efforts to facilitate President Franklin Roosevelt's New Deal, Capitol Hill handed over sweeping legislative powers to the chief executive and his agencies. The division of powers, and the federal inertia that followed it, were purposefully short-circuited.

Congress came to regret this nearly wholesale delegation of its lawmaking authority, as it saw its power shrink in comparison to what came to be known by the late 1960s as the "Imperial Presidency." But Congress has been unwilling to take its lawmaking powers back, especially as incumbents realized that the abdication actually helped them get reelected. If bureaucrats make the laws, after all, they are the ones who get blamed for the costs and inconveniences those laws might cause. Lawmakers avoid that blame by not legislating and, in turn, gain credit by fixing problems the laws and the bureaucracy have caused for their constituents.

The expansion of bureaucracy facilitates this game, which shows no sign of letting up. A slew of agencies and commissions was given birth in the early 1970s. The Environmental Protection Agency, Federal Railroad Administration, National Highway Traffic Safety Administration, National Oceanic and Aeronautic Administration, and Postal Rate Commission were all founded in 1970 alone. Two years later lawmakers set up the Consumer Product Safety Commission, and 1973 witnessed the creation not only of the Occupational Safety and Health Administration (OSHA), but of the Mine Safety and Health Administration as well. The Economic Regulatory Administration was started in 1974, the Nuclear Regulatory Commission in 1975, the Federal Grain Inspection Service in 1976, and the Office of Surface Mining in 1977. Each new agency represented an expansion of federal power, an expansion made possible by Congress' delegation of legislative authority to the agencies.

Some of the agencies were given broad mandates and even broader discretion. So loose were the outlines of the responsibilities of the EPA, for example, that it was able to recreate itself in the late 1970s. Officials at the agency, recognizing that public health concerns were more politically powerful than purely environmental worries, changed the regulatory focus of the EPA from one of protecting the environment to one of protecting human health from environmental hazards. The move was a spectacular success, transforming the agency from a regulatory backwater to a bureaucratic powerhouse with its fingers in nearly every aspect of commercial and private life.[5] Only recently—after any number of EPA-encouraged environmental panics have gone bust and as the public has expressed concern about the environment per se — has the EPA moved back toward its original mandate of protecting the environment.

Some agencies had their mandates spelled out for them far more explicitly. But even in instances in which Congress left its creations with little discretion, lawmakers still officially delegated power for the making of the laws, a ritualized passing of the buck. OSHA is a case in point. The statute that created OSHA laid out in strict detail what regulations the agency might promulgate. Yet, when those regulations were issued, lawmakers expressed shock and outrage at the economic costs OSHA was imposing on businesses. Distinctly absent were any mea culpas.

Congress had required OSHA to take every existing industry guideline on health and safety, and make it a federal regulation. As the legislation was being developed and debated, though, the number of industry guidelines, as well as their specificity, had gone through the roof. Business hoped that, if they could point to a copious list of strict self-imposed regulations, Congress would not feel the need to create new government rules. Instead, Congress responded that, if all those guidelines were already in place, business wouldn't mind having them codified as federal law.

And so OSHA was given the task of compiling business guidelines and making them federal rules. When the agency did just that,
and the rules began to pinch, OSHA took the heat. Rather than
blame Congress, business looked to legislators for relief, and called
on them to rein in the agency's zealous regulations. By expanding
federal powers and promoting onerous regulation, Congress had not
brought itself under criticism, it had cleverly created for itself new
clients for constituent service: businesses who needed relief from
OSHA. Congress came through for its new clients, holding hearings
to pressure the agency to soften the impact of the rules. By late 1978
OSHA did so, announcing it would revoke en masse 928 regulations
that it admitted were not needed.[6]

Sometimes legislation so thoroughly delegates power that it is
hard to see why lawmakers even bother to show up for work. Take
the Worker's Family Protection Act of 1991, sponsored by Sen.
James M. Jeffords, a Vermont Republican. The bill not only delegates to agencies the questions of how and whether to respond to
the "problem," the legislation leaves it up to bureaucrats to decide
whether the problem even exists.

The bill tells the National Institute of Occupational Safety and
Health (NIOSH) to collect information on cases across the country
in which workers have inadvertently exposed their families to toxic
chemicals by wearing contaminated clothes in their homes. The
Institute would be given two years to review the cases and compile
a list of current practices used to keep workers from contaminating
their homes.

While putting together this report, NIOSH would be charged with
creating a Worker's Family Protection Task Force comprised of all
the interested parties (sound familiar?), such as industrial hygiene
experts, business associations, labor representatives, environmentalists, and officials from the various agencies involved in the issue
—including OSHA, the Agency for Toxic Substance Disease Registry (ATSDR), and the EPA. The Task Force was to review the
NIOSH report to find out if any extra information was needed. If
so, the Institute would have up to four years to conduct whatever
studies were needed to fill in the data gaps.

After this six-year process, the buck would pass to the Secretary of Labor who would have responsibility for reviewing the final NIOSH report and deciding what should be done to head off future incidents of home contamination. The Secretary would have the discretion to decide if regulations were needed at all, and, if so, would have three more years to put those rules in place. In essence, the elaborate, decade-long procedure established by the legislation comes down to a mandate to see if there is a problem, then, if need be, do something about it.

The strategy behind this pseudo-legislation is not unappealing. Jeffords' staffers say that, by giving the Secretary of Labor the final say on workers' home safety regulations, they hope to head off a power grab by the EPA. For example, if a worker were to wear tainted clothes home from a site designated for cleanup under the Superfund Law, which is administered by the EPA, that agency would then have the leeway to declare the worker's house itself to be a Superfund site. Given that Superfund has become a black hole of environmental litigation, stopping the EPA from applying the law in any new ways is an eminently sensible goal.

But consider the way this goal is pursued. The problem is that four or five agencies have the discretion to get involved in the issue, and each of them may just do so. That of course would lead to piles of inconsistent regulations and lots of litigation. The problem is that rather than cutting back on the authority of these agencies, Congress opts to make one of the agencies (in this case, the Department of Labor's OSHA) stronger by expanding its discretion. In other words, too much delegated legislative authority is fixed by delegating more legislative authority. It is like treating cirrhosis of the liver with whiskey.

The New Deal and the New Social Regulation

Though the pace accelerated in the seventies, Congress has been delegating legislative authority for a long time. Some of the earliest large-scale delegations of legislative authority were in tariff laws. As early as 1890 Congress gave the President the power to stop the importation of several specified commodities if he found that the exporting countries levied "unreasonable" duties on American products. If the President suspended trade in a good—namely sugar, molasses, coffee, tea, or hides—congressionally mandated duties would thenceforth be applied to the product. The Tariff Act of 1922 went much further, giving the President the power to set duties at whatever level was needed to compensate for cheaper overseas production costs. Neither of these tariff laws was struck down for unconstitutional delegation of power, though both were challenged. It was not until the 1930s, in the throes of Franklin Roosevelt's battles with the Supreme Court, that legislation would be thrown out for impermissible delegation.[7]

Indeed, the New Deal took the practice of congressional delegation of lawmaking powers to new heights and new applications. In 1933 Congress passed the National Industrial Recovery Act, which gave the President almost unlimited authority to regulate the economy by setting out and enforcing codes of competition (or perhaps more accurately, codes of non-competition). The Supreme Court first invalidated a section of the Act, and then tossed out the rest of the law in a second case. In the latter ruling the Court concluded that "the discretion of the President in approving or prescribing codes, and thus enacting laws for the governing of trade and industry throughout the country, is virtually unfettered. We think that the code-making authority thus conferred is an unconstitutional delegation of power."[8]

Alas, the wariness the Justices expressed about giving the President and his agencies legislative powers was short-lived. After Roosevelt's Court-packing scheme, and with the onset of World War II, the Supreme Court was willing to tolerate almost any congressional delegation of authority. One such transfer of lawmaking powers was the Emergency Price Control Act of 1942. Upheld by the Supreme Court in 1944, the Act created an Office of Price Administration headed by a Price Administrator who was given the power to set prices that "in his judgment will be generally fair and equitable and will effectuate the purposes of this Act."[9]

By the 1960s, congressional delegation of authority was so widespread that it was hard to imagine the federal government operating otherwise. "The necessity of broad administrative discretion in the legislative area is recognized," wrote Peter Woll in his 1963 book *American Bureaucracy*. "There is simply no other way to conduct the business of government given its present scope and complexity."[10] Thus, Congress' delegations of legislative power allowed the federal government to grow geometrically. Once the federal government's new scope and complexity came to be assumed a necessity, limitations on congressional delegation of authority could not be imagined.

Woll expressed some discomfort with the expanding power of the executive branch, but concluded that the growth of the bureaucracy was a good thing; the agencies would become a fourth and "equal partner with the President, Congress, and the judiciary," thus strengthening our constitutional democracy. By the end of the decade, however, others were expressing a much less sanguine view of the new power of the presidency and the bureaucracy.

Activists in the New Left movement, so influential in the 1960s, found themselves cut out of the iron triangles of the day. Big Government, born of the New Deal and World War II, had become an establishment of "corporate liberalism" they argued, controlled by big business and the military. Those closed triangles of power put the lie to democracy, they said, because all the important laws and decisions were being made behind closed doors.

One obvious response to the loss of democratic control entailed by a huge federal bureaucracy would be to call for Congress to reclaim its rights and responsibilities as a lawmaking body. But that was not the platform of the New Left, nor of the public lobbies that grew out of the New Left movement. Congress simply does not have the capacity, both because of its size and—more importantly—the restraints inherent in a democratic process, to run a large federal government legislatively. The complaint of the public lobbies was not about the size or scope of government but about who controlled it. The public lobbies did not want to dismantle the federal machinery; they just wanted to get their hands on the levers. Their argument was that the bureaucracy needed to be "democratized" by opening up the regulatory process to citizen action. Agency-made law would be democratically legitimate because representatives of citizens would help shape the regulations.

They may not have succeeded in opening up the bureaucracy, but they certainly succeeded in getting a piece of the action. In the flood of legislation creating new regulatory agencies in the 1970s, the public lobbies were there not only to help write the laws, but also to be sure that they were given a voice in how the real laws—the rules and regulations made by the agencies—were to be written. Citizen groups were given standing under environmental and consumer laws to challenge agencies in court, to sue the government when they thought rules were too lenient or too late in being written. And with citizen-suit provisions, the public lobbies were given standing to act as their own attorneys general, to bring lawsuits directly against businesses they accused of polluting or making dangerous products. And as we saw in Chapter Two, the groups may even return to Congress for help in publicizing their lawsuits.

The underpinning of this new arrangement was the dubious assumption that "citizen groups" are interchangeable with citizens in a democracy. But are they? Does an environmental regulation worked out by an agency in consultation with "interests"—business and environmentalist — necessarily represent the regulation that would have been made if the public had voted on it? Who, after all, made Ralph Nader the "representative" of consumers? At least Members of Congress represent their constituents by virtue of having been elected; public lobbies represent the public only by virtue of saying so.

One of the most powerful critics of this new Washington establishment has been Theodore Lowi, who argues that the United States has entered a "Second Republic," a regime defined by principles of "interest-group liberalism." Citizens are no longer what are represented in Washington; groups or classes of citizens are. This has been made possible by the congressional delegation of lawmaking power to the agencies. As Lowi puts it, "Modern law has become a series of instructions to administrators rather than a series of commands to citizens."[11]

The Consumer Product Safety Commission (CPSC), one of these seventies' creations, demonstrates some of the problems with this approach. Originally it was charged by Congress with eliminating unreasonable risks to consumers caused by faulty or flawed products. Congress did not define what was reasonable and what was not, nor did it set any standards for judging product safety. "All Congress did was to assume that the agencies in their own wisdom would be able to provide such standards,"[12] Lowi has noted.

But the CPSC did not provide standards. Instead the agency decided to rule on a case-by-case basis. In the absence of rules, the CPSC was free to act by fiat. The lack of rules gives the agency more power. In fact, it is unrestrained, except by the need to satisfy the clients—Congress and the public lobbies—who helped give it that power. "The agency began with an almost unlimited mandate from Congress, and it can go on avoiding limits on itself by the simple expedient of not issuing rules of general legislative content," Lowi writes.[13] Given that there are no standards for businesses to adhere to, the particular judgments of the CPSC cannot be justified in any objective legal sense. So it is left to the courts, when reviewing a CPSC ruling, to try to discern or write some rule on which to justify its decision. Courts end up having to write the laws not necessarily out of judicial ambition but because no one else, neither Congress nor the agencies, has been willing to do so.

This institutionalized buck-passing persists, especially with high-profile laws that amount to little more than the legislation of nice sentiments. Such is the case with the Americans with Disabilities Act (ADA). As we saw in Chapter One, the legislators maneuvered their way out of an amendment that would have given small businesses tax credits to offset the costs of complying with the disabilities law. The main argument against the credits was that no one knew how much they would cost. If the law was at all clear on what would be required of businesses, Congress ought to have been able to estimate the costs of compliance. Lawmakers have at their disposal personal staff, committee and subcommittee staff, and a variety of number-crunching research arms from the Congressional Research Service to the General Accounting Office and the Congressional Budget Office. Yet with all those staffers and all their computers, legislators couldn't arrive at a guesstimate for ADA's cost to small business.

Certainly it was not for lack of analytic skill. Congressional researchers can do statistical backflips with the best of them. The problem was twofold. For one thing, lawmakers didn't want to talk too explicitly about the actual costs of the bill, and so they did not go to very great lengths to get the numbers. For another, even if they had, they would have found that the core of the law was too soft; it couldn't support the structure of cost projections. How can you project the cost of the bill's requirements, when the bill doesn't spell out what those requirements are? Under the law, public accommodations (e.g., hotels, restaurants and such) have to be made accessible to the handicapped, but only if the changes are "readily achievable." Asked to define readily achievable, Sen. Ted Kennedy explained that businesses would have to do what was "easily accomplishable and not involving much difficulty or expense." But who is to say what is "easily" accomplished, or what is "much" expense? The businesses affected? One or more federal agencies? Congress, in later hearings? The courts?

The same vagueness afflicts the bill's section on employment. Businesses are required to provide "reasonable accommodations" to workers with disabilities as long as that doesn't cause the firm "undue hardship." Sen. Tom Harkin, the Iowa Democrat who led the fight for the ADA, tried to define what undue hardship meant when asked on the Senate floor if the provision would require, for example, that a company provide a full-time reader for a blind employee. "If it is IBM, perhaps that is not a big deal. But if it is a small pharmacy,... that's a different story," he answered.[14] What kind of guide is that? How are medium-sized businesses to know if they are abiding by the law? Though a law is hopelessly vague, at least the agencies are in a position to make the law by issuing regulations. But in the case of the ADA, even the agencies involved have balked on defining the key terms, explicitly leaving it to the courts to decide.

The final rules for the ADA set out by the Equal Employment Opportunity Commission (EEOC) simply paraphrase the ambiguities in the wording of the law. A few examples are given to illustrate what might be considered a "reasonable accommodation," but even the examples are couched in uncertain terms. Consider this illustration given by the EEOC:

Suppose an individual with a disabling visual impairment that makes it extremely difficult to see in dim lighting applies for a position as a waiter in a nightclub and requests that the club be brightly lit as a reasonable accommodation. Although the individual may be able to perform the job in bright lighting, the nightclub will probably be able to demonstrate that that particular accommodation, though inexpensive, would impose an undue hardship if the bright lighting would destroy the ambience of the nightclub.[15]

The key phrase here is "will probably." Even in the few examples the EEOC gives to shed light on the vague law, it equivocates. In practice, it will be up to a federal bureaucrat to decide what kind of lighting is essential to a particular nightclub's ambience. For businesses prosecuted under this section, their trials are pure Kafka: they can't be told what law they have broken because the law won't be made until the judge hands down his decision.

Similarly, a guide to businesses on the new employment requirements of the ADA, compiled by the National Legal Center, suggested that firms would know in a decade or so what was demanded of them.

Because the Act is so far-reaching, yet vague, ADA litigation will require reviewing courts to look closely at agency interpretations all along the regulatory process. As a result, and with much legal gloss, ten years from now the employment community will have an understandable, or at least predictable, framework with which to work in complying with the ADA. Until then, employers and persons with disabilities alike face an uncertain and somewhat painful learning process.[16]

Painful and expensive. There is no way to estimate the costs to individuals, businesses, and the economy as a whole that come from a decade of legal uncertainty and litigation. It's not just the price of hiring lawyers. Uncertainty and the litigious battles that result sap the energies of those caught in the legal maw; ask anyone who's spent a day contesting a traffic ticket. The litigation over the ADA promises to be some of the most extensive and costly ever. The lawsuits got off to a slow start, mainly because the law only allowed plaintiffs to recover their legal fees, thus giving little incentive to take legal action. But when the Civil Rights Act was passed in 1991, it included a section allowing plaintiffs in ADA cases to receive compensatory and — the lawyers' goldmine — punitive damages. Lawsuits will undoubtedly follow fast and furious.

The vagueness is justified, say lawmakers, in the interests of flexibility. We don't, after all, want rigid and heartless laws that pull up the flowers as well as the weeds. But not all flexibility is created equal. The power of a Governor to issue a pardon is one type of legal flexibility, built to ensure that the application of law doesn't go awry. But that kind of flexibility is only negative: Governors do not have the power to punish those whom the system has declared innocent. The flexibility of federal agencies, by contrast, is often positive. Agencies have been given powers not only of judge, jury, and executioner by Congress, they have been given the power of legislators as well. They get to make the law up as they go along.

Consider the Bureau of Alcohol, Tobacco, and Firearms (BATF). Officially the agency has no power over how alcoholic beverages are advertised, but that doesn't stop the bureau from punishing manufacturers whose advertising offends vocal interest groups. Time and again, the agency approves a product, and then rescinds that approval when interest groups complain about the way the product is marketed. PowerMaster malt liquor is a case in point. The agency first approved and then pulled the brew off the market after activists argued that the high-alcohol product was targeted at the poor. The same thing happened to Crazy Horse malt liquor. After complaints that the malt was being marketed to American Indians, who suffer high rates of alcoholism, the BATF revoked its clearance of the product. Concerns of Native Americans were not the reason given for the change of heart, however. Somehow the BATF became suddenly concerned about small technical issues in the wording on the label.

The quality or morality of these products is not the issue. The point is that the BATF's flip-flops show how wide agency flexibility gives power, not only to bureaucrats, but also to the vocal organized interests that develop issue networks with them. While it's easy to blame the federal agencies, Congress bears the primary responsibility for looking no further than a cute sound bite. In the case of the ADA, for example, Congress could easily have created a "reasonable accommodation" standard that was objective, yet which also took into consideration the limited resources of smaller businesses. It might have said that no businesses would be required to spend more than 1 percent (or some other figure) of its gross receipts on meeting the demands of the act, but such an approach was explicitly rejected. It's not that legislators don't want to run the show. They just don't want to be held responsible when the scenery falls down and the curtains catch fire.

In practicing this back-stage management Congress employs a number of strategies to control agency decisions. Reg negs and confrontational hearings are two. Through the '70s and into the early '80s there was an explosion in what were called "legislative vetoes." In a pure expression of backwards legislating, Congress gave itself the power to veto rules or decisions of federal agencies. One house of Congress could issue a resolution of disapproval and so invalidate an agency action. This inversion of the legislative process was so baldly unconstitutional that it was finally ruled out of bounds by the Supreme Court in *Immigration and Naturalization Service v. Chadha*.[17] That 1983 case sent Congress spinning, leading to congressional proposals for constitutional amendments to override *Chadha* and a slew of new unofficial legislative veto provisions crafted to slip around the Supreme Court's decision. The most common of these new vetoes are informal (though binding, if an agency wants to avoid all-out warfare with Capitol Hill) instructions to consult with congressional committees before making managerial or regulatory changes.

Committee and conference reports provide another main avenue for Members of Congress to tell agencies to do what the lawmakers themselves were unable to. The reports committees issue along with bills cannot be amended on the House or Senate floor as the actual legislation can. For this reason committee reports are a favorite place to stash pork projects or favors to interest groups: items that might not survive if they had to be voted on.

Reports also give Congress a head start on influencing regulatory decisions. By the time legislation comes out of the conference committees that try to reconcile House and Senate versions of a bill, the language is usually so convoluted that only the most diligent lawyers (and ones with a few months to spare at that) could possibly make heads or tails of it. Almost no one, not even the sponsors of the bill, let alone the conferees who voted on it, know everything that is in a given package. The compromise language is put together by staffers, who are notorious for throwing in little changes that their bosses never notice. For those lawmakers who want some sort of clue as to what they are voting on, a conference report is written to outline and paraphrase the legislation. Written by the majority staff, conference reports also give Democrats, who currently hold that majority, a chance to get started putting their "spin" on the bill. The legislation might be vague because a definitive compromise could not be reached. But the conference report can explain that, in principle, the conferees meant for that vague language to be interpreted in a clear and specific way. Not surprisingly, the interpretation given in the conference report is usually that preferred by Democratic staffers.

These reports are one part of a Capitol Hill game called "Making Legislative History." Through this means, Congress seeks to extend its control to the courts as well as to executive agencies. For decades courts, when confronted with obscure or otherwise indecipherable language in a law, would look to the so-called legislative history of the act to figure out how to interpret it. That means judges would read the statements given by key legislators to find out what they were really getting at. Drafts and revisions of the bill would be examined to see how the legislation evolved. All that information would then be used to decide the case. What this means for lawmakers is that they can slip into the so-called legislative history all sorts of things that they cannot, for political reasons, actually put in the bill. Now, after every important piece of legislation is passed, lawmakers insert undelivered speeches in the *Congressional Record* outlining their interpretation of the bill — to make instant legislative history. The bill itself may be incoherent, but every

Member seems to have an explanation of the meaning, and one that he expects the agencies and the courts to follow.

With so many lawmakers pushing their interpretation of a bill through instant, even retroactive legislative histories, even more confusion follows. And so the Democratic leadership has tried to get control of legislative histories, to be in a position to write it all themselves. As with the ADA, the 1991 Civil Rights Act left the most fundamental issues vague and uncertain. Republicans and Democrats could not agree on a compromise to clarify the standards of "business necessity" and "job relatedness" that would give businesses justification for choosing one job applicant over another. Instead, a provision was slipped into the bill saying that the only real legislative history would be an interpretive memo entered into the *Congressional Record* on October 25, 1991. That memo, of course, laid out the interpretation favored by the Democratic leadership. Not that it mattered. Members of Congress from both parties still rushed to toss their own legislative histories into the mix, hoping to push policy their way.

Associate Justice Antonin Scalia has addressed this problem, and has been leading the Supreme Court to reject legislative histories. Inasmuch as the bill is the actual thing lawmakers voted on, it follows that the bill is what should be applied as law. In his opinion in *Blanchard v. Bergeron*, Justice Scalia outlined exactly how legislative histories are used by staff to transform legislation at the last second into the favored policies of lobbyists or the staffers themselves. The particular question Scalia addressed was whether the citation, in a committee report, of a list of court cases, meant that the Supreme Court had to consider the opinions in those cases to be part of the new law being passed. Scalia scoffed at the idea.

> As anyone familiar with modern-day drafting of congressional committee reports is well aware, the references to the cases were inserted, at best by a committee staff member on his or her own initiative, and at worst by a committee staff member at the suggestion of a lawyer-lobbyist; and the purpose of those references was not primarily to inform the Members of Congress what the bill meant ... but rather to influence judicial construction.

The Justice then nails the point home.

> What a heady feeling it must be for a young staffer, to
> know that his or her citation of obscure district court cases
> can transform them into the law of the land, thereafter
> dutifully to be observed by the Supreme Court itself.[18]

Consistent with this logic, the Supreme Court has ruled that, if
agencies are given discretion in a bill, they cannot be challenged
for making regulations that, though consistent with the vagaries of
the bill, run counter to the positions staked out in some legislative
history.[19]

The courts' general shift to the right, together with specific
rulings such as that on legislative vetoes and agency discretion, has
signaled Congress that it can no longer count on the courts the way
it once did. In the '60s and '70s, lawmakers could pass vague and
incoherent statutes knowing that the courts would be more than
happy to write the laws themselves, and that the results would jibe
with an aggressively liberal policy. No longer. According to Philip
Harter, the lawyer who drafted the reg neg law that now governs
the making of many regulations, Congress became interested in reg
neg in large part as a way to keep regulatory decision-making out
of the hands of unfriendly judges.

Now, it might be easy to conclude from Congress' actions on the
regulation front that the institution is simply incapable of clarity.
But when it comes to pork, Congress somehow finds the strength
of specificity. Legislators don't want to avoid responsibility for
pork; in fact, they want their names pasted all over the projects.
When a new traffic interchange or strip of road is at stake, watch
how easy it is for Members to get clear and specific. The detail can
quickly become ridiculous, such as this item in the Intermodal
Surface Transportation Efficiency Act of 1991 (also known as the
highway bill):

> (x) CHAMBERSBURG, PENNSYLVANIA. — Not later
> than 30 days after the date of the enactment of this Act, in
> Chambersburg, Pennsylvania, at both the intersection of
> Lincoln Way and Sixth Street and the intersection of
> Lincoln Way and Coldbrook Avenue, the Pennsylvania

Department of Transportation shall include an exclusive pedestrian phase in the existing lighting sequence between the hours of 8:00 and 8:30 a.m. and between the hours of 2:45 and 3:45 p.m. on weekdays.[20]

It is hard to see what business it is of the federal government to be directing the crosswalk signals on Lincoln Way, but at least there won't be a decade of expensive and contentious litigation trying to figure out what Congress meant.

The Enforcers on the Hill

With vague delegations of authority, the regulatory fights never end. And the longer they go on, the fewer niceties govern the fisticuffs. One of the most troubling developments in Washington over the last decade has been the criminalization of policy disputes. The punishment lawmakers hand down for bureaucrats and administrators who cross them goes far beyond the humiliation of a dressing down in nationally televised hearings (though that is always a good start). The Ethics in Government Act, with its strict conflict-of-interest provisions and the menacing presence of that Frankenstein monster, the independent counsel, has become the prime weapon for the enforcers on Capitol Hill. Administration officials who buck Congress increasingly find themselves accused of some conflict of interest, or better yet, the *appearance* of a conflict of interest.

Here's how the game works. A powerful Member of Congress is displeased with the way an agency is using the power that has been delegated to it; specifically, the Member is unhappy with a particular official who is responsible for regulations that he doesn't like. So the lawmaker has his committee staff issue subpoenas for any and all agency documents they can get their hands on. Staff attorneys then pore through the files to find any indiscretion by the agency official or his subordinates. The mere appearance of an impropriety will do, of course. The staff often gets help in such fishing expeditions from bureaucrats in the agency who don't like their boss' policies. The official is then called before a congressional hearing where he is accused of any number and manner of crimes and is challenged to defend himself. If the official is unrepentant, his sworn testimony is then painstakingly scrutinized for any misstep or misstatement that can be construed as misleading or lying to Congress. As with the mere appearance of a conflict of interest, an omission that merely seems to mislead Congress is enough for accusations of perjury. If the official is particularly obstinate and has still not backed down, an independent counsel is dispatched, thus burying the offending administrator in a legal catacomb that will take years and millions of dollars to escape.

Theodore Olson ran afoul of the powers on the Hill. As part of the struggle between Reaganites and environmentalists in the early 1980s, Congress was investigating EPA Administrator Anne Gorsuch-Burford. Reps. John Dingell, the Michigan Democrat, and Elliott Levitas, a Georgia Democrat, both demanded that the EPA hand over its most sensitive Superfund enforcement files. The administration refused, with Olson, the head of the Justice Department's Office of Legal Counsel, making the argument for withholding the documents as an executive privilege. After that fight was over, lawmakers exacted their revenge. Olson was called to testify before New Jersey Democrat Rep. Peter Rodino's subcommittee on a Justice Department authorization bill, where Olson was grilled about the withholding of the Superfund documents. Two years later, his statements at that hearing were the centerpiece of a 3,129-page report written by congressional staff about the document fight. Rodino called for an independent counsel to investigate Olson's statements and actions, as well as those of two other Justice officials. Under congressional pressure, Attorney General Edwin Meese appointed an independent counsel to investigate Olson, though he refused to target the other two officials. Olson was locked into years of litigation and over a million dollars in legal fees, even though the prosecutor admitted that she thought Olson was most likely innocent. (The investigation was eventually closed without charges.)

Given experiences like Olson's, other administration officials bow to Congress even when they have done no wrong. Until he was driven out of the job in January 1992, Allan Hubbard was Executive Director of the Council on Competitiveness chaired by Vice President Dan Quayle. At the height of his travails, Hubbard and the Council were being investigated by six congressional committees led by six different Democrat lawmakers: Reps. Henry Waxman, John Dingell, John Conyers, and Ted Weiss, as well as Sens. John Glenn and Ted Kennedy. Hubbard's crime? According to legislators, he suffered from conflicts of interest. In reality Hubbard found himself under fire for "ethical violations" simply because the Council was cutting in on what the lawmaker's considered their turf.

The Council on Competitiveness was created in 1989 by President George Bush. Its mission was to review proposed regulations in order to stop or revise rules that would unnecessarily hurt American business. That meant, of course, throwing a wrench in the machine that, until then, had ensured that only Members of Congress, public-interest lobbies, and their bureaucratic friends had any say in the regulations made by federal agencies. Concentrating on regulations being proposed by the EPA, the Council was instrumental in stopping that agency from issuing rules requiring recycling at municipal waste incinerators and inhibiting the incineration of car batteries. The Council also pushed to grant old power plants a reprieve from Clean Air Act regulations if they were in the process of being refitted with new equipment.

By the summer of 1991, the Council's work had provoked indignant shrieks all over Capitol Hill. "There's no legislative authority for what they're doing," complained Rep. George Miller, Chairman of the House Interior Committee, "It's a serious breach of the separation of powers." Rep. Gerry Sikorski called it "treasonous." "Too much of our hard work is being ignored or reversed," he said. And Rep. Waxman accused Hubbard and his staff of being a "polluter star chamber."[21]

These were warning shots across the bow. When the Council ignored them and persisted in reviewing Clean Air Act and other environmental rule-making, the hit men on the Hill brought in the heavy artillery: ethics. First came a complaint by Waxman and others that the Council was interfering in the regulatory process. Then the suggestion from public-interest lobbies, such as the Ralph Nader groups OMB Watch and Public Citizen, that the regulatory process was being "subverted" in secret on behalf of business interests. Dingell weighed in with a demand that all correspondence between the EPA and the Competitiveness Council be surrendered to his investigators, so the documents could be searched for hints of wrongdoing. Dingell's fishing expedition was rejected, on the grounds that the Competitiveness Council was a White House operation and thus enjoyed the protection of executive privilege.

Now Congress was out for blood.

Waxman was the trigger man. "Regulatory Advisor Has Stake in Chemical Firm" cried the Waxman-inspired headline in the *Washington Post*. Hubbard not only had made regulatory decisions that benefited him financially, a slew of articles implied, he had done so with the knowledge of the Vice President. "Quayle was wrong— legally and ethically—to give his chief deputy at the Council, Allan B. Hubbard, who owns a chemical company, a blanket waiver from our conflict-of-interest laws," asserted Waxman. "This waiver allows Hubbard to participate in clean-air regulatory decisions that directly affect his financial interest. . . . Hubbard has acted inappropriately—and probably illegally—in making regulatory decisions that affect his financial holdings."[22]

Ultimately Hubbard resigned as Director of the Council on Competitiveness and took a lower-visibility job on Vice President Quayle's staff. Hubbard stepped down not because he had done anything wrong, but because the congressional assassins had announced that he was in for the kind of senseless criminal prosecution that destroys the lives of administration officials foolish enough to take on Capitol Hill. Hubbard did indeed own stock in a chemical company—a specialty firm that makes car polishes—but the firm was not affected by any of the regulations with which Hubbard was involved. The most damning conflict the congressional inquisitors could trump up was that five years or more into the future the company might conceivably come under some Clean Air Act regulations. In other words, it wasn't even the amorphous charge of an "appearance" of a conflict of interest (that magic crime proved by the charge itself), but rather with the *appearance* of a *potential* conflict of interest many years in the *future*. This is akin to being arrested for "sort-of looking like the type of person who might someday be tempted to shoplift." There is no defending against such ridiculous charges, especially when the calumniators have at their disposal special prosecutors and are unfettered by libel law or due process. To anyone who knows how Congress works, Hubbard was wise to give up and go.

In her excellent book on the new politics of ethics enforcement in Washington, *Scandal*, author Suzanne Garment suggests that the "Prosecutors on the Hill" attack administration officials largely because they can. The victims of their assaults don't have the kinds of rights before congressional inquisitions that they would in a real court, and lawmakers have so many staff aides that they can go through the minutiae of their targets' lives. But there is something else going on in addition to the development of a culture of scandal. Victims of congressional lynching are not random; they are almost all officials who have resisted the Hill's imperial power.

The struggle between Congress and the White House has become one long gangland war. Like Mafia dons vying for control of a town's criminal enterprises, Members of Congress dispatch political hit men to rub out administrators who move in on their turf. Mafia justice is ruthless and violent because there is no legal process for mobsters to work out their differences. When a regular business-man breaks a contract, he gets sued and the courts make him pay up. But criminals can't turn to the law to enforce their contracts— "Your Honor, the defendant did not deliver the shipment of heroin that my client had paid him for, in clear breach of contract"—and so must enforce deals themselves, usually with the barrel of a gun. In a lawless society, deals are enforced brutally, and assassination is the favored method of dispute resolution.

In its own way, Capitol Hill has become as lawless as organized crime. The lawless Congress avoids passing decipherable laws, choosing instead to delegate powers to the federal bureaucracy. That delegation leaves little legal structure for legislators and the exec-utive to work out their policy differences. The Constitution provides a legal process for the making of law, a process that allows the separate branches to fight over policy without killing one another. If Congress passes a bill the President doesn't like, he can veto it. And if lawmakers can muster the votes, they can override his veto, and he has to live with it. The process makes clear who wins and who loses, and the issue is resolved. Either the bill becomes law or it doesn't. But now, law is largely made, not through the normal legislative process, but through the rulemaking process of the regulatory agencies. And, unlike the lawmaking process, which has a clear end point, regulatory battles, like that over ethanol, go on and on. And even when agency rules have been promulgated they can be changed. In the struggle between Congress and the President to control the crucial making of regulation there is no legal process, and so Congress has turned to character assassination as a means of getting what it wants.

It is through these policy-inspired prosecutions that Congress enforces its will in the lawless environment it has created. Members do not need to pass comprehensible laws to get their way. When reg negs are not suitable, the bureaucrats who make the laws can be bullied, and any administration official who tries to intervene can be eliminated with a charge of lapsed ethics. The result is that Congress manages to run the Washington establishment while avoiding any accountability for it.

Perhaps the best way to begin restoring respect for constitutional divisions of power is to take away the ethics cudgel from the prosecutors on the Hill. And the best way is to allow the independent counsel provisions of the Ethics in Government Act, which expire in 1992, to remain dead. If Congress insists on resurrecting the independent counsel monster, then the law should apply to Congress exactly the way it applies to other branches. The corrosive way in which ethics accusations are used on Capitol Hill illustrates why Congress should never be exempt from the laws it passes. Lawmakers can distort and corrupt the law in any way they please, because they know that the monster cannot be turned against them. If the White House subpoenaed all of the correspondence and notes of meetings between Rep. Waxman's staff and public-interest groups or between Rep. Dingell and industry lobbyists and then launched an investigation into every appearance of a potential future conflict of interest among the legislators or their staffs, Members would doubtless think twice about using those destructive tactics again.

If Congress is denied its monopoly on ethics persecution, the President will be in a position to assume accountability for the regulations that he signs. Philip Harter, the administrative law professor who devised the regulation-negotiation procedure now being used to haggle out EPA rules, disputes the charge that reg neg gives lawmaking power to special interests and leaves no room for accountability to the voters. The President, Harter points out, still has to sign his name on the line before any regulation becomes official. The President can choose not to create a rule, and can defend his choice if that is what the voters want. That's fine in theory. In practice, however, it doesn't work, because Congress assassinates any administration official who encourages the President to ignore negotiated regulatory proposals.

Once free of the fear that his officials will be ambushed by the Hill mob, the President should deny Congress any say in the administration of the laws it has passed, either in the making or implementation of regulations. The President would have the Supreme Court on his side. In its ruling on the Gramm-Rudman-Hollings Deficit Reduction Act, the Court said the Constitution "does not contemplate an active role for Congress in the supervision of officers charged with the execution of the laws it enacts." The Court further concluded that "once Congress makes its choice in enacting legislation, its participation ends. Congress can thereafter control the execution of its enactment only indirectly—by passing new legislation."[23]

The result would not be a continuation of the partisan gridlock that has paralyzed Washington, but, instead, its elimination. A return to legislative means entails a process by which gridlock is avoided; avoided because there are clear winners and losers. By contrast, in today's endless regulatory struggles, factions are always in a stand-off. Policy battles are never resolved. And eventually public debate is poisoned. The return to legislation would defuse that bitterness, a vitriol that is mistakenly blamed on "divided government," that is, the control of Congress by one party and the presidency by another. The problem is not that Congress and the White House disagree on policy, but that there is currently no rule-governed way for the two to fight out their differences.

The argument here is not the short-sighted one that the President should run the show; indeed, some conservatives wrongly place all their hopes with the executive merely because the White House has tended in recent years to be in Republican hands, whereas Congress has been dominated by the Democrats for four decades. To say that the President should have control over the discretionary actions of the federal agencies is not an argument for increased Presidential power, quite the opposite. Congress is jealous of its prerogatives and has gone to great lengths to retain control of the legislative power it ostensibly delegates to the agencies. If lawmakers knew that by delegating their authority they were truly giving it up, they would be far less likely to hand over their legislative responsibilities. The power of the executive and his agencies would be reined in then, and legislative decisions would be made on Capitol Hill where there would be some hope of democratic accountability.

Faced with the impossible task of legislating all the details that now fill the Federal Register, that compilation of agency decision-making that now takes up 67,000 pages each year, lawmakers would have to reassess the shape and responsibilities of the federal government. To begin with, even with more staff, legislators simply could not keep up with the demands of the leviathan. Just as significant, big government would no longer work to the lawmakers' electoral advantage. Instead of being able to blame bureaucrats for injurious laws and grab credit for applying Band-Aids, lawmakers would get voters' disapprobation. This is not only the best way to reduce the size of the federal government, it is the only way.

Congress should legislate, and nothing more. That is its constitutional role, and it is only by abdicating their lawmaking responsibilities that lawmakers gave birth to the giant administrative state in Washington. If Congress cannot get its way through non-legislative activities, such as bullying hearings and investigations or pressure on bureaucrats — the "micro-management" that conservatives have so long complained of — it will find itself forced to return to its proper role. Demanding that Congress return to its legislative role is not a call for a weakened Congress or an "Imperial" President. If anything, Congress has more power when it exercises its legislative rights directly and unambiguously. But that power entails responsibility. Unambiguous legislative action can be understood by voters, who are then in a position to hold their representatives accountable. A Congress that was democratically accountable would no longer be a Congress in need of reform.

4
STAFF INFECTION

*People asked me how I felt about being elected to
Congress, and I told them I never thought I'd give up that
much power voluntarily.*

> —Rep. Norman Dicks (D-Wash.), on his elec-
> tion to Congress after spending eight years as
> an aide to Sen. Warren Magnuson (D-Wash.)

Neil Sigmon is one of the most powerful people in Congress.
But Sigmon is neither a Senator nor a Representative. He is a
member of the congressional staff, who, from his perch on the
House Appropriations Interior Subcommittee, exercises de facto
control over a sizable corner of the federal government. For, like
aristocrats of old, today's lawmakers think it beneath them to handle
money, even the taxpayers' money, themselves. Instead, the purse-
strings are held by their legislative lackeys, such as Sigmon. With
the purse-strings comes power.

Sigmon's job is to write the final version of the Interior
Department's appropriation, fleshing out in legislative language the
broad agreements made by the lawmakers. This gives Sigmon great
discretion in how the taxpayers' money is spent: Dropping or adding
a few words can move tens of thousands of dollars into or out of a
government program. No surprise, then, that Sigmon sometimes

pursues his own policy preferences, or even acts to punish those who have displeased him.

Gerry Tays is one bureaucrat unlucky enough to have displeased Sigmon. Tays used to write the "Notes from the Hill" column in the National Park Service magazine, *The Courier*. One day Tays inserted a little jab against Congress into his column. "Having assured themselves a significant pay increase while retaining many of the 'perks' attendant to being a Member of Congress," he wrote, "they made the nation safe again by recessing for the Christmas holidays in late December."

Harmless, you might think, even trite. Yet Sigmon didn't think so. He felt his bosses had been slighted and launched a personal crusade against Tays. According to the *Washington Post*, Sigmon dressed down no less than four Park Service officials, including Deputy Director Herbert S. Cables, Jr., spokesman George Berklacy, *Courier* Editor Mary Maruca, and Tays himself. All of them grovelled, apologizing to Sigmon for that most unpardonable of sins, criticizing Congress. To appease Sigmon's wrath, Tays was sacked from his job at the paper and reassigned to a position where he wouldn't get into trouble. The Park Service assumed this would be the end of the matter.

But even all this kowtowing was not enough to assuage Sigmon's sense of outrage. When he got his hands on the next year's appropriations bill, he slashed $75,000 from the budget of the Park Service's Public Affairs Office—the precise amount used by that office to publish the *Courier*. Sigmon's congressional bosses never even noticed his petty act of revenge, and the Park Service survived: Ultimately they found funds elsewhere to continue the publication. Still, Sigmon had sent his message. As an unnamed staffer told the *Post*, "From time to time, signals are sent to the agencies when they've been bad."[1] You can bet that the *Courier* will have no more criticisms, however trivial, of Congress.

Sigmon's vendetta may have been particularly mean-spirited, but it is by no means unique. Senators and Representatives have little time, and even less inclination, to peruse the thousands of bills that are produced each session. In 1991 there were 4,702 bills introduced in the House of which 248 were enacted. Of the 2,136 bills introduced in the Senate that year, 182 were approved.[2] With so much activity, Members are forced to rely on people such as Sigmon, whom they trust to represent their best political interests. In exchange, committee staffers become what congressional scholar Michael Malbin calls "unelected representatives," making decisions routinely affecting hundreds of millions of dollars.

Such power is a heady intoxicant, and it is what attracts thousands of young college graduates to Capitol Hill. While the pay may not match that of their friends on Wall Street their power greatly surpasses it. Indeed, the ambition of Hill staffers can be far more insidious than greed in a businessman. John Jackley, a former congressional staffer and author of *Hill Rat*, tells of a conversation with a staff aide unimpressed by the tale of an investment banker who had bet one-million dollars on a single hand of the game Liar's Poker: "I can do ten mil with report language and not even have to ask the chairman," he said. "Who cares about keeping the money? ... It's a lot more fun to shove a hundred mil up someone's a -- and then knock off for the rest of the day for a cold one."[3] For many young congressional staffers, government is not something one does *for* the people, but rather what one does *to* the people.

Lawmakers tolerate such arrogance by their minions for a variety of reasons. For one thing, many are arrogant themselves, and their staffs' actions and attitude seem innocuous by contrast. Even more important, many lawmakers have become creatures of their staffs. When legislators ask questions at hearings, more often than not, their every remark has been scripted in advance by staff aides. What about follow-ups? Look for a staffer to lean over and whisper it into the Member's ear. Most legislation gets its start at the desks of staffers. Even when lawmakers give their aides broad outlines, the staff fills in the text. And when it comes time for that text to be voted on, few lawmakers will have read it, though again their aides will be there to tell them whether they ought to vote yes or no. It is not uncommon to see legislators rushing in for a roll call, looking for a staffer to flash a thumbs-up or-down so they will know how to vote.

The reason most often given for the growth and influence of staff is that Congress is just trying to match the executive branch, datum for datum. Once upon a time, for instance, Congress relied almost completely on the Department of Defense for estimates of military costs, and the Office of Management and Budget for estimates on economic growth. After Watergate, Congress moved to seize power back from what was characterized as an imperial presidency, and one of the key sources of presidential power Congress attacked was the executive's virtual monopoly on detailed information about government programs.

Congress might have cut back on the President's informational and bureaucratic resources. They chose instead to compete by erecting a parallel congressional bureaucracy. There were only 2,030 members of the House and Senate staff in 1947, a number that grew to 3,556 within 10 years. By 1972 there were 7,706 staffers, and in the short space of four years that number leapt to 10,190. The crowd of Capitol Hill assistants stabilized by the late 1970s, and in 1989 the total number of staff aides was at 11,406.[4] Much of this increase was in committee staff. In 1965 the House had 571 aides working on committees. By 1985 that number had reached 2,009. On the Senate side the number increased from 509 to 1,080.[5]

Many of these new staffers were deployed in Members' offices, with many going to district offices to drum up constituent service work as we will see when we look at the power of incumbency (Chapter Eight). But much of the staff went to the burgeoning committees, creating a shadow bureaucracy, one that helps explain why cutting spending is so hard in Washington: For every corner of every federal program, there is not only a gaggle of bureaucrats desperate to protect and expand their turf, there are one or more congressional staffers who also have a stake in the program's existence. The bigger a program a staff aide oversees, the more power and importance he has. No aide, then, wants to allow, let alone propose, cutting spending in a program under his control. Lawmakers, at least, have their fingers in many pies, and thus are not necessarily threatened personally by the reduction or eradication of a program they are involved with. For many staffers, though, the particular program they oversee is their whole political existence, leading them to protect it viscerally.

To match the analytical resources of the executive branch, Congress also devoted staff to new analytical bodies of its own. These bodies, and the staff that comprise them, have grown tremendously in power. The most dramatic example is the Congressional Budget Office (CBO), created in 1974. At first the CBO was primarily an informational body, generating economic forecasts independent of the executive branch's Council of Economic Advisers and the Office of Management and Budget (OMB). In 1985, however, the Gramm-Rudman-Hollings Deficit Reduction Act put the CBO on a level with the OMB by requiring it to join the OMB in providing the estimates used to pick the points at which automatic spending cuts would set in. Yet another congressional agency, the General Accounting Office (GAO), would have the final say. This gave the congressional staffers at the CBO and GAO unprecedented power over where, and how much, federal money would be spent. Though the Supreme Court eventually disallowed the CBO and GAO roles in setting spending cuts, public competition between the CBO and the executive branch's OMB continues. The agencies' estimates of the federal budget deficit have differed by as much as $50 billion in one year. Wall Street reacts to predictions by both groups, giving the number-crunchers even more influence. And the taxpayer foots the bill for everything.

Although they don't have as high a profile as, say, their colleagues on the CBO, committee staffers also exert tremendous control over the day-to-day decisions of the government. Originally committee staffers were meant to be the bipartisan bureaucrats, assisting busy Members in the details of researching issues, writing bills, scheduling hearings and meetings, and negotiating the finer points of legislative disputes. As their numbers multiplied, staff involved themselves more and more with the details of every federal program, staking out their policy turf. Not content to oversee the status quo, staffers have become entrepreneurial, always searching for new issues to engage the interests, whether political, electoral, or legislative, of their congressional bosses. The staff aides given the most power are those whom lawmakers can trust to pursue their interests for them. Staffers have become the entrepreneurs behind the entrepreneurs, and as such have earned the right to be the only ones who actually read the legislation that lawmakers regularly vote on.

Indeed, if Members themselves had to draft legislation, it would likely be less complicated and obtuse than it is today, for the simple reason that Members have neither the time nor the patience to put together thousand-page bills. Staffers, on the other hand, have both. Legislation consequently becomes a creature of staff, with twists and turns that only they understand and details that only they know how to exploit.

Members also rely on the committee staff to keep a bill moving forward. If a would-be law fails to pass during its first session, as most do, it is largely up to staff to keep the measure on the agenda, by scheduling meetings and hearings about the bill, gauging support and opposition, and working out compromises and forming coalitions.

So powerful are committee staffs that Senators have personal aides on each committee on which they serve. These operatives are called "S. Res. 60" aides, after the 1975 bill which created them. The arrangement is often criticized because it politicizes the committees with a new, partisan layer between committee staff and the Members. But the need for committee aides responsible directly to Senators is a result of the legislators' recognition that they have handed perhaps too much power to staffs. To get control of those staffs they—what else?—add another layer of staff, this time a layer more responsible to individual lawmakers. But the extra layer only reinforces the tendency of delegating responsibility to aides. With each Senator having his own man on the committee staff, those staffers then conduct the debates and work out the compromises that Senators, once upon a time, would have fought out themselves. The result is, of course, even more power for the unelected and invisible staff.

The 1987 Highway Bill is a typical result of this process, too long for individual consumption or comprehension. The hot political aspects of the $88 billion bill were easily reduced to evening news sound bites. But when the bill reached a conference committee there were hundreds of points of contention. Of these, staffers recommended that Members deal directly with 18 major ones. Sixty smaller issues were highlighted for consideration by Members with a particular interest. That meant there were two to three hundred points to be negotiated by staff alone.[6]

Members of Congress have put up with this explosion of staff not only to compete with the executive branch but also because it helped break apart the seniority system that put power in the hands of a few lawmakers. The old system was not without its advantages; congressional policies were more unified and coherent, and the White House could negotiate with Capitol Hill more easily, having to deal with only a limited number of people. The drawback was that congressional decisions were made in smoke-filled rooms by gerontocrats and their iron-triangle buddies. Younger lawmakers played along, rubber-stamping the decisions of the elder powers, hoping that they would be around long enough to someday assume the positions of power themselves.

The reforms of the 1970s demolished that system. Power was wrested from the entrenched and conservative committee structures and spread around to individual Members. Individual Members consequently took on more staff. In the new system, knowledge, not longevity, was at the core of power. The more staff a Member had at his disposal, the more power he could wrest from the old congressional establishment and the executive branch. Thus the constant addition of ever more staff, to the point where it has outstripped even the explosion of congressional office space, leading to sardine-like conditions in most Hill offices.

These newly expanded staffs have in turn facilitated the diffusion of power in Congress. Almost every Member, for example, now has an aide responsible for foreign affairs. Thus, lawmakers don't have to rely on the Foreign Affairs Committee. Indeed, the growth of staff has so helped to fragment power in Congress that there are over 100 different committees and subcommittees claiming jurisdiction over the Department of Defense alone. At least 74 have some say in drug abuse policy. More than 110 committees and subcommittees have some jurisdiction over the Department of Housing and Urban Development (HUD). Those committees are full of staffers pushing for projects their bosses favor. True oversight gets lost in the shuffle. How else can we explain the fact that Congress failed to expose the HUD scandal — in which sweetheart deals were packaged for friends of the agency's officials—until after the fact, even though HUD was receiving 2,425 telephone calls a month from Members of Congress and their staffs.

The growth of staff has been expensive in budgetary terms as well. As former Sen. William Proxmire, the Wisconsin Democrat, pointed out in awarding his famous "Golden Fleece" to Congress, "Added staff is... used to justify new buildings, more restaurants, added parking spaces, and greater support personnel." The legislative branch budget has soared by more than 3000 percent since 1946 and is now well over $2 billion.[7]

With all this staff, and all these resources, it might seem that Congress has no excuse for not doing its job well. In fact, the expansion of staff has had an inverse effect on efficiency. As Members and senior staffers pursue their interests, basic oversight tasks are often left to junior staffers, sometimes high school or college interns. Take a February 4, 1992, letter to the Defense Department. President Bush had just announced a moratorium on all new regulations pending a review of existing rules to see if they should be revised or revoked. Rep. John Conyers, head of the Committee on Government Operations, did not want the administration to think it could start playing around with regulations without hearing from Congress. The Michigan Democrat thus sent vaguely threatening letters to the head of every department and agency demanding the names and titles of any employees who were to be a part of the President's regulatory review.

The letter arriving at the Department of Defense, however, was addressed, not to Defense Secretary Dick Cheney, but to "The Honorable John G. Tower, Secretary of Defense." Although former Sen. Tower had been nominated for that position at the beginning of the Bush administration, after a nasty battle he was not confirmed. More to the point, Tower had been killed in 1991 in a plane crash. A Conyers spokesman says it was a simple mistake: The intern drawing up the letters got the wrong mailing list (which means that several other letters were misaddressed as well). What makes it more telling is that these letters were intended to ensure that only Congress control regulatory law. The rulers on the Hill who want to micromanage the federal government can't even get the right name for the Secretary of Defense.

In fact, as committee staff has grown in influence, they have imitated their bosses in looking to turn the hard work over to others. Often this means using statistics that have conveniently been provided by advocates of one policy or another. Sometimes it means letting special interests write the first draft of a piece of legislation. The more staffers there are, the more legislation they end up proposing, to justify their existence if nothing else. But this means they never get ahead of the work curve. Always understaffed, then, aides are all too often beholden to lobbyists of diverse stripes for help in putting bills together. In addition, because staffers are far more accessible than Members, the more staffers there are, the more access special interests can get (especially if the lobbyists are, as is usually the case, themselves ex-staffers). As Mark Bisnow, once an aide to Sen. Robert Dole, has pointed out, "The presence of specialized aides on each representative's staff has multiplied contact points for peddlers of influence... the thousands of lobbyists in Washington, many former staffers, would have little to do if they depended on personal audiences with Congressmen."[8]

Indeed, lobbyists and special-interest representatives sometimes court staffers more assiduously than they do Members. Washington restaurants do a booming business on all the lunches being bought for aides who have a direct say on legislation. Special interests and corporate lobbies fly congressional staffers around the globe on exotic "fact finding" missions. To be sure, these trips usually include a series of meetings and tours of relevant areas. But it's remarkable how often they coincide with, say, an NCAA basketball tournament. During one such tournament in New Orleans, a senior staff assistant on Illinois Democratic Rep. Dan Rostenkowski's Ways and Means Committee, James Healey, found himself brunching at Brennan's with representatives of Freeport-McMoran Inc. Healey was asked what they talked about. "It was an extremely general conversation," he answered. "What else would you talk about over brunch when you're having a Bloody Mary and going to a [Georgetown] basketball game from there?" Fair enough. Then again, Healey was also at the time working on legislation that meant millions of dollars for his hosts.[9]

Until recently most staffers faced even fewer limits than their bosses on accepting gifts and honoraria from interest groups. Although most staffers like to keep a low profile, that doesn't mean they don't jump at the chance to get on the lucrative lecture circuit. There are groups, such as Washington Campus, that regularly book speaking engagements for key aides.

William Pitts is a good example. An aide to House Minority Leader Robert Michel, he was profiled in 1989 by *The Wall Street Journal*. In 1988, the aide to the Illinois Republican had accepted $17,000 in honoraria. Just prior to the *Journal* interview he swore off accepting any more. But the list of corporate contributors to Pitts was nonetheless interesting, including $2,000 from H. Ross Perot's oil company, H.R. Petroleum, and another $2,000 from Perot himself.[10] If honoraria are ethically dubious for Members of Congress, they should be all the more so for staffers, who, after all, are the only ones who actually know what is in many of those bills that Members pass without ever having read them.

But free trips, lunches, and speaking fees are not the only ways staffers cash in. Although they may not make much money while on the Hill, the pay is sweet when they leave to "go downtown," or join a Washington lobbying firm. Even better, staffers planning to leave the Hill can create jobs for themselves by playing with the legislation they write, making it so complex that only they, for a consulting fee, can unravel it. This indeed is how Section 89 of the 925-page Tax Reform Act of 1986 was given birth. A 30-year-old Capitol Hill lawyer named Kent Mason wrote the section under the pretense that corporate fringe benefits were being unfairly distributed to company executives. The provision imposed tax penalties on companies that didn't include low-paid and part-time employees in their health and pension plans. The measure was bound in so much red tape that it virtually promised full-time employment for those who could advise businesses on how to collect, analyze, and present the data needed to comply with the law. Nor was all that effort a one-time expense. The data had to be provided every year.

One estimate concluded that American businesses would have to assign 2,000 full-time workers per year to comply.

So huge and complex was the Tax Reform Bill that no one even noticed Section 89. The chairman of the Small Business Committee, Rep. John LaFalce, a New York Democrat, organized a hearing only after it had become law and several small business owners complained they had to spend $24,000 to $60,000 in consulting fees just to figure out what Section 89 meant. Mason, who three months before the law was to take effect joined the Washington law firm Caplin and Drysdale, was eager to direct some of those fees his way. Had the Section 89 scam not been exposed, and the provision not repealed, Mason would have made a small fortune counselling businesses on how to comply with the law he had devised.[11]

The Mayor of HUD

The greatest cost to the political system, however, is not staffers getting rich, it's the way increasing staff power perverts the legislative process and intrudes into the daily operations of executive agencies. One aide notorious for wielding his power to control the tiniest details of the executive branch is Kevin Kelly, the top staffer on the Senate Appropriations Subcommittee which approves spending for the Department of Housing and Urban Development (HUD). Answerable to Maryland Democratic Sen. Barbara Mikulski, Kelly is effectively the author of the annual appropriations bill for HUD and several other agencies. Such is Kelly's power that, not only do executive branch employees hesitate to tangle with him, most House Members also take pains not to offend him.

Over the last few years Kelly has been at odds with HUD Secretary Jack Kemp, who came to the HUD with the mandate to clean it up after a particularly embarrassing scandal. The previous Secretary and some of his assistants had used HUD's discretionary fund to dole out juicy favors and pet projects to cronies and friends. Secretary Kemp moved to eliminate the kind of discretion that was abused, making all decisions involving HUD funds competitive rather than political. A point system with performance goals was set up to evaluate applications for funding. The projects with the most

points were to be the only ones funded. This also meant there would
be no room for pork projects back in the home district. Congress
complained; Kevin Kelly went to work.

Kelly agreed to Kemp's plan to eliminate discretionary spending
by the Secretary. But, instead of eliminating the funding altogether,
he turned it to his own use, becoming the gatekeeper for congressional pork projects. When Members asked Kelly for money for
their districts, he did not write the pork projects into the actual
appropriations bill. Instead, he slipped them into the committee
report that accompanied the legislation, a report that no one could
change once it left Kelly's hands.

Secretary Kemp resisted Kelly's first attempt to control his budget through the report, which is never actually voted on. Because
committee reports are not officially binding, HUD's General Counsel, Frank Keating, advised Kemp that he could ignore the line-item
projects in the committee report. Kemp did just that. The following
year, Kelly placed an item in the appropriations bill requiring the
Secretary to adhere to recommendations in the accompanying committee report. To make his point, Kelly also punished Keating for
giving the Secretary the advice about ignoring line-item projects by
deleting the funding requested for nearly 50 lawyers that were to
have been added to his staff. Several years later, Keating was still
in trouble in the Senate. Despite a long record of civil rights activity,
his nomination to be a federal judge was held up over transparently
absurd charges of insensitivity.

Congressional staff see nothing wrong in this way of doing
business. A Senate Appropriations Committee aide points out in
Kelly's defense that there has been a tradition of following committee report language as "the letter of the law," going back nearly 30
years. (Like Keating, most executive branch legal advisors dispute
this claim.) The aide argues that legislating through committee
reports is valid because the reports have to be approved by committee members, and the documents are, after all, public. By using the
report language instead of the actual text of the bill, Congress gives
executive departments the flexibility needed to manage efficiently.
Just as lawmakers are relieved of going through the full and tedious
legislative process, so too the executive agencies can get approval

expeditiously for programs by asking friendly committee staff to include them in the committee report.

As long as they play along, that is. Handing power to staff aides to make big-money decisions in the committee report may allow for occasional efficiency, but the main result is the augmented importance of staffers like Kelly. Not only are department officials at a disadvantage, so too are Members of Congress, who are put in the role of supplicants, begging the Kellys of Capitol Hill to include their pet projects. A Republican staffer on the Senate Appropriations Committee says that, as Kelly has amassed power, access to him has become more difficult. Minority staff requests generally are limited to one audience per year with him.

Kelly has also foiled attempts to reform the entrenched bureaucracy at HUD. The staff at HUD, as might be expected from any bureaucracy, was not eager to accommodate Kemp's reforms, especially since those reforms meant taking away much of their power. Knowing that bureaucrats feel more affinity with their congressional masters than with their ostensible bosses within the department, Kemp tried to ensure that career workers would not be in a position to hold up key reforms. One of the Secretary's plans for dealing with this problem was to move officials who did not get with his program into the backwaters of the department, where they could not hinder his efforts at change.

Ever since HUD was established in 1966 the Secretary has had the authority to move his employees around throughout the department as he wished. Most other agencies have the same flexibility. But it wasn't that easy for Kemp. One reason bureaucrats are loyal to their congressional overseers is that the Hill can protect them. The HUD employees Kemp wanted to marginalize turned to Kelly for help.

Kelly responded. As long as the appropriations for HUD came for the department as a whole, Secretary Kemp had the freedom to emphasize certain offices within the department and starve out those who stood in the way of change. Unlike the tradition of adherence to committee reports, Kelly felt no compunction in sweeping away this traditional arrangement. First he began writing the appropriations bill in seven sections, one for each division of

HUD. In its new form, the bill includes not just the salaries and expenditures for the seven sections, but the number of employees who must work in each.

But Kelly didn't stop there. Although a database is standard in virtually all businesses, particularly those the size and scope of HUD, when Kemp tried to put one in, the appropriators refused to supply the money. This was not mere window-dressing: One reason Kemp wanted to update the archaic record-keeping system at HUD was that it was this sloppy system that enabled his predecessor, Samuel Pierce, to dole out the money at the height of the previous HUD scandal. In addition to stopping the new database, Kelly added the following provision to the HUD appropriations bill: "No funds may be used... for details of employees from any organization in the Department of Housing and Urban Development to any organization included under the budget activity 'Departmental Management.'"[12] In other words, Kemp could not even, on a temporary basis, assign additional HUD employees to clean up the management mess he had inherited.

Mary Brunette, a senior policy advisor to Kemp, learned the hard way the consequences of tangling with Kelly. As Assistant to the Secretary for Policy, Brunette played a key role in Kemp's efforts to reform the Department and to oppose Kelly's pork. When Brunette was nominated for promotion to Assistant Secretary for Public Affairs, Kelly used the occasion to try to put her out of a job. While the confirmation was pending, the initial draft of the appropriations bill was put forward. The entire budget for public affairs had been eliminated. While funding for the office was eventually restored, though with a one-third cut in its budget, Brunette's promotion was delayed for months by Kelly's vendetta.

Lawmakers come and go, but key staffers like Kevin Kelly rarely leave, thus becoming the institutional memory of their committees. If Sen. Mikulski loses or gives up her position as chairman of the subcommittee, her successor will inherit Kelly. And he will be happy to do so. Kelly is the only person who, practically speaking, can write his subcommittee's appropriations bill. Along with the power that comes from being the only mechanic who understands the machinery, staffers like Kelly enjoy leverage over pet projects and the power to put people out of jobs. If this doesn't make them the most important people in Washington, it at least makes them *think* they are.

When a group of HUD executives called for a meeting to work out some of their grievances, Kelly demanded that the department send a limousine to pick him up. HUD officials reminded him that the subway stopped practically in the basement of their building, and besides it was forbidden to use the HUD motor pool for such matters. These are the kinds of fights that set the pecking order in Washington. And it is a fight that Kelly was bound to win: He held out until special permission was secured from the Deputy Secretary. In the end, a car was sent.

The Wolf Pack

Perhaps the most visible manifestation of the unchecked might of unelected congressional staffers was the confirmation of Clarence Thomas. When Judge Thomas allowed his name to be put in nomination for the Supreme Court, he certainly expected a fight. After all, he was a conservative appointed by a Republican President and needed the approval of a liberal Senate Judiciary Committee dominated by Democrats. But never did he expect the mock trial that ensued. And the truth is, neither did most of the Senators.

The public was right to feel that there was something rotten in the way the whole thing was handled. What they didn't know, however, is the degree to which the Anita Hill-Clarence Thomas confrontation was engineered by staffers. Immersed in trysts with special-interest groups and lobbyists, staff aides staged the Anita Hill affair from start to finish. Despite their abuses, moreover, they have largely escaped blame.

So embarrassing were the leaks of confidential Senate information on Anita Hill, the Senate voted to launch an inquiry. Ultimately however, the investigation of Temporary Special Independent Counsel Thomas Fleming was hamstrung by Senators unwilling, as ever, to allow scrutiny of their own operations. Otherwise we might now know exactly how the whole thing happened. Although Fleming was unable to prove beyond a doubt who was responsible, he did reveal more than Capitol Hill would have liked, and more than the media were willing to admit.

To begin with, Fleming traced the machinations by which staffers "outed" an unwilling Anita Hill. They wooed Hill with promises of confidentiality and anonymity, and then spread her tale through the staff network and into the ranks of the anti-Thomas interest groups. They made sure that everyone in a tight circle of staffers, activists, and journalists knew about her allegations. Then they used the fact that "everyone knew" (a situation they themselves had created) to pressure her to come forward and testify.

Hill's name and telephone number originally were unearthed by the Alliance for Justice, a leftist group working against the Thomas nomination. Leaders of the organization heard, from a man who had known the mystery woman at Yale, about a victim who allegedly had been sexually harassed by Thomas. The victim, whose name quickly would be discovered by the Alliance, was described as a University of Oklahoma law professor who had worked with the Judge while he was at the Department of Education and the Equal Employment Opportunity Commission (EEOC). The Alliance turned the lead over to Ohio Democratic Sen. Howard Metzenbaum's Judiciary Subcommittee on Antitrust, Monopolies and Business Rights. The subcommittee's Chief Counsel, William Corr, assigned it to a staffer from Metzenbaum's Labor Subcommittee, Gail Laster. (It remains unclear what business a Labor Subcommittee staffer had investigating the conduct of a Supreme Court nominee.)

Laster was unable to turn up information that would corroborate the story. To the contrary, women with whom she spoke, who had worked with Thomas at the EEOC and the Department of Education, had no complaints against him. Laster still had not spoken to Hill when she told a Metzenbaum investigative-staff powwow that she had drawn a blank. Her colleagues at the meeting agreed that she should get in touch with Hill.

Far from offering to testify, Hill was not even willing, initially, to provide leads. But congressional staffers knew they could coax or coerce her into the spotlight. Just five days before the nomination hearings began, staffers, and public-interest groups opposing

Thomas' appointment, knew that with Anita Hill they had an ace. The only question was how to play the card.

Laster found that she and Hill had a mutual friend, Kim Taylor. After seeking approval from her supervisor, James Brudney, Laster told Taylor about the situation. This was the first of many outings of Anita Hill. From the beginning, committee staffers were determined to weave a web around Anita Hill that would draw her into addressing the Judiciary Committee. Brudney, Chief Counsel to Metzenbaum's Subcommittee on Labor—and a friend of Anita Hill from Yale Law School — was at the center of the scheme. After Laster had laid the groundwork, Brudney took over. While a number of staffers knew about Hill's existence, it would take seasoned political judgement to weasel the charges into public. This is where Brudney came in.

In the *Almanac of the Unelected*, Washington's guidebook to staff, Brudney is characterized as an expert on labor issues who worked extensively on a number of workers' rights bills. After clerking for Supreme Court Justice Harry A. Blackmun in 1980-81, he became an associate at a Washington law firm for four years before returning to government. By definition his job description wouldn't have him dogging court nominees. But, as a staffer who worked on the Thomas nomination for the Minority points out, "Don't get too caught up in the official positions of these people, when they decide to go after someone they're like a pack of wolves."

Another Metzenbaum investigator, Bonnie Goldsmith, met with George Kassouf of the Alliance for Justice to receive a briefing on Thomas' alleged personal improprieties, including details on the Hill story that the Alliance had gotten from Judge Susan Hoerchner, an old friend of Hill. Bonnie Goldsmith passed the information along to Ricki Seidman, chief investigator on Sen. Edward Kennedy's Labor and Human Resources Committee. Seidman had been hired by the Massachusetts Democrat from the liberal activist group People for the American Way shortly before. Her explicit task was to dig dirt on Thomas. Her salary? $82,000 for the year.

Seidman called Anita Hill on September 6, 1991. Although Hill was evasive, Seidman wrung out of her "some oblique comments

about victims of sexual harassment." Word of this conversation was
relayed to Kennedy's chief of staff. At this point, Senators themselves were still in the dark about Hill's allegations. The investigation was proceeding on staff initiative alone.

Seidman continued to talk with Hill. The day before the confirmation hearings began, Miss Hill started to give in, telling the
Kennedy staffer she would be willing to share her experiences with
the committee, though she was reluctant to cooperate with an FBI
investigation. Seidman listened as Hill described a vague pattern of
comments made to her by Thomas that might constitute sexual
harassment. This was sort of a down payment for the staffers. They
now had solid grounds for pursuing Hill's testimony. The matter
came full circle when Seidman suggested to Hill that she might be
more comfortable discussing the matter with Brudney, "a person
she knew."

What followed were several conversations during which Brudney
leaned on Hill to present her charges to the Judiciary Committee. It
appears, however, that Brudney overestimated his persuasive abil-
ities. They first spoke on September 10, the day the confirmation
hearings were to begin. The clock was running. Lobbyists, interest
groups, and staffers had put together such a formidable arsenal of
inquiry that Thomas would be on the stand for five straight days,
the second-longest testimony by a Supreme Court nominee in
history. That fact alone prevented a vote from having come sooner,
before Anita Hill would ever have surfaced.

When Hill continued to express reluctance about going to the
committee, Brudney, along with other Metzenbaum staffers, decided to let the Senator in on the chase. He was the first elected
official to be informed. Metzenbaum was not nearly as eager as the
coterie of staff. He recoiled early in the presentation and insisted
that the accuser, whose name he still didn't know, would have to
raise her charges with the Judiciary Committee. Not only that, he
said the "charges were too serious for a single member or staff." He
then bolted the scene.

And so Brudney again went to Hill to tell her how essential her
testimony was if they hoped to prevent Thomas from being confirmed. Hill thought about it overnight and finally agreed to speak

with a member of the Judiciary Committee. But nothing happened. Not being a member of the Judiciary Committee staff, Brudney was unaware that complainants were required to initiate contact with the committee. Nevertheless, they soon straightened this out, and the next day, September 12, Anita Hill left a message for Judiciary Committee staffer Harriet Grant, formally initiating contact.

When Grant called back, Hill again expressed her reluctance to step forward. She continued to fear that her testimony would not be believed by the committee. Brudney was told of Hill's hesitation and again initiated a series of conversations with her. He claims these discussions were meant to provide support and to relate that he thought Harriet Grant had misunderstood the conditional request for anonymity. Hill tells a different story. She insists that Brudney was leaning on her.

On September 18 Brudney tried a different tack, bringing yet another actor into the drama. He explained the situation in thinly veiled hypothetical terms to Susan Ross, a Georgetown law professor who specializes in sexual harassment issues. Brudney was getting desperate and wanted Ross to convince Hill that her charges might constitute sexual harassment. The Thomas hearings were sliding by, and barring a dramatic turn the nominee was going to make it past the committee.

Professor Ross agreed to speak with Hill, so Brudney gave Hill her name. At about the same time Brudney apparently talked with Kennedy staffers about his concern that the Judiciary Committee was failing to pursue Hill's allegations due to a misunderstanding about the scope of Hill's request for anonymity. Kennedy's staffers in turn contacted two aides to Sen. Pat Leahy, a Vermont Democrat. Leahy's chief Judiciary staffer, Ann Harkins, realized that enough people involved with the investigation knew of Hill's charges that "disclosure could embarrass the committee if nothing more was done." This was the point of no return Brudney had been striving for. They needed to involve as many people as possible in case their activity blew up in their faces. But they had to pick allies who would not go public, or prematurely derail their progress with Hill. Yet Sens. Leahy and Biden, provided with briefings of the allegations, decided that nothing more should be done unless Hill voluntarily came forward. With word out among interest groups all over Washington, the committee staffers knew too much was at stake to let the Hill affair quietly go away. Again, they decided to have Brudney put the squeeze on.

By the time Brudney called again, Anita Hill had spoken with Professor Ross. On September 20, the final day of the Senate hearings, Hill agreed to cooperate with an investigation of the charges she had made. Hill sent her now-famous affidavit detailing her complaint against Judge Thomas to the Judiciary Committee first on September 23, and followed it up with a corrected version on September 25. Perhaps already sensing that their staffs were out of control and not wanting them to run wild with such a sensitive document, Senators on the Judiciary Committee made sure that no one made copies of the Hill affidavit. This meant that, after all his work bringing Hill forward, Brudney did not himself have access to her statement. So he went around the committee and called Hill directly, telling her he needed a copy of the affidavit to assist him in writing a memo for Sen. Metzenbaum. She sent him an unnotarized, unsigned copy.

An FBI report on Hill's charges was also available to the Senators on the Judiciary Committee, but most were satisfied with a briefing from Chairman Biden on the basis of the allegations. Not until Anita Hill, along with Kim Taylor, a Stanford law professor, and others (including Harvard Law Professor Laurence Tribe) pushed the committee staff was the affidavit circulated among the Members. It is clear from the Fleming Report that the Senators knew of the affidavit and the FBI report, but also realized that an eleventh-hour complaint regarding a 10-year-old allegation in a sitting judge's personal life would never hold up.

But staff had brought Hill forward, and they and their activist allies were not about to let the matter drop. Defying the wishes of the Senators and Anita Hill, the affidavit was leaked to Nina Totenberg of National Public Radio and its contents were divulged to Timothy Phelps of *Newsday*. As the Fleming Report emphasizes, James Brudney had the only unsigned, unaccounted for copy of the affidavit. Though Totenberg has been tight-lipped about who passed the document to her, it is apparent that the copy she had was neither signed nor notarized: she spent five days trying to verify the authenticity of her copy. It certainly appears that Brudney was Nina Totenberg's source.[13]

But, instead of pursuing an investigation of Brudney, Senators opted to do nothing. For all their rhetoric, the Senators knew that there probably was no legal violation in leaking the affidavit. Once it was established that it was this affidavit, and not the FBI Report, that had been leaked to Totenberg, a subsequent inquiry would have dealt more with the integrity of the Senate than with any legal violations. Therefore, Senators refused Fleming's request to require Totenberg to answer questions about the matter. The most important thing for Congress was not to find out who had done the wrong thing. The most important thing was to sweep the Thomas/Hill affair under the carpet as soon as possible.

Staffers escape unscathed in such instances because they are unaccountable except to their bosses, who are reluctant to rein them in because this same staff makes it possible for the Member to function. Even more than Senators or Representatives, who are at least exposed to some degree of public accountability at the ballot box, staffers work behind the curtains. They are the new rulers on Capitol Hill, a nameless, faceless mandarinate that pulls the strings and feeds off the worst impulses of the institution they claim to serve. Whether it is the outing of Anita Hill or micromanaging HUD, no amount of new rules or ethical guidelines will change staff behavior. After all, such rules as do exist are ignored. The remedy is obvious: Cut staff. Cut it by a quarter. Cut it by half. But the very dependence that staff encourages makes it far from likely that Members will reduce staff size absent a sustained public clamor. So what are we waiting for? Let the clamor begin.

5

THE GRANDIOSE
INQUISITORS

Admit Nothing. Deny Everything. Make Counter-accusations.

—Washington Motto

Joseph Monticciolo could have used that advice when he appeared before the Government Operations Subcommittee on Employment and Housing to talk about the influence-peddling at the Department of Housing and Urban Development (HUD). Monticciolo had been the New York Regional Administrator for HUD, and was on Capitol Hill to testify about the partisan lobbying efforts that had corrupted the agency.

Rep. Tom Lantos started out nicely enough. The California Democrat asked Monticciolo to explain how he felt about the way HUD had been run. Lantos had more than a passing interest in this subject, inasmuch as he was heading an investigation into whether firms that hired former Reagan administration officials to lobby the agency received sweetheart deals. So, he not only put forth the question, he suggested the answer he was looking for. "You are appalled?" said Lantos, expectantly.

"Yes, sir," Monticciolo replied.

"Are you also surprised?"

"Yes. I think we all have built perceptions of things, and we know there are political issues being dealt with... [the problem] goes back to Johnson and Nixon and Ford and Carter. I mean, it's no different —the process—in terms of political [pressures]. I'm certain that many members even of this committee have inquired of HUD, have asked HUD to consider issues, to reconsider issues, to legitimately support their constituents' efforts in dealing with projects and issues."

Ooops. Monticciolo had just made the cardinal mistake: He had implied that Members of Congress extort favors for their constituents and campaign contributors from the agencies they oversee. This is one of those aspects of life inside the Capital Beltway that everyone knows but no one speaks about. And Lantos was not about to let it be spoken in front of him.

"Are you suggesting that if Congresswoman [Marge] Roukema approaches a HUD office on behalf of a project in her district, that is analogous to [former Secretary of the Interior] James Watt getting $300,000 for a phone call?" he snapped.

"Oh, absolutely not. Absolutely not," Monticciolo said, realizing the gravity of his mistake.

"Well then, would you like to rephrase your last few sentences, because they didn't... didn't strike a very reasonable chord?"

Monticciolo became flustered. "Well, I wasn't dealing with... I never dealt with those individuals. I never dealt with them. I had no relationship with them."

The witness had good reason to be flustered. Rep. Lantos reminded him that an offended lawmaker can be a very vindictive lawmaker. "But you're under oath, Mr. Monticciolo," he said. "We are conducting this hearing in a very cordial fashion. But you have to be precise in the statements you make."

"I apologize if I tried... " Monticciolo fumbled.

"So you would like to back up and start all over again?" asked Lantos helpfully.

"In terms of our role in terms of dealing with the issue, certainly there were... "

"You are not answering my question, Mr. Monticciolo, and I will direct you to answer the question."

"Would you please... rephrase the question?"

"I will, and please listen when I ask questions."

Capitol Hill has become a land through the looking glass, where listening to the question really means giving the right answer. The right answer, in turn, is the one the lawmakers want to hear. What they never want to hear is any suggestion that they themselves might be to blame. Not only do they not want to hear it, as Lantos demonstrated, they will not even tolerate having it suggested.

Hence, some good advice to those unlucky enough to find themselves before a congressional committee: Blame anyone but a Congressman. If the hearing is about irregular defense contracts, blame the contractor or blame the bureaucrats, but by no means blame the legislators who encouraged the Defense Department to favor a dubious contractor. If agricultural products sent overseas as foreign aid are diverted by Third-World kleptocrats, decry the behavior of the Department of Agriculture or the Department of State, but certainly not the farm-state lawmakers who harassed the bureaucrats into arranging the foreign grain sales.

But the public may not buy such fine distinctions. Anyone truly interested in ferreting out the shenanigans at HUD would naturally be just as curious about political pressure from Members of Congress as from lobbyists. James Watt may have been paid $300,000 for calling in favors, but then Members of Congress get paid for dealing in favors all the time. Producing favors, one part of a well-developed congressional constituent-service racket, is a key element of getting reelected. Producing favors builds political good will at home and prompts campaign contributions that bulk up the reelection war chest. And when a Congressman puts in a call to HUD on behalf of a buddy or campaign contributor, there are no hearings into corruption, no nasty innuendoes on the evening news. This is their job, they say.

Take, for example, the later questioning of Monticciolo by Connecticut Rep. Christopher Shays. Asking about any contacts New York Sen. Alphonse D'Amato, a fellow-Republican, had with Monticciolo's office, Shays might have queried whether there had ever been any political pressure that Monticciolo thought inappropriate. Instead, he asked his questions in a way guaranteed to elicit the appropriate response. "Is it your testimony that [Sen. D'Amato] never asked to promote any project?" asked Shays, quickly adding, "and see, there is nothing wrong with a Senator asking to promote a certain project, so I don't have any problem with that."

"I don't either," Monticciolo agreed, "because certainly I've had elected officials call me to promote projects all the time."

"Right. So there's nothing wrong with that."

"No sir."

Back up a moment. Congress launches an investigation into whether political favors tainted projects at HUD. The inquisitors are told by a top official that he was regularly pressed — by elected officials, no less — to choose one project over another. Instead of following the lead, and scrutinizing the interference by Members, the inquisitors badger the witness into agreeing that this particular variety of political pressure is okay.

This is the way congressional investigations work. And it should come as no surprise. The Founding Fathers did not envision the Congress as a prosecutorial body, but rather as a legislative one. Investigators and prosecutors are, in the best of worlds, as neutral and objective as possible. Members of Congress are by definition neither. Lawmakers are partisan people with political agendas. That can be said of some prosecutors as well. But such political ambitions are seen as a fault in a prosecutor, and the justice system is designed to protect the innocent from abusive, politically motivated prosecutions. The procedural niceties that provide those protections (such as due process or the right to an attorney) are not recognized in front of the prosecutors on Capitol Hill, making the political nature of their investigations all the more troublesome.

Investigations have become the preferred method of addressing policy questions on Capitol Hill because only one side can be challenged. Thus does Congress resort to investigations in every type of battle with the administration. If the President criticizes Congress for wallowing in perquisites, legislators neither defend their perks nor rely on simple criticism of the perks enjoyed by the executive branch. Instead, they hold hearings to "investigate" the administration's perks. If Congress is embarrassed by choosing the wrong side on a contentious public question, investigations can be used to turn the tables. After Congress misjudged the public mood on the war with Iraq, for example, it quickly moved to show that it was really the President who wanted to appease Saddam Hussein. Thus the "investigation" into a non-scandal dubbed "Iraq-gate." (It is fitting tribute to the political pathologies born of Watergate that every one of Washington's so-called scandals now, in due course, has "-gate" in its title.)

Investigations can be, and are, used simply to discredit political enemies without any hard evidence. Iraq-gate was typical: a ploy by Democrats to taint a Republican President in an election year while casting a more favorable light on wartime waffling by Congress. Similarly, in 1992 the House launched an absurd "October Surprise" investigation. No remotely credible evidence existed to support the implausible charge that then-Vice Presidential candidate George Bush travelled to Paris in 1980 to ask Iran to hold American hostages through the election (so that Jimmy Carter's reelection bid would be scuttled). But talk of evidence misses the point. Congressional investigations are not about reaching conclusions. They are about forming clouds.

"It just didn't seem very important at the time."

Earlier President Bush was the subject of another congressional smear, this one the Senate investigation into alleged links with Panamanian drug smugglers. Again, there was no credible evidence to back up the wild charges, and this itself should dispel the notion that Congressmen or their staffs can act as impartial investigators. The Panama inquiry, launched by Sen. John Kerry, ultimately focused on the Bank of Credit and Commerce International (BCCI) through which former Panamanian strongman Manuel Noriega had laundered his drug profits. The Massachusetts Democrat's handling of the matter reveals the partisan nature of such investigations and raises profound questions about whether Members of Congress can pursue investigations without skewing them to favor political allies and protect campaign contributors. Certainly our Founding Fathers never intended to hand prosecutorial power over to people with this kind of blatant political agenda.

In the summer of 1991, a scandal broke in Washington newspapers: Clark Clifford, *éminence grise* of the Democratic Party and advisor to four Presidents, appeared to be the front man for BCCI in its illicit ownership of the Washington-based First American Bank. Clifford, as President of First American, had assured Federal Reserve regulators that Middle-Eastern investors in his institution were independent of the foreign-owned BCCI. As it turned out, the investors were actually quite dependent on BCCI; the bank had given them the money with which they made their proxy investments. When this was revealed, Clifford claimed he had been duped along with the regulators. That is not to say that Clifford was uninvolved with BCCI. In addition to heading First American, he was the Washington lawyer/representative of the international bank.

When the scandal hit, some in the media began to ask questions about Sen. Kerry's investigation into drug-money laundering. The probe by the Senator's Subcommittee on Terrorism and Narcotics had identified BCCI as the money-laundering agent for Manuel Noriega. Yet somehow the investigation failed to expose the First American connection. Why? Though denied by the principals, rumors circulated that Kerry's chief investigator, Jack Blum, had been called off, perhaps by Kerry's committee boss, Rhode Island Democrat Claiborne Pell, when he got too close to exposing Clifford.

Faced with criticism over an obviously flawed investigation Kerry did the obvious thing: He launched a new investigation. Of course, the Senator was uninterested in reviewing his own failed effort. Instead he asked why someone else—the Justice Department or federal banking regulators — had not unearthed or acted on information that First American was surreptitiously owned by BCCI. In the late summer, Kerry accused Bush administration officials of bowing to political pressures brought to bear by friends of Clifford.

"What is amazing, and I guess frustrating, to a lot of us is that BCCI's day of reckoning was so long delayed," said Kerry. "We are inevitably left with the question of whether the mere presence—

and I emphasize, left with the question — of whether the mere presence of these influential people was sufficient to keep lawyers and accountants and regulators from doing their jobs for so long."

Kerry's attack posture did the trick. Instead of being asked about the failings of his own investigation, the Senator was trumpeted as the last honest man, finally seeing the fruits of his tireless and thankless efforts. Perhaps the biggest kudos came from *Washington Post* columnist Mary McGrory, who declared Kerry the "man of the moment" and fantasized that the Senator "may walk around at home late at night murmuring 'at last, at last.' "

So successful was this blame-passing strategy that as late as November of 1991 Kerry was still berating the Bush White House for dropping the ball on BCCI. "If I had a grand jury instead of a congressional committee," the Senator told a panel of Justice Department prosecutors at a November 21 hearing, "this case would have been wide open in the early months of 1989."

Maybe. Then again, maybe not. In the early months of 1989 Kerry had just accepted $5,000 in campaign contributions from Clifford and his associates. Kerry accepted the money even though his assistant Jack Blum had learned six months earlier of the illegal ownership of First American by BCCI. Blum says he had been told of the subterfuge no later than June 1988, by Manuel Noriega's personal banker at BCCI, Amjad Awan. This was three months before a crucial meeting in which, according to the official chronology of the affair handed out by the Kerry subcommittee, Blum met with Clifford to discuss BCCI documents. At the September 1988 meeting, Clifford appeared in his capacity as a lawyer for BCCI. Blum was present, as the chronology states, but so too was Sen. Kerry, who was not listed as a participant. Kerry spokesman Jonathan Winer says it was a simple oversight that the Senator was not listed. It was "not an attempt to mislead or misinform anyone," he claims.

At the meeting, Clifford asked Blum and Kerry to back off BCCI. He told them that the bank was an upright institution and the investigators' requests for documents from BCCI had become harassing.

Blum admits that he knew Clifford was not telling the truth. The evidence he had discovered about BCCI and First American showed that Clifford either was lying when he said BCCI was clean, or had been bamboozled into thinking his clients were on the up and up. Yet, neither Blum nor Kerry confronted Clifford with what they knew. Blum defends this by saying that the First American connection "just didn't seem very important at the time." So much for the notion that Kerry and his staff were ready to blow the lid off the BCCI-First American connection if they had only been given the chance. Kerry's and Blum's failure to pursue what they knew about First American and BCCI, either in person with Clifford, or months later in the official investigation report published by Kerry's subcommittee, can be explained in a number of different ways. None reflects favorably on the Senator's investigation, or on congressional investigations in general.

One explanation is that the First American connection simply *wasn't*, as Mr. Blum asserts, very important at the time. The investigation may have ignored Clifford because he had no connection with then-Presidential candidate George Bush. "The whole tenor and thrust of the investigation into Panama and Manuel Noriega was to tie Noriega to the CIA and through the CIA to George Bush," says a Republican member of the Kerry subcommittee staff. Nothing the investigation unearthed about Clifford pointed to George Bush, the staffer says. So it was ignored.

The Clifford information might not have been ignored by the Republican staff on the committee. That is, if they had been told about it. But they had not. The only check on congressional investigations to keep them from degenerating into machines for pure partisan attacks is that they are ostensibly bipartisan. Democrats have staff to work on the investigation, but so do Republicans. If one side ignores politically inconvenient information, the other side can pick it up and run with it. At least that's the way it's supposed to work. But in fact, with such investigations the Minority staff is regularly cut out of the loop. When Blum interviewed Amjad Awan in June of 1988, Republican staff were not present. In September of that year (around the time of Blum's and Kerry's meeting with Clifford), Blum held an official, on-the-record deposition of Awan.

Not surprisingly, he did not ask the witness about First American. Because the Republican staff had not been present at the initial June interview with Awan, they did not know to ask about it. The Republican staff apparently was purposefully kept in the dark.

The twists of the Kerry investigation into BCCI show how marred such investigations are by their partisan slant. Not only are they designed to dig, manufacture, or merely imply, dirt about political opponents, they simply ignore wrongdoing by political allies. Far from getting at the truth, congressional investigations are taxpayer-funded exercises in "opposition research," that pleasant Washington euphemism for mudslinging.

The Kerry investigation, and its failure to chase leads regarding Clifford, raises further, more-troubling questions. Did the congressional investigators let Clifford off the hook because he was a Democratic icon? Or perhaps because the banker and his partners were donating heavily to the campaigns of Kerry and other Democrats? The Senator brushes off the last charge. "What's the story here, that John Kerry sold out for a couple of thousand bucks?" he asks. "Come on."

The question may not be that easy to dismiss. When asked why Sen. Kerry accepted Clifford's contributions at a fundraising party even though the banker should have been an object of the Senator's investigation, Kerry spokesman Jonathan Winer tries out a variety of answers. At first, Winer maintained that Kerry didn't know the donations were being made. "Kerry's campaign staff and Kerry's investigative staff were not in communication regarding the event," he said. "Hence there was never anybody who put together investigative work on the one hand and fundraising work on the other hand, because those two functions are appropriately kept separate." But the donations were made at a fundraising party for Kerry hosted by Democratic maven Pamela Harriman at her house. To be a guest at the party, one had to be a contributor to Kerry's campaign, and no doubt Kerry saw that Clifford was there.

When this question is put to him, Winer tries out another explanation for his Senator's behavior. "In October of 1988 we had an allegation," he says. "We had a variety of other allegations which were at that time not proven. One does not take action on the basis of unproven allegations."[1]

That legalistic answer misses the point. If Kerry were an investigator in any real sense of the word, it was his job to look into the allegations that had been raised against Clifford. Yet the Senator's spokesman maintains that, so long as the allegations remained unproven, it was perfectly fine for the Senator to accept Clifford's money. At the least this suggests the potential for a grave conflict of interest: that it was in the Senator's interest not to chase down the First American connection, because to do so would have meant having to forego thousands of dollars in campaign funds (at a time, Winer admits, when Kerry was strapped for political cash). You don't have to argue that Kerry was bought off to recognize that it would have been in his interest to overlook the discovery that ultimately became the juiciest part of the BCCI scandal.

We don't yet know whether there was in fact a conflict of interest. The question is: How would Congress judge Kerry if he and Blum had been administration officials who gave a political patron a pass because "it just didn't seem very important at the time"? Doubtless it would have provoked a multitude of ethics investigations into the matter, and likely the appointment of an independent counsel (who would have chased the two for years until the victims had run out of cash with which to pay their defense attorneys). Luckily for both Kerry and Blum, they are denizens of Capitol Hill. Not only do lawmakers rarely turn on their own, there simply isn't the structure for doing so. The independent counsel law does not apply to Congress, and legislators are not generally allowed, under the rules of courtesy that govern congressional debate, to question the integrity of their colleagues. To be sure, there is the occasional inquest by the Senate Ethics Committee. But these are few and far between, and on the rare occasions they are undertaken (the Keating Five) it is even more rare that the punishment extend beyond wrist-slapping.

Investigating Congress

Even when serious questions are raised about their behavior, Congressmen look for excuses rather than answers. Look at how the House of Representatives handled the scandals that enveloped its Bank and Post Office. Since 1952 the General Accounting Office (GAO), in its audit of the House Bank, detailed the fact that Members were writing piles of bad checks. Either the Bank was keeping horrible records, messing up the accounts of Members who wrote checks thinking they had positive balances, or Members were bouncing checks at an alarming rate. In 1961 this came to 5,221 checks, worth $610,000.

When the GAO audits began to be available to the public in 1977, the problem still had not been addressed. So that it would not become a public scandal, the GAO changed the language in its report. In 1958 the audit had said that "aside from the doubtful legality of accepting overdraft items and holding them for rather lengthy periods of time, the accounting control over the items is not adequate." In the 1977 audit, rubber checks were viewed much more kindly. "Amounts due from Members represent checks drawn on and cashed or paid by the Sergeant at Arms but not charged to Member's accounts.... The Sergeant at Arms monitors all such items daily, and no financial losses have occurred under these procedures."[2]

The part about losses was true. But the ability to bounce checks at will allowed Members to float themselves interest-free loans during the campaign season. Under banking laws and Federal Election Commission rules, such a check-kiting scam is unquestionably illegal. But somehow this too just didn't seem very important at the time to the leaders of the House. When the scandal hit, Members reacted with an investigation by a subcommittee of the House Committee on Standards of Official Conduct. At first the subcommittee tried to keep the names of most who had bounced checks out of the newspapers, offering to release the names of only the 24 most flagrant abusers. Under pressure from upstart freshman Republicans, the entire list was finally released (a list that embarrassed long-time GOP as well as Democratic incumbents). But as far as the House was concerned, that was about it for the investigation. Names had been named. According to congressional leaders, the attendant loss of face was the worst punishment an incumbent could receive.

Of course, there is worse. Losing office through scandal may be bad, but losing office and going to jail is even worse. And some may be doing just that. Attorney General William Barr appointed a special counsel—that is, an independent prosecutor authorized by the Justice Department, rather than one appointed under the Ethics in Government Act, which does not apply to Congress—to investigate the Bank and Members' accounts.

"Politics!" scream the Members. This is a curious charge coming from Capitol Hill, because it implies that whereas congressional investigations of the administration are not politically motivated, however tenuous the charges, any Justice Department investigation into their wheelings and dealings amounts to dirty tricks. The most vocal case has been made by the chairman of the House Banking Committee, Rep. Henry Gonzalez. The Texas Democrat filed (and lost) a suit to stop the prosecutor from gaining access to the Bank's records. Although the Representative did not himself bounce any checks, he claimed that the administration could use information from Members' private financial records to punish Members who went against the President's policies.

"What will be the effect on the Members if they know the government holds the records of all their financial transactions in its hands?" Rep. Gonzalez asked. "Knows all the political affiliations, charitable contributions, or even religious views each Member financially supports? Isn't that really the purpose and effect of these subpoenas?"

The Texan has a point. We don't want the Federal Bureau of Investigation to become a rogue sub-government, protecting its fiefdom by blackmailing Members. Nor do we want an Internal Revenue Service that avoids reform by auditing the tax returns of any Member who dares criticize the agency. But, if it is wrong for executive agencies to intimidate lawmakers, by making them indictment bait, then it is just as wrong for Members to extort acquiescence from the administration by conducting witch hunts against officials who displease them.

In fact, the game continues to be stacked in Congress' favor. The FBI treats Congress with kid gloves, and for a reason. The last FBI investigation to snag a few Members was the ABSCAM bribery scandal. Such was the retribution against the Bureau by Congress that former agents who had been involved in the investigation say that it would never be undertaken today. Without the Ethics in Government Act's conflict-of-interest hammer, moreover, the administration has little in the way of weapons with which to bully congressional foes.

This is quite the contrary for Members wishing to beat up on the executive branch. Members of Congress regularly use their hearings as bullies' pulpits, charging, often as not, people who are innocent of any wrongdoing with criminality. Sometimes it is done to assassinate political enemies, sometimes just for the publicity the scandals generate for lawmakers. These were jointly the prime motives of Sen. Joseph McCarthy in his investigation into communist infiltration of the U.S. Army. McCarthy's hearings, and those conducted earlier by the House Committee on Un-American Activities, have become symbols of the abuse of government power. In textbooks and movies the viciousness of these inquests is blamed on the anti-communist fervor of the congressional prosecutors. But what the hearings displayed were not the claws of the anti-communists, but the inherent faults of congressional investigations. Sen. McCarthy did indeed set a new standard for shameless irresponsibility in congressional probes. But it is a standard that guides the prosecutors on the Hill to this day.

Indeed, our new McCarthyites are even more dangerous than Tailgunner Joe. McCarthy's excesses caught up with him, and he was finally shut down. Today's McCarthyites are much too careful for that, and are thus not easily stopped. In addition, even if one or another legislator is thwarted, there is another would-be star investigator waiting in the wings. Because of the "reforms" of the 1970s, today almost every majority lawmaker is the chair of some committee or subcommittee. That means there are hundreds of Members with their own stages on which to play McCarthy.

Who Lost Iraq?

In the summer of 1992, Congress was engaged in a classic set of investigations, looking into whether the Bush administration encouraged Iraq's invasion of Kuwait by favoring Iraq in its war with Iran, and helping Saddam Hussein build up his army. By the spring, with the Presidential election season already in full swing, five different congressional committees were investigating so-called Iraq-gate. Henry Gonzalez (the same Representative who is otherwise exercised about separation of powers issues) was using his Banking Committee to investigate loans that the United States guaranteed for Iraq to purchase American grain. Rep. Charlie Rose, a North Carolina Democrat, was looking at the same Commodity Credit Corporation (CCC) loan guarantees from the vantage point of his Agriculture subcommittee. So too was Vermont Democratic Sen. Patrick Leahy, with his Agriculture, Nutrition and Forestry Committee. And Rep. Doug Barnard, a Georgia Democrat, was using his Subcommittee on Commerce, Consumer, and Monetary Affairs to determine whether the Commerce Department was right in allowing Iraq to buy heavy trucks that could be used for military as well as civilian purposes. These four legislators appeared in early June as witnesses at a sort of meta-investigation being held by Texas Democratic Rep. Jack Brooks, chairman of the House Judiciary Committee. The four were there to call for the appointment of (what else?) an independent counsel.

A formal request for an independent counsel can be made by half of one party's Members on either the House or Senate Judiciary Committee. The only catch is, they must specify a criminal offense. Misjudgment in foreign policy, however egregious, is not criminal. But Members are not that easily daunted. They fell back on the old standby that served them so well in the Iran/Contra affair: the charge of lying to, or misleading, Congress. The call for an independent counsel was being made because Agriculture Department (USDA) officials involved in the CCC program told a congressional committee that no "undue political pressure" had been placed on the USDA to authorize the loan guarantees. In truth, the White House and the State Department had been lobbying the USDA to allow the credits, as a way of supporting the Iraqis in the years before the Gulf

War. Whether or not this amounted to "undue" pressure is a judgment call. But the prosecutors on Capitol Hill were in no mood for judgment calls. When Members smell blood, they become a most punctilious lot.

When America's relationship with Saddam Hussein began to deteriorate in the months before Iraq's invasion of Kuwait, it also emerged that an Italian bank, known as BNL, that had handled most of Iraq's U.S.-guaranteed loans had been cooking the books, helping Iraq to use the loans in illegal ways. The USDA responded by holding up the commodity loan guarantees to Iraq. At Rep. Brooks' Judiciary Committee hearing, it further emerged that political pressures were brought to bear on Agriculture to give Iraq a break notwithstanding Saddam's cheating. What made this interesting is that the pressure to push forward with credit guarantees for Iraq came not from the White House but from Congress. In fact, it came from Judiciary Committee Chairman Jack Brooks himself.

The reason has to do with the nature of foreign aid. Far from providing relief for starving foreign children, foreign aid today is mostly about subsidizing domestic industries. The credit guarantees to Iraq were a case in point. Under the CCC program the United States did not give Iraq food or money; what it did was make it possible for Baghdad to get low-interest loans because Uncle Sam co-signed the bank papers guaranteeing that the loans would be repaid. In return, Iraq (or any other country using CCC loans) would have to buy American grain with the money. The bedrock support for such foreign aid plans, then, comes not from the diplomatic community or the State Department, but from the farmers who get to sell the grain.

Brooks represents Texas rice growers. As it turns out, he tried to ensure that these constituents would not lose out on a lucrative market. Thus the letter he wrote to Agriculture Secretary Clayton Yeutter on May 7, 1990, a mere three months before Iraq invaded Kuwait. At Rep. Brooks' committee hearing, a senior Republican, Illinois Rep. Henry Hyde, displayed the letter, barely disguising his glee as he read:

Dear Secretary,

We are writing to inquire about the status of USDA approval of a $500 million GSM 102 export credit guarantee allocation for Iraq. We understand that due to alleged transaction irregularities committed by the Atlanta branch of an Italian bank, involving the GSM credit guarantee program, that further allocations to Iraq have been held up by the Department of Agriculture. While we would never want to hurt the integrity of the GSM credit guarantee program, the withholding of these credits will have a significant economic impact on our area. As I'm sure you're aware, Iraq is the 12th largest importer of U.S. agricultural products and a large export market for United States rice and wheat. Not only is the Houston area involved in rice growing, but the Houston ports play a key role in the exportation of rice and wheat. . . . We look forward to coming to an understanding with regard to this situation.

Between puffs on a well-chewed cigar, Rep. Brooks responded calmly that he had only meant to find out if the USDA was being diligent enough in investigating the problems with the Italian bank. "We just wanted to know when the Department of Agriculture foresaw the investigation of the credit guarantee program, as it pertains to Iraq, coming to a conclusion."

Rep. Charlie Rose, who was appearing before the committee, was not nearly as calm when Hyde read a letter that Rose had signed, a year before the Gulf crisis, which urged the Department of Commerce to encourage and finance the sale of American-made heavy trucks to Iraq. The issue in the hearings had been whether the Commerce Department had misled Congress by designating trucks sold to Iraq as civilian-use goods (and thus not subject to strict export controls). The trucks could be, and many were, converted to military use. The way some Democratic lawmakers had put it at the hearing, the trucks all but turned the Gulf War in the favor of Iraq. "I'm sure for the thousands of American servicemen and servicewomen," said Rhode Island Rep. Jack Reed, "they were thinking many nights why they were out there in the Persian Gulf, and also probably thinking — sleeplessly — where all those trucks came from."

With this background, it was no wonder Rose was so embarrassed when Hyde read from his letter. "In recent years," the letter read, "the Iraqi government has made a concerted effort to court Western investment, with the West Germans and Japanese being most responsive to these overtures. American corporations are already present in Iraq, but given the business opportunities that exist there, as well as the strategic importance of the Middle East, we believe that our government must help in expanding this presence [by financing the truck sales]."

Now, Hyde did not reveal who had written the letter until after he had finished reading it for the committee. As he began reading, however, Rose, who was sitting at the witness table, smiled a sheepish smile of recognition, as though he knew the letter and remembered that he had signed it. But if he did remember having signed it, that is certainly not what he told the committee.

"I didn't sign that letter," Rep. Rose jumped in.

"Someone forged your signature to it?" Rep. Hyde asked.

"Well, my staff signed the letter, but they never checked with me. And how did you get those... "

"You repudiate that letter, then?"

"Absolutely. How did you get it, Henry?"

"You do?" Hyde persisted.

"Where did you get both of those letters, because the administration... "

"I'm going to follow the Nina Totenberg rule," Rep. Hyde said, the crowd laughing, "and not tell you where I got that."

"All right. The administration... " Rose said, looking for some way of making counter-accusations.

"But I'm shocked that your staff would forge your signature to something."

"Well, I am too. I am too."

"And I hope you'll take appropriate action," Hyde chided.

"I have."

"Good."

"It will never happen again."

When Charlie Rose, the tell-tale smirk not yet erased from his lips, bleated that he had never signed the letter calling for a joint venture to produce heavy trucks with the Iraqis, he provided the House Judiciary Committee with real grist for an investigation. Either members of Rose's staff were forging documents (the very charge being levelled against staff at the Department of Commerce), or Rose was lying to Congress (ironically, the accusation being made about officials from the Department of Agriculture). One way or another it seems that something criminal was going on.

Of course, there was no investigation launched, no special prosecutor appointed, in the Rose affair. In fact, it was all forgotten by the next day. The confrontation between Henry Hyde and Rose was a trivial embarrassment, nothing more, rendered all the more trivial because it made no splash in the press. For one thing, no one thought for a minute that Rose had actually signed the letter. This is not to say that the North Carolina Democrat didn't approve the application of his signature to the document; just that Congressmen, in the age of autopens, do not bother with the details of signing or even reading —let alone writing—their own correspondence. The practice is not simply a convenience, as Rose proved. By giving their staffs the keys to the autopen, legislators maintain what has come to be known in Washington as "plausible deniability." Pressing Rose about his claim that his staff had "forged" the letter would have meant discussing the fact that few Congressmen see all the correspondence that goes out the door with their "signatures"; not a topic lawmakers are eager to take up in a public hearing.

What if Rose did sign the letter? Or what if he had read it and given his aides the go-ahead to plug in the autopen? Wouldn't that mean Rose had just lied to Congress? Isn't that the cardinal sin for which executive branch employees are hounded until they are utterly impoverished? Yes. So why did the Judiciary Committee let the ball drop? The investigation would have been quite straightforward: Bring in Rose's administrative assistant and team of legislative assistants and ask which one of them autopenned the letter.

Then ask the staffer whether he had gotten approval from Rose. Simple.

But even so, there was no basis for investigating Rose. One of the manifold privileges of being a Congressman is that it means one can lie to Congress with impunity. So says the Constitution, which gives legislators immunity from prosecution based on their statements in Congress. Rose might have had his wrists slapped by his colleagues under the rules of the House, but fundamentally they just don't care. There is a callous disregard for the truth on Capitol Hill. As we have seen, votes are regularly manipulated to bamboozle the public. Witch hunts are orchestrated to ruin political enemies regardless of their innocence. Hypes and scares are foisted on the nation at immense cost for no greater purpose than to get media hits for ambitious legislators. Lawmakers wax messianic about the saving virtues of bills they never have — and never will— read.

Congressmen have institutionalized lying. They are members of the Ruling Class, and have created for themselves a decadent culture of deceit.

All the more ironic, then, that the main weapon in the congressional armory is the charge of "misleading Congress." "Lying to Congress" can be hard to prove and thus is not the charge of choice. "Misleading" Congress is much easier because all lawmakers have to do is to say they got the wrong impression from some testimony — of course, lawmakers would never fib about what their "impressions" were — and then blame it on the witness. Even when Members really did get the wrong impression, they never ask whether it was their own fault: Legislators often don't understand the answers they are being given because they don't even understand the questions they are asking. At the average hearing, lawmakers are simply reading from cue-cards handed them by their staffs. Nonetheless, the charge of misleading Congress provided one of the bases cited by House Judiciary Committee Democrats in their July 9, 1992, call for an independent counsel to investigate Iraq-gate.

Left completely out of the call for an investigation was any mention of the role Judiciary Committee Chairman Brooks and other Democrats played in keeping U.S. funds flowing to Iraq.

Pointing out Brooks' garden-variety hypocrisy is not to imply that some investigation of the administration's tilt toward Iraq is not in order. The State Department continued to support Saddam Hussein well after the evidence had piled up about Iraq's ruthless ambitions. Hussein's use of chemical weapons against the Kurds in northern Iraq should have been reason enough to abandon efforts to moderate through grain sales the Hussein regime. But such mistakes are not criminal. They may be wrong, and it may be quite proper to criticize such policy flaws. But the proper realm for such disputes is of course the political, not the legal.

Were Congress to hold public hearings looking into the diplomatic blunders building up to the war with Iraq the policy failures could be exposed, and the administration would have a chance to defend its actions. If the public agreed that the mistakes made by the administration were crucial, then the voters would be in a position to punish the President by not returning him to office. Indeed, there were a number of hearings like that, both during the hostilities with Iraq and afterward, in which legislators grilled State Department officials and tried to dump the blame for the war in their laps. But the hearings were not the political successes Democrats were looking for. April Glaspie — the diplomat who appeared to have given Hussein the green light for invading Kuwait by saying the United States didn't care about Arab border disputes — aggressively fended off her congressional attackers in her Capitol Hill appearances.

That is why lawmakers turn to the independent counsel provision, why they criminalize policy disputes: An open airing of the issues does not guarantee a win for Capitol Hill. A policy debate means lawmakers have to defend their own policies and actions. If they cannot convince the voters that their policies were right, then they lose the argument. But by relying on criminal proceedings, legislators are freed from having to explain their policy choices. Instead, policy questions are reduced to punctilious matters of procedure. And of course the only ones who have to answer for their fidelity to procedural niceties are the inmates of the executive branch.

For Congress this is a "heads I win; tails you lose" proposition. If the independent counsel is able to find some wrongdoing—no matter how technical or trivial—on which he can base a conviction or even an indictment, the headlines scream that the administration and its officials were not only wrong, they were scandalously, morally, criminally wrong. But if the officials are exonerated, it is not because their Capitol Hill rivals have been shown up. The prosecutor may get some grief for letting the officials slip by, or on the other hand for using abusive tactics, but that blame never finds its way back to the Congress that empowered him. Independent counsels and the criminalization of policy disputes that they represent, are simply one more way that Congressmen grab credit and avoid blame.

This was the lesson on the Hill from the Iran-Contra hearings. Lawmakers had a great scandal on their hands, and raced to exploit it through nationally televised hearings they expected would discredit the policy of supporting the Nicaraguan Contras, and, better yet, demolish the confrontational Reagan administration. But the show was derailed when administration officials threw away the script that the congressional directors had written, and started to improvise their lines. Lt. Col. Oliver North, far from apologetic at being caught, proclaimed his actions as the heroic execution of a "neat idea." Lawmakers came off as bullies of questionable patriotism. Capitol Hill not only failed to make the case against North and his cohorts stick, lawmakers themselves got burned as North used the hearings as a forum to debate the virtue of helping the Contras. And later, the fact that North's testimony to Congress was under a grant of immunity helped him escape a criminal conviction.

If lawmakers were burned in their Iran-Contra hearings, then full-blown Iraq-gate hearings would promise to be a congressional debacle. To begin with, the prosecutors on the Hill might start to look a little bit ridiculous making the argument that Saddam Hussein constructed the fourth-largest military in the world with a few hundred million dollars scammed off the top of agricultural aid programs. Lawmakers had a hint of how silly they could end up sounding with Rep. Reed's statement that American troops were suffering sleepless nights worrying about the origin of Iraqi trucks. But far more damaging to the case that Congressmen might want to make in Iraq-gate hearings was the fact that Charlie Rose and

Jack Brooks were not the only legislators applying pressure on the administration to give Iraq a break.

And who knows what else a thorough investigation—one that looked into legislative branch actions as well as those of the executive—might turn up. Brooks admitted as much during the press conference he held to announce his call for an independent counsel. The Attorney General could appoint (instead of an "independent counsel" such as Lawrence Walsh, who was authorized under the independent counsel statute) a special prosecutor. One main difference in appointing a special prosecutor, such as the one given the task of investigating the House Bank, is that his tenure can be limited by the Attorney General. Given the spectacle of Lawrence Walsh and his never-ending Iran-Contra investigation, the somewhat less formal special prosecutor might seem prudent. But the main difference between the types of investigators—from Congress' point of view, at least—is that an independent counsel would look only at the actions of the administration. A special prosecutor would probably look into the actions of the would-be secretaries of state on Capitol Hill as well. For that reason, Brooks was emphatic that a special prosecutor should not be appointed, saying at his press conference:

"A special counsel has no guidelines. He just goes off willy-nilly, hires a bunch of lawyers, and starts investigating everybody, and grabbing records, and nobody knows where he's going, or what he's planning to do."

One can see why Congressmen don't want to be the object of an investigation. The letter signed by Rose had also been signed by every other member of the North Carolina congressional delegation, except Sen. Jesse Helms. On the same day, the same group of legislators wrote a similar letter to the Export-Import (Ex-Im) Bank, from whom financing for the project was being sought, encouraging the lender to fall into line. Volvo-GM, the company interested in selling trucks, is headquartered in North Carolina. The truck deal would also have meant jobs for Volvo-GM workers in Utah. Not surprisingly, the congressional delegation of that state also wrote to Deputy Secretary of State Lawrence Eagleburger and the Ex-Im Bank.[3] Even more numerous were letters complaining about the, albeit tardy, actions of the Bush administration to restrict agricultural credit guarantees to the Iraqis, called the GSM program. In addition to their own correspondence, several lawmakers passed along the concerned letters of their rice-growing constituents.

With all of this political pressure coming from Capitol Hill pushing for the administration to ignore evidence that Saddam was playing a shell game with the money he was borrowing, it is no wonder that legislators have focussed on calling for an independent counsel. Any open airing of the U.S. government's policies toward Iraq could not help but embarrass Congress as much, if not more, than the administration. Far better to set up a criminal investigation that will pay attention only to the actions of the administration.

Congress' apologists, given the slew of embarrassing letters written by lawmakers urging trade with Saddam, have tried to shift blame to the administration. (Remember the motto—"Admit Nothing. Deny Everything. Make Counter-accusations.") If only legislators had been told everything that was known by the administration about Iraqi arms dealings, then they would never have pressed for continued grain sales or joint truck ventures. The fault then is with the Bush administration for not acting fast enough on its investigation of the GSM loans, and for not passing its findings around Capitol Hill.

Even if that were the case—and it isn't—Congress would deserve much of the blame. Through the criminalization of policy differences, Congress has given the administration good reason to be tight-lipped. When any statement is potential grist for an independent counsel investigation into the misleading of Congress, is it any wonder that administration officials become non-committal, trying not to say very much at all? We have seen it happen with nominations to the Supreme Court. Since lawmakers have taken to using the statements of nominees in bad faith as nothing but tools for discrediting them, would-be justices have stopped making statements. Clarence Thomas pretended to have never thought about abortion. David Souter breezed into Washington without a paper trail, never having made much in the way of a statement in his life.

These are the predictable consequences of the vitriolic atmosphere Congress has created. Once upon a time, lawmakers could be consulted about judicial appointments, because Senators did not simply use the consultations as an opportunity to compile damaging information with which to impugn nominees. So too, Capitol Hill was once better trusted with sensitive foreign policy information. If legislators wish to be given more thorough briefings, perhaps they should reconsider the criminalization of policy disputes, which has poisoned the relationship between the executive and legislative branches and continues to stifle communication.

Congress today is a place where show trials are the norm, where prosecution substitutes for legislation, and where the language of justice is misused to eliminate enemies. This noxious habit has poisoned Washington, driving good people out of public life, particularly in the executive branch. To be appointed to a serious post in the administration means to be questioned, queried, lectured, hectored, harangued, insulted, impugned, libeled, slandered, leaked against, charged, indicted, tried, and, ultimately, either found guilty or be forced to resign anyway because the public thinks you are. But the corruption of the system has also had a deleterious effect on Congress itself. Rather than engaging in serious, and balanced, inquiries into faulty policies, a process that might lead to valuable lessons for the future, Congress reflexively grasps for a hide to nail to the wall. The world's greatest deliberative body has become the world's most infamous accusatory one, and Americans are disgusted with the process at the same time they are transfixed by the flying accusations.

Thus, it may be just as well for Congress, and it is certainly better for the health of the American political system, that Attorney General William Barr refused to launch the criminal probe Rep. Brooks requested. Barr replied to Brooks in great detail,[4] pointing out that the Democrats' request failed to allege any specific crimes, didn't offer any evidence to support their vague allegations, and did not identify the officials who were to be investigated. The accusations simply did not meet the standards Congress itself had established in the independent counsel law. But Barr's broader point was about the evils of mixing politics and criminal law: it undermines our system of justice at the same it poisons political debate.

If the independent counsel law is not renewed, the congressional inquisitors will have lost their ultimate weapon. But more fundamentally, Congress should get out of the business of conducting criminal investigations. If Congress won't, the executive branch should expand on Attorney General Barr's Iraq-gate response and just say no. When Congress asks policy questions, administration officials should answer to the best of their ability, but when Congress attempts to "investigate," they should politely decline to play along.

Aside from the noxious political results, congressional meddling has not infrequently endangered genuine prosecutions. Rather than playing the role of amateur sleuths, congressional committees should be required to hand over evidence of criminal activity to real prosecutors, who will be more interested in punishing wrongdoing than in scoring political points. To the extent that they do pursue criminal accusations, committees should be required to do so in closed hearings. This would serve both to protect the rights of the (often innocent) accused and to remove the incentive to fling criminal accusations strictly for their publicity value.

While the grandiose inquisitors will obviously resist these changes in the ground rules, the public can judge a Member of Congress' commitment to reform by his willingness to rein-in the partisan investigatory machine.

6

OTHER PEOPLE'S MONEY

I didn't become a United States Senator to sit around and worry about the fine details.

—Senate Budget Committee Chairman James Sasser explaining that he doesn't like math.[1]

Of all the battles over federal spending, few are more revealing about congressional mores than the fight over the Corporation for Public Broadcasting (CPB) during the spring and summer of 1992. The controversy began as an effort by conservative Republicans to chastise the Public Broadcasting System (PBS) for airing left-leaning, counter-cultural, and quasi-pornographic programs. By the end, the debate had shifted to whether the federal government should be in the business of paying for television shows in the first place. In a time of staggering budget deficits and out-of-control spending, the ultimate triumph of those who argued in favor of shelling out $350 million a year to air BBC reruns helps illustrate why reforming congressional spending habits appears next to impossible.

Though only a tiny portion of the federal budget, public broadcasting illustrates perfectly the division between the elites who spend and the taxpayers who foot the bills. Indeed, if ever a federal beneficiary qualified as a welfare queen, it is public broadcasting.

The federal subsidy accounted for only 17 percent of public radio and TV budgets in 1992, with the rest coming from individual, corporate and foundation donations and state and local governments. More to the point, its viewers are more than capable of paying their own way. A rate card sent out by Washington, D.C., public television station WETA to potential advertisers boasted that the average household net worth of contributors to the station was $627,000, with an investment portfolio of $249,000. One in seven WETA contributors had a wine cellar; one out of eight was a millionaire; one in three had been to Europe within the past three years.

The stations serving such impoverished audiences receive all manner of government assistance. Take the Educational Broadcasting Corporation of New York, which operates the PBS station WNET. In fiscal year 1989, various government agencies gave the corporation grants totalling $30 million. Of this, $16.7 million came from the federal government via the CPB, $220,000 from the National Science Foundation, $155,000 from the National Endowment for the Humanities, $116,000 from the National Endowment for the Arts, $69,000 from the National Aeronautics and Space Administration, and $43,000 from the U.S. Postal Service. An additional $10 million came from New York state government agencies and $560,000 from the state of New Jersey.

The Educational Broadcasting Corporation used these funds to pay their staff members lavish salaries. In the 1989-90 fiscal year, WNET Executive Producer Lester Crystal received salary and benefits of over $400,000; President Trustee William F. Baker received $275,000 in salary and benefits; and George Page, executive producer and host of the "Nature" series, received $240,000 in benefits and salary. At least 12 other WNET officials—an executive vice president, six senior vice presidents, and five vice presidents —received six-figure packages of salary and other compensation. Even the station's chief publicist, Senior Vice-President for Public Affairs Ruth Ann Burns, received $118,471 in salary and $35,541 in benefits.

One reason PBS and its affiliates can afford hefty salaries is that some of its programming is highly profitable. Big Bird has become big bucks. The Children's Television Workshop, which produces *Sesame Street*, grosses approximately $100 million a year in royalties, licensing and subscription revenues on Sesame Street books, lunchboxes, dolls, arena shows, towels, sheets, shampoo, diapers, bicycles, videos, pajamas, and other products. The Children's Television Workshop has over $51 million in stocks and bonds in its investment portfolio; its highest-paid employee, Divisional President William W. Whaley, received $641,224 in salary and benefits in 1991.

Yet, despite its obvious profitability, the Children's Television Workshop receives $14 million per year in government grants. On top of this, it even applied for $20 million in funds designated to help Russia free itself from Communist tyranny. What did the Children's Television Workshop have in mind? Broadcasting *Sesame Street* to Russian children.

During the debate over PBS funding, columnist George Will was among the first to question the propriety of taking money from working people to subsidize the pleasures of the upper middle class. The lack of success in ending a transfer of resources from poor to rich did not, he suggest, bode well for other spending reforms. "If something as marginal as public television successfully defends its subsidy," wrote Will, "[budget] cuts can come only at the expense of Americans less affluent, educated, articulate, and skillful at lobbying than public television's aggressively moralistic constituency."

In the Senate, Republican Leader Robert Dole of Kansas led the fight, arguing that large increases in public broadcasting subsidies are a luxury that the nation cannot afford in hard times. "America is broke," he said. "We simply cannot pay for all the good things we have to have. We simply cannot afford all the good things for the inner cities, our military bases, our farms, our schools, hospitals, the unemployed, America's highways, mass transit, the elderly, and yes, even for all the good things for public broadcasting."

But the defenders of public TV were undaunted. Public broadcasting is educational, they said, and America can't go around cutting spending on education at a time when our children's test scores are down. Some of the more honest among them even owned up to the real reason they supported public television spending: good old-fashioned pork. There is either a public radio station or a public television station in every congressional district.

Sen. Lloyd Bentsen opted for the educational-value defense. The Texas Democrat was ecstatic over the programs that KLRU-TV in Austin, KMBH in Harlingen, and KERA in Dallas broadcast in the schools, such as KERA's program to "instruct child care providers on the use of *Sesame Street* to teach preschool-aged children."

Massachusetts Democratic Sen. John Kerry provided an even more explicit example of how essential PBS was to the folks back home by relating the sad story of Ruth Anne Dingee, a constituent from South Boston. Dingee is a retired church organist. Disabled, alone, and in a wheelchair, she spent her days at home watching the tube. "Ms. Dingee has a lot of time to watch television," Sen. Kerry said. "But she doesn't have cable and she says most of what is on commercial TV distresses her. She says that when she became disabled and her world became smaller it was public television that opened it up again. Public broadcasting took her to places she could not otherwise go, broadening her education and deepening her mind .... She doesn't have to pay someone to take her out to movies because the world comes into her home via public television."

On the merits of these arguments, the defenders of the billion-dollar PBS system don't seem to have much of a case. Why should pre-school teachers be turning to *Sesame Street* rather than teaching the children themselves? But the knock-down argument against the public broadcasting subsidy is that public broadcasting doesn't need it. Defenders themselves routinely pointed out that the federal government accounts for only 17 percent of the budget, the implication being that it was a bargain for the taxpayer. But logic points in the opposite direction. If the federal share of the enterprise is so small, then public broadcasting should have no trouble doing without it. A little more fundraising, and a variety of new efficiencies, and PBS should still be able to produce shows like its epic Civil War series. And Mrs. Dingee would still find the world coming to her via her television set.

In the end, however, only 11 Senators voted even to limit spending increases for PBS. The lop-sided vote for this pork-for-the-well-heeled bill suggests why it is so hard to cut spending. As with every other item on the federal budget, public broadcasting has a constituency. In the broadest sense, that constituency is made up of everyone who watches the *McNeil/Lehrer Newshour* or *Masterpiece Theatre*. This audience enjoys public radio and television, and they aren't about to see its subsidy cut back without raising a fuss. They are joined by a second constituency: all those for whom public broadcasting represents a job. These latter people have the most reason to mobilize in defense of the public broadcasting budget, and mobilize they did. Is it any coincidence that George Will's main sparring partner in debates about PBS funding was Bill Moyers, who makes his living almost exclusively as public TV's in-house middlebrow intellectual? Likewise Robin McNeil, co-host of the *Newshour* with his name in it, could be heard on public radio deriding those who would cut public broadcasting funds as narrow-minded ideologues.

Against this the vast body of taxpayers who neither work for public broadcasting nor enjoy its programming remained virtually silent. A few people offended and angered by PBS documentaries celebrating such things as the lesbian and gay counter-culture did get involved. But their reasons were ideological rather than financial. Taxpayers as a group were not heard.

Not that this was much of a suprise. The entire public broadcasting bill added up to $1.1 billion over three years. A lot of money, yes, but divide it among the 112-million taxpayers in the country, and the elimination of the public broadcast subsidy would provide the average taxpayer with a savings on his federal tab of only $3.27 a year. It's just not in the interest of a normal citizen to fly to Washington, pay for a hotel, and spend all day waiting in a stuffy Senate hearing room to testify against PBS just to save $3.27 on his tax bill. It doesn't even make financial sense for residents of Washington: Cabfare alone would easily amount to more than the three-years' savings.

The Joy of Spending

This is the age-old dilemma of special interest spending. The benefits flowing from the spending are focused, while the costs are spread out. It is the beneficiaries, then, who always win the day. Take a penny from each taxpayer, and none will notice it. Give that million dollars to one person, however, and he will most certainly notice it. Conversely, give taxpayers back their pennies and again they won't notice, let alone thank you. But take away the beneficiary's million dollar present and his hollering will be heard for miles.

Nearly every congressional spending program operates the same way. Each taxpayer shares the costs; a select group reaps the benefits. For each program, then, it is the beneficiaries who have reason to speak up, and it is they who nearly always dominate the debates. When the question is subsidies to Amtrak, rail employees and passengers make their way to the mikes. When the question is farm subsidies, farmers. Art subsidies, artists. If given a chance taxpayers might opt to reduce their taxes as a whole by, say, setting the total spending level first. That was the idea behind the Budget Act of 1974: Set overall spending levels first as a way to get control of the federal budget. But the Budget Act had few real impediments to spending, and Congress does everything it can to ignore even those. As a result, spending is considered on a program-by-program basis so that in any particular instance it is not worth the taxpayer's while to fight. In each case, then, the program's beneficiaries win out, and the federal budget grows and grows.

This explains the strange phenomenon author James Payne found when he came to Washington trying to understand federal spending. Payne looked at hundreds of congressional hearings, expecting lively debate and perhaps even a little drama. Instead he found everyone in agreement. Now, Payne was not examining Congress' more flamboyant hearings, those used as soapboxes by legislators eager to keep their names in the papers with alarmist health hoaxes. Rather, he reviewed the bread-and-butter hearings, the ones in which the real work of Congress is done, the hearings of committees in charge of spending money. At these, there were no fireworks, just a succession of witnesses who favored whatever spending bill was on the table.

Payne studied dozens of hearings on 14 different spending bills working their way through Congress. Out of some 1,060 witnesses testifying about the bills, he found only seven opposed to either the program or the spending that keeps it afloat. A mere 39 witnesses were ambivalent, expressing support for some spending and opposition to other money requests. The vast majority—over 1,000 of the 1,060—were there to propose, encourage, or defend spending.

In his book *The Culture of Spending*, Payne rejects, at least in part, the common view that Members rather cynically conspire with bureaucrats and interest groups to spend money in ways that benefit every side of the so-called iron triangle. He argues instead that generally well-meaning, earnest lawmakers come to the Hill and are met by a phalanx of outstretched hands. Like a lottery winner set upon by needy unfortunates, all the stories of hardship sound compelling. Members find it hard to refuse. In this way, they are drawn progressively into a "culture of spending"—the longer one stays in Congress, the more likely one is to be a big spender.

Payne may be a bit too generous in his assessment that Congressmen are disposed neither for nor against spending until they arrive in Washington, where they are brainwashed by a barrage of funding requests. Congress is most able to do things when it spends money, and so legislators who want to demonstrate some accomplishments are inclined to pull out the federal checkbook from the get go. But Payne is right to note that Members are driven by what they hear from constituents, and that generally what they hear from constituents is "gimme."

Although he does not explain why only those who favor spending manage to make themselves heard, Payne's research does give clues. Of the 1,014 advocates of spending Payne noted at congressional hearings, nearly 47 percent were federal employees. An additional 10.5 percent were state and local government officials. Members of Congress accounted for 6.1 percent of the witnesses. Most of the private-sector groups who testified, he discovered, were large organizations (the Sierra Club, the AFL-CIO, Planned Parenthood) dependent to some degree on federal handouts. Such witnesses defend spending because they have a direct stake in it. These incentives are what some have termed the commons problem.

The Tragedy of the Commons

For centuries, English farmers grazed their cattle on public pastures. These plots were called "commons," because the land was owned and maintained in common by the community. Though the farmers were by no means incompetent at their trade, they would repeatedly put too many animals on the commons. Overgrazing led to cows which weighed less, produced less milk, and were prone to disease. The farmers knew that overburdening the commons resulted in lower production and thus lower revenue than if the public pastures were managed sensibly. They knew they risked losing their overcrowded and underfed livestock in ruinous epidemics. Yet they still put too many cows on the commons.

Economist Garrett Hardin explained why in an essay, "The Tragedy of the Commons."[2] Each farmer receives the full benefit, in milk or meat, of every cow he puts on the commons. The farmer is only responsible, however, for a share of the upkeep of the fields. If there are 10 farmers in a particular village each pays one-tenth of the cost of maintaining the commons. Yet each gets all the profit from his own cows. For the farmer considering whether to expand his herd there is a simple economic calculation, one that always leads to the same answer. When a farmer adds a new cow he gains all the profit to be had from that cow, but he incurs only one-tenth the cost of its upkeep. So it is always in each farmer's interest to add as many cows as he can afford to buy. The result? Disaster.

This paradox has become known among economists as the commons problem. When costs are divorced from benefits, no one has reason to exercise restraint. To the contrary, everyone grabs for benefits. As more and more benefits are snagged, costs are driven out of sight. Think of it as going out to a restaurant with a group of friends who decide to divide the check evenly. Even if the group would like to keep the bill down, each person has an incentive to order the most expensive thing on the menu. Among friends, social pressure may be enough to keep everyone eating hamburger. But let one person order filet mignon, and all bets are off.

Federal spending is just such a dinner. We are gorging ourselves because not one of us has been asked to pay his own tab. So the shouts for more and more services escalate and Congress is happy to play along. The logic of the commons is such that by handing out money, Congressmen earn the focused gratitude of beneficiaries, while the distress of taxpayers is fragmented. Pork projects are profoundly wasteful, and most taxpayers would be willing to forego pork if everyone else did the same. But as long as local spending is funneled through Washington, no one complains when his Congressman brings the bacon home. Naturally Members of Congress relish the electoral gratitude that comes with this job. So they perpetuate a federal commons.

How else can we explain the persistence of such boondoggles as sugar subsidies. There are about 11,029 sugar-beet farmers and 1,900 sugar-cane growers in the United States who receive about 22 cents a pound for their sugar from the government, substantially more than the world market price of about 8.5 cents per pound. In effect, each sugar-beet farmer gets a subsidy of about $25,000 and each sugar-cane grower gets $119,000, all in all about $2.5 billion from taxpayers each year. In addition, corn growers, given the artificially high price of sugar, can sell high-fructose corn syrup at a price of a few cents per pound below the price of sugar.

When Congress asks whether it should continue sugar subsidies, the overwhelming chorus cries yes. Again, it's simply not worth the average taxpayer's effort to cut a program that adds only $22 a year to his grocery bill. At least it's not worth as much to the average taxpayer as it is to the average sugar-cane grower who stands to lose $119,000 if the subsidy is nixed. And certainly it's not worth as much to the average taxpayer as it is to corn-processing giant Archer-Daniels-Midland, one of the richest and most influential lobbies on Capitol Hill. Not only do such subsides make it worthwhile for beneficiaries to speak out when the subject is raised on Capitol Hill, they make it virtually imperative that they already have a lobbying presence to guarantee that the gravy train continues.

In 1989 Congress discovered, quite by accident, how to dismantle the insidious logic of the commons. With the Medicare Catastrophic Coverage Act, Congress reversed the cost/benefit equation. A broad population (senior citizens as a whole) was given the benefit of big-ticket health insurance, while a segment of that population (wealthy senior citizens) was saddled with the costs.

Wealthy seniors screamed. Why should they have to pay $800 dollars a year for insurance they already had? (A $3.27 change in one's tax bill may not be enough to engender action, but $800 will generally do the trick.) Had the costs been spread around as usual, wealthy seniors no doubt would have been happy to sign up for the federal insurance, even though it duplicated policies they already had. But when asked to pay, seniors were forced to ask whether they could get their coverage elsewhere at a better rate. They could, and they let their legislators know it.

Almost overnight those who favored spending were shouted down by those opposed. Of the 2,173 letters Wisconsin Republican Rep. Steve Gunderson received about the Catastrophic Care Act, 2,172 urged repeal. Of the 3,807 letters sent to Rep. Bill Paxon, a New York Republican, not one supported the program. The House, not surprisingly, voted 360-66 to repeal the act just months after it had gone into effect. The logic of the commons was broken. For the first time, a major federal entitlement program was dismantled.

Here, then, is the answer for controlling federal spending: insofar as possible, tie costs to benefits. Congress saw the result, but the lesson they took was to keep costs as far away from benefits as possible. After the catastrophic care reversal, Members vowed that if they ever tried to bring the program back they would be sure to make the financing "fairer." Which is to say, they won't dare stray from the logic of the commons again.

Lawmakers not only tolerate the logic of the commons, they exploit it for their electoral advantage. To make sure legislators get full credit, Congress has structured spending so that they can get their pictures taken handing out the checks. Consider what has happened to federal highway spending. The bill that authorized the creation of America's interstate highway system, the Federal-Aid Highway Act of 1956, was just 32 pages long. The section of this

bill that described how the interstate highways would be funded and
built took up only 11 pages of this text. The legislation was broad
and general. No state, county, or locality was mentioned in the bill.
Compare that with the highway bill Congress crafted in 1991, the
Intermodal Surface Transportation Efficiency Act. In addition to the
298 pages of small-print text in the bill itself, the accompanying
conference report goes on for another 186 pages.

Packed into the bill is project after project of pork amounting to
billions. Each Member was happy to sign off on the total bill, as
long as he knew his own project would be included. Indeed, such
was their zeal to take credit that Members insisted their names or
those of their relatives and patrons be placed on these projects.
Section 1083 of part A, for example, declared a Pennsylvania
highway to be the "J. Clifford Naugle Bypass" and a lock and dam
on Louisiana's Red River the "Lindy Claiborne Boggs Lock and
Dam." Section 1083(d)(1) of the bill declared "the boat ramp
constructed on the left bank of the Mississippi River at River Mile
752.5 at Shelby Forest in Shelby County, Tennessee, shall be known
and designated as the 'Joseph Ralph Sasser Boat Ramp,'" in honor
of Democratic Sen. James Sasser's father. Taking no chances,
Section 1083(d)(2) reads that "a reference in any law, map, regulation, document, record, or other paper of the United States to such
boat ramp shall be deemed to be a reference to the 'Joseph Ralph
Sasser Boat Ramp.'"[3]

This practice is limited neither to Democrats nor to transportation
projects. Pennsylvania Rep. Joseph McDade is the ranking Republican member of the House Appropriations Committee, which gives
him a great advantage when the pork is doled out. Why else would
the federal government be paying for the Steamtown National
Historic Site, which McDade has tried to make the nation's repos-
itory for steam trains. Called a "white elephant" by a dismayed
National Parks Service, federal dollars for Steamtown were first
slipped into an appropriations bill by McDade in 1986. Under
protest, the Park Service began to renovate the site. But the boondoggle soon began to go over budget. One bridge cost $7.5 million
to repair. Not only was the project expensive, it was dangerous: So
rickety were the trains that at one point eight passenger cars decou-

pled from an engine while travelling at 50 miles per hour. Yet each
year McDade managed to slip in amendments at the last minute
giving Steamtown more money. Over five years this made up a tidy
sum: $40 million.

Yet even this largesse was not enough. In the fall of 1991 McDade
introduced a bill that would give Steamtown an additional $40
million to complete the project, and $6.5 million a year to run it.
"We've got too much money invested to kill this project now,"
McDade argued. "Think of all the money we'd be wasting!" Think
of it, indeed.

Still, Rep. McDade is a piker compared with Sen. Robert Byrd.
The Democratic Sen. makes no bones about his quest to lavish
federal money on West Virginia: His stated aim is to garner $1
billion for the state during his current six-year Senate term. As
chairman of the Senate Appropriations Committee he can do it, too.
Few appropriations bills get out the door without being loaded
down with West Virginia pork.

Frequently working in conjunction with West Virginia's House
Members, Byrd has come close to his billion dollar target in only
four years. *Congressional Quarterly* reports that in 1991, Byrd and
his staffers managed to add earmarked projects in nine out of the
13 major appropriations bills, including $195 million in the trans-
portation bill, $48 million in the bill funding the Departments of
Commerce, Justice, and State, $88 million in energy and water
projects, and $46 million in defense and military construction
projects. Although the Senator was blocked in his efforts to move
much of the Central Intelligence Agency to West Virginia, he did
manage to capture an FBI fingerprint lab worth $185 million. That
bit of pork had a domino effect: $12.3 million in highway funds to
build roads to the lab and $48 million for new automated fingerprint
equipment.

Local colleges have been prime recipients of Byrd's generosity
with our tax dollars. Some $65 million went to West Virginia
University and Wheeling Jesuit College. Funding for the schools
came from the budgets of several federal programs, including the
Department of Health and Human Services, the Centers for Disease
Control, the Energy Department, the Environmental Protection

Agency, the Department of Transportation, the Agriculture Department, and the National Aeronautics and Space Administration (NASA). To put this in perspective, the $41 million NASA gave Wheeling Jesuit for a National Technology Transfer Center and a Classroom of the Future is more than 10 times the college's endowment and three times its annual budget.

Yet NASA officials did not want, or need, a National Technology Transfer Center, since the agency already has nine laboratories that distribute research findings to industry. But lawmakers such as Byrd don't even make a pretense of working toward national objectives. According to Leonard A. Ault, deputy director of NASA's Technology Transfer Division, the grant to Wheeling Jesuit got its start when Byrd's staffers asked NASA to do "something about technology transfer in West Virginia." NASA then conducted a study looking at "a role West Virginia might play" in this field; three years later, Wheeling Jesuit got its grant.

The scandal is that Wheeling is no exception. More and more of the money that Congress gives to colleges and universities is allocated on the basis of political muscle rather than educational or technical merit. According to the *Chronicle of Higher Education*, at least $684 million in the fiscal year 1992 budget was "earmarked," specifically designated by individual Members of Congress in non-competitive grants to home-state colleges and universities. *National Journal* reports that such funding may amount to $1 billion annually—a substantial increase from the $50 million spent on earmarked higher education projects a decade ago.

Like most pork, earmarked education projects are no bargain. Robert Crease looked at three examples of education pork in *Science* magazine, finding not only that the projects were not leading-edge efforts, but, in fact, they didn't even exist except as checks drawn on the federal treasury. The National Center for Chemical Research at Columbia University, which received annual grants from the Energy Department totalling $23.7 million between 1984 and 1988, is a case in point. Crease, who had attended Columbia, had no idea that such a center existed. Neither did the university's public information office. No piece of stationery existed with a National Center for Chemical Research letterhead. The money was actually used to renovate the Columbia University chemistry building. "I don't know what the phrase 'National Center' really means," Columbia chemistry professor Nick Turro told Crease. "If someone were to ask me to show them the Chemistry Center, meaning the part funded by the DOE, I would show them the renovated part."

Or take the $220,000 grant the Department of Energy made in 1989 to Rural Enterprises, Inc., (REI) of Durant, Oklahoma, to develop a "transferring technology demonstration project." The funds were used by REI to aid small businesses in southern Oklahoma. That "aid" consisted of handing out Energy Department reports to about two dozen Oklahoma businessmen. An REI newsletter Crease examined had no mention of its technology transfer program. But it did, he noted, "contain pictures of one of Oklahoma's U.S. Congressmen and a full-page insert about one of the state's U.S. Senators."

A third Energy Department grant Crease looked at, a $14.8 million award to St. Christopher's Hospital in Philadelphia, was given with the objective of developing a medical center for children that would feature "new evolving energy source technologies." This center was indeed built—but without any new technologies. A St. Christopher's spokesman explained that they had decided to make the center one that emphasized energy conservation.[4]

Obviously, larding up home district projects and helping one's colleagues do the same is an easy way to build loyal constituencies at home and make friends on Capitol Hill. Cutting pork, by contrast, is a quick way to make enemies. It is not just that other Members become angry when their pet projects are threatened. To challenge pork is to question one of the most venerable traditions of the institution. Cutting spending in this way is seen as an affront, a display of bad manners, a legislative faux pas. When Rep. Harris Fawell led a lonely effort to strip pork from an appropriations bill, the Illinois Republican was told that he was "insulting" the 59 members of the House Appropriations Committee.

An "insulted" Congress is not a comfortable place for the offending Member. Rep. Jim Slattery is one who learned his lesson the hard way. The Kansas Democrat led a successful effort to block a half-million-dollar grant to restore the birthplace of bandleader Lawrence Welk. His reward was an angry blast from the sponsor of the Welk effort, North Dakota Democratic Rep. Byron Dorgan, and a warning from Rep. Jamie Whitten, Chairman of the House Appropriations Committee. Chairman Whitten informed Slattery that his Kansas projects might well be doomed if he didn't shape up. And shape up he did. Soon Slattery announced that the Welk fight had so wearied him that he would in the future confine his budget-reducing activities to one or two major (and no doubt, more socially acceptable) goals, such as ending funding for the B-2 bomber.

Defenders of pork argue that it is just a way for taxpayers to get back the money they send to Washington. But the impression that pork is some sort of windfall is false. One should not be grateful just to get back what ought to have been one's own money all along, especially after it has been laundered through the Washington spending machine. It would be akin to describing an income tax refund as a gift from the government.

There are two main problems with Congress as the nation's spending middleman. To begin with, sending tax dollars to Washington and then having them sent back is profoundly inefficient: there is the cost of federal tax collection; the cost of the federal bureaucracy; the cost of complying with federal paperwork; the cost of navigating red tape; the costs associated with lost flexibility; and the cost of delay. In other words, doing business with Washington is ruinous because of the federal government's overhead. As of 1990, the federal government had for the last four years taken more money from the states than it returned.[5] Then again, the very idea that the federal government could give *more* money to the states than it takes from the citizenry is a testament to the power of deficit spending. We have given Congress a national credit card with which lawmakers get to play Santa Claus. Unfortunately, some day *we* will have to pay the bill for all our presents.

The second, and more important, reason to resist funneling money through Washington is the fact that it is by controlling money that Congress exercises its greatest powers. Handing our money over to Washington then asking for it back is rather like turning our bank accounts into a trust fund, and asking Congress to give us

money only when Members deem it in our best interest. Free
citizens should shudder at the thought of such a paternalistic arrangement. And even if we didn't feel competent to govern ourselves, would we want to entrust such powers to Congress?[6]

Spending is not a simple matter of either funding a program or
not. Increasingly, Congress has divided programs and departments
into smaller and smaller pieces, until lawmakers can determine the
minute details of administration. Bureaucrats and executive branch
officials know that their jobs can be written out of existence if they
displease Congress. With that threat, the modern Congress has
perfected the techniques and ambitions that Woodrow Wilson described in *Congressional Government* in 1885. The legislative
branch, Wilson wrote, "has entered more and more into the details
of administration, until it has virtually taken into its own hands all
the substantial powers of government. It does not domineer over
the President himself, but it makes the Secretaries its humble
servants."

The more spending, the more scope for congressional power. And
Congress has never been shy about amassing what power it could,
doing so gradually, almost imperceptibly: "It is safe to say that
Congress always had the desire to have a hand in every affair of
federal government," Wilson wrote, "but it was only by degrees that
it found means and opportunity to gratify that desire, and its activity,
extending its bounds wherever perfected processes of congressional
work offered favoring prospects, has been enlarged so naturally and
so silently that it has almost always seemed of normal extent, and
has never, except perhaps during one or two brief periods of
extraordinary political disturbance, appeared to reach much beyond
its acknowledged constitutional sphere."[7]

Since Wilson's time the staff and other resources of Congress
have exploded, exacerbating the problems he recognized. But far
more than the growth of staff, the growth of the federal government
overall has given Congress its real opportunity to expand its power.
Money is power, and Congress now deals in far more money than
ever before. Nearly every dollar lawmakers hand out comes with
strings attached, and those federal strings are strangling businesses,
private organizations and state and local governments.

The 1991 Highway Bill, for example, not only came larded with pork, it was stuffed with demands states would have to meet to get their money. Some of the stipulations were about how the money had to be spent: Under Section 18 of the Act, states are ordered to spend 5 percent of the highway money available in fiscal year 1992, 10 percent in fiscal year 1993, and 15 percent from fiscal year 1994 onwards in an effort to establish an intercity bus system.[8] But many of the demands were only obliquely related to the spending. That is, Congress said: If a state wants to get its money, it has to pass laws to accomplish favored social goals.

Since the advent of automobiles, state legislatures have been considered competent to determine what counts as drunken driving, and to prescribe appropriate punishment. Today, Congress wants to make those determinations, and so set up a program of grants to prevent drunk driving. To receive their full share of the monies, states are required to make their drunk driving laws conform to Congress' standard. States that enact laws declaring drunk any drivers whose blood alcohol content is over 0.08 percent get 5 percent more money; states that declare drivers under the age of 21 drunk if they have a blood alcohol content of over 0.02 percent get another 5 percent. States which ban the possession of open alcoholic beverage containers in vehicles (except on chartered buses with more than 10 passengers) get a further 5 percent bonus. Another 5 percent goes to states that enact laws requiring drivers to undergo a blood alcohol test if a police officer thinks they are drunk. Still another 5 percent comes to states that hit drunk or drugged drivers with a mandatory license suspension of 90 days for the first offense and one year for the second. Lastly, an additional 5 percent grant goes to states that buy video equipment for police to detect drunk drivers.[9]

Living up to Congress' demands means not only the loss of state and local discretion, it also means an avalanche of paperwork as state and local officials are forced to prove that lawmakers' specifications are being met. John Meyer, a political scientist at Stanford University, looked into the effect federal education funds had on local school districts in the 1976-77 school year. He found that federal education programs other than Title I created four and a half times as much paperwork as comparable state funds. Title I funds were 19 times more difficult to administer than state programs. Princeton's Jane Hannaway observed school administrators overseeing federal grants in a city of 500,000 and found that these administrators spent 64 percent of their time in meetings and twice as much time pushing paper as did their colleagues with non-federal responsibilities.

Spending gives Congress the leverage to make demands of states and localities. More and more, however, Congress is commanding the states to use their own money for programs that federal lawmakers don't even pay for. By 1980, Congress had passed 36 laws requiring state and local government action without providing the money to pay for it; 22 of these laws were passed in the 1970s. The cost of these "mandates" on state and local governments is far from insignificant. When the Rehabilitation Act of 1979 required, for example, that public transit systems be accessible to handicapped people, the Chicago Transit Authority complained that the mandate would cost the city more than it had invested in rapid transit since the system was founded in 1890.

Initially the Reagan Administration attempted to reduce such regulatory burdens on cities and states. The Office of Management and Budget estimated that 1981 reforms consolidating dozens of federal programs saved state and local governments 5.9 million work hours annually. But the attempts to reduce regulations fizzled. In 1985 the Supreme Court refused to review a lower court decision declaring the federal mandate process on states constitutional, even when no funds are attached.[10] Congress proceeded to impose even more mandates on state actions: including 27 statutes requiring states to enact major changes in their laws in the 1980s.[11]

The appeal for Congress in passing mandates is that, once again, they can grab credit and dodge blame (and the bill). Since Congress can no longer afford new programs, and is unwilling even to limit the growth of easy targets such as public broadcasting, if lawmakers want to sponsor new initiatives, they have to pass the costs off on someone else. The states are an obvious answer. Lawmakers are able to deliver for special-interest groups by requiring that the states satisfy the groups' desires. Yet when the bill comes due, it is not

Congress that has to come up with the money by raising taxes, cutting other services, or imposing new regulations. For Congress, mandates are the perfect way to spend other people's money.

And a lot of money it is. Medicaid, the federal/state program to provide health insurance to the poor, has been a favorite target for mandates. For example, in 1989 Congress required the states to extend the program, previously limited to those legally defined as poor, to children under six in families with incomes up to one-third above the poverty line. In 1991 Congress decided it hadn't gone far enough and ordered states to phase-in coverage for children between ages six and 18. Such mandates, along with general health care spending increases, boosted the share of state budgets devoted to Medicaid from 9 percent in 1980 to 14 percent in 1990—costing states more than $32.4 billion.[12]

The pace of congressional mandates on states has quickened. As of April 1992, bills before Congress would impose 150 new federal mandates upon the states, requiring states to do everything from creating commissions on domestic violence to testing infants for hearing loss. The National Conference of State Legislatures estimates that these bills, if enacted, would cost states at least $1.7 billion, with most of the costs coming under the Child Welfare and Preventive Services Act, which would cost states $997 million in expanded Medicaid benefits. The National Governors Association estimates that federally mandated spending will consume 28 percent of state budgets by 1995.

The Shell Game

When not fobbing the costs of its programs off on the states, Congress finds other ways to mask the money it spends. A favorite is to put a program "off-budget," so that, at least in theory, neither its assets nor its liabilities count as part of the federal budget. In practice, however, while the liabilities are taken off the books, often some assets are left as part of the budget, to make the deficit look smaller. Such was the case with the savings and loan bailout. The Resolution Trust Corporation (RTC) created by Congress in 1989 to manage the bailout, borrowed money to pay another government

agency, the Federal Savings and Loan Insurance Corporation
(FSLIC), for the assets of failed S&Ls. The money borrowed by the
RTC is off-budget; only the interest paid on the loans it takes out is
considered a cost to the government. Yet all of the borrowed money
given to FSLIC by the RTC was treated as revenue added to federal
coffers. Paying for the S&L disaster, then, appeared to reduce the
deficit rather than add to it. In the real world, this is called cooking
the books, and people go to jail for doing it.

Trust funds are another deficit-reducing trick. For years Congress
has been assessing special taxes for highways, airports, and, most
notoriously, Social Security which bring more money into the trust
funds designated for these programs than is paid out in benefits. The
result: a lower deficit. The problem is, there are no real trust funds,
merely some accounting entries at the Treasury Department. When
baby boomers start to retire or highways crumble, there will be no
real money in the trust funds and taxes will have to be raised to pay
the bills. Once again, these sorts of financial practices are illegal,
unless of course you happen to be the United States Congress.

With all these ruses to shift costs and hide spending, you may
wonder at the furor over budget cuts, particularly under President
Reagan. Of course, those "cuts" were another trick. Along with the
hidden spending increase, Congress has perfected the phony spending cut. The most pervasive—and cynical—tool for making phony
cuts is something known as the "current services baseline." When
lawmakers pass an appropriation bill and pat themselves on the back
for cutting spending by millions of dollars, chances are Congress
has just spent more than it did the year before. How can Congress
spend more and yet claim that it has cut spending? The spending
level legislators use to match their new bills against (the "baseline")
is not the amount that was spent the previous year. Instead, they
project automatic annual increases in every program for inflation,
population growth, and other factors. These estimates are routinely,
and purposefully, high. When the real bill is completed, therefore,
it is likely to be less expensive than the bogus bill estimated in the
current services budget. A cut, then, is when Congress doesn't spend
as much more money as it thought it might.

Congressmen get so much mileage out of spending money that it is no surprise that they are not willing to rein themselves in. Nor will they stand for an executive branch getting any ideas along these lines. It turns out, for instance, that sending some veterans to private doctors and hospitals might save as much as $500 million per year. But, because privatization would mean less control by legislators, Congress passed a law prohibiting the Department of Veterans Affairs from even considering such proposals. Similarly, the executive branch is not allowed to study whether government-owned dams should charge free-market rates for the electricity they produce. Congress has barred the Farmers Home Administration from asking recipients of new loans whether they have ever defaulted on previous loans. Then there are marketing orders, a system of limits on the amount of citrus fruit produced in the United States which allows wealthy growers to charge artificially high prices for oranges and tangerines. In the early 1980s, the Office of Management and Budget (OMB) began to study how the citrus market would be affected if marketing orders were abolished. Congress did not want to know (or already knew, but did not want it to become common knowledge). So lawmakers passed an amendment barring the OMB from studying marketing orders, and they have continued to pass this amendment every year for nearly a decade.

Between the political incentives to increase spending, and Congress' bag of tricks, cutting the budget will not be easy, especially in the area of entitlements, where increases in spending are triggered automatically. Given that the logic of the commons gives the organizational advantage to those who favor spending, putting the burden of proof on cost-cutters means entitlement programs will rarely be slowed, let alone cut back. But, if welfare and other entitlement programs had to be funded anew every two or five years, they would have to be defended. This would at least give the advocates of savings a chance.

To be successful the advocates of savings have to be more far-reaching in their goals. Primarily this means looking to eliminate programs outright rather than simply cutting them back. As long as a program remains in existence, the constituencies for that program's spending will stay organized and continue to lobby for more spending. During the early days of the Reagan Administration, Congress did acquiesce in some budget cuts, but lawmakers were careful only to reduce spending in many areas, not to eliminate programs. Like a bit of cancer a surgeon leaves behind, as long as the program remains, one can expect that more lavish spending on it will return. The public broadcasting subsidy, which was cut under Reagan, is a perfect example.

Still, until Congress reforms its budget process there will be no stomach for cutting programs. Today, Members set an overall budget figure, but it is meaningless, because they are allowed to violate that number at will. To break the logic of the commons, a real budget total must be set each year. If the total amount the federal government is going to spend is determined first (as many states and virtually all households do), only then to be followed by how much will be allocated to each program, the advocates of savings might have a chance to make themselves heard. Taxpayers would have an incentive to get involved if their overall tax bill was at stake, rather than just a $3.27 increase.

While it is easy to get lost in the complexities of the congressional budget process, there are a few reforms worth mentioning. Changing the budget resolution passed each year from an internal congressional document into a real law, signed by the President, would make it more difficult for Congress to get around the spending totals it sets. Getting rid of the automatic spending increases incorporated in the "current services baseline" would produce a more honest budget and reduce slightly the bias toward spending growth. Rep. Christopher Cox's "Budget Process Reform Act" includes these and other useful reforms. Another approach that was tried and actually worked to limit spending and the deficit was the Gramm-Rudman budget law. When it really began to pinch, however, that law was dismantled. This is the problem with statutory limits crafted by Congress: They can too easily be undone. It is like tying Odysseus to the mast with slipknots.

An amendment to the Constitution requiring that the federal government spend no more money than it takes in would force Congress to face up to the question: How much money do we want to spend? Advocates of spending know that a balanced budget amendment would bring taxpayers into the annual spending debate, challenging the one-sided chorus that is now heard. It should be no surprise then that beneficiaries of any and every program banded together to thwart a balanced budget amendment, which Congress finally voted down in the summer of 1992. They knew that such an amendment—which would demolish the logic of the commons by requiring costs to meet benefits—would have removed the advantage they have in spending debates.

A balanced budget amendment or a presidential role in the budget process would force Congress to set budget totals and stick to them. At least then we would get a chance, each year, to put a cap on federal spending. Like a limit on the total number of cows we allow on our commons, it is the only way we may have to keep Congress from overgrazing.

7

NOT-SO-INNOCENTS ABROAD

I'm not for good government. I'm for pretty good government.

—Sen. J. Bennett Johnston

As war with Iraq began to appear more and more likely in late 1990, Senate Armed Services Committee Chairman Sam Nunn was as visible in the media as President Bush and his advisors. The Georgia Democrat staged a remarkable series of hearings featuring retired senior military officers and former Secretaries of Defense all saying that a battle to liberate Kuwait would fail; that Saddam Hussein's army was just too strong. And if by chance we did succeed, the witnesses predicted, it would be only at the cost of tens of thousands of American lives. Some Senators were even moved to morbid speculation about how many body bags the Pentagon had ordered.

Despite the Senate's fears, the American people backed military action, and Congress eventually voted to support it. But Nunn's shows, staged for domestic political consumption, had other audiences too: America's allies in the Gulf, and its enemies, including Saddam Hussein himself. Overseas, Nunn's hearings made America look indecisive and unreliable. Among the allies this made it more difficult to secure firm commitments to join in military action. In Baghdad they concluded the United States lacked resolve, and that Bush's threats could be ignored.

Nunn and his colleagues had not started out as doubters. When the Senate Armed Services Committee met in September 1990, President Bush was in the process of moving troops into the Saudi Arabian desert. And Senators could not express strongly enough that they were behind the operation. Their only concerns were about how soldiers' hazardous duty pay and vacations would be handled and about whether the allies involved in the effort were going to foot their share of the bill.

"From the first days after the Iraqi invasion," said Nunn, "I believe that President Bush and the administration have handled this crisis well."

Secretary of Defense Dick Cheney and Chairman of the Joint Chiefs of Staff Colin Powell sat at the witness table and were quizzed, not primarily about the wisdom of the Gulf policy, but about such side issues as whether servicemen would have to pay postage to mail letters home. Sen. John Glenn urged Cheney to provide war-time privileges to the soldiers stationed in Saudi Arabia. "These benefits could include," the Ohio Democrat said, "imminent danger pay, free mailing privileges, income tax relief, and overseas savings options."

Sen. J. James Exon, a Nebraska Democrat, was worried that Saudi Arabian customs officials were censoring the mail that American troops were receiving.

The only foreshadowing of the hearings to come two months later were questions by Sen. Al Gore, who pressed Cheney to outline whether the defensive force in Saudi Arabia would take the offense if Saddam Hussein, the military dictator of Iraq, did not leave Kuwait. "Now, do not misunderstand me," said the Tennessee Democrat. "I support what we have been doing, but I have some questions about how it is going to work." Gore asked Cheney for specifics on how the United States would escalate its response if Saddam Hussein acted in a variety of ways. Not wanting to show Hussein the allies' hand, Cheney was vague.

The November 1990 round of Senate hearings on the U.S. response to Iraq's invasion of Kuwait was not the exercise in support for the President that hearings in September had been. By then Bush and Cheney had doubled the U.S. force in Saudi Arabia to over 400,000. The number was far more than that needed solely for a defensive posture, creating the possibility, and perhaps probability, that troops would be sent into Iraq. Senators were not so eager to support that kind of action, and put together hearings chock full of doom- and nay-sayers to argue that an allied war in the Gulf would be a catastrophe, and that the American public would never tolerate it.

Retired Air Force General David C. Jones, a former Chairman of the Joint Chiefs of Staff, warned that by threatening Iraq rather than just deterring its aggressive instincts, the United States risked "exceeding the tolerance of some members of the [allied] coalition." Keeping 400,000 troops in a foreign desert indefinitely, he added, would destroy their morale, forcing the President into a use-it or lose-it situation. The country would either have to fight or back down, economic and political isolation of Iraq would not be given time to work.

Former Secretary of Defense James Schlesinger and former Chairman of the Joint Chiefs of Staff, Admiral William J. Crowe, Jr., also urged restraint. Schlesinger argued that threatening Saddam would only strengthen his resolve. "If the United States conveys the impression that it has moved from the original international objectives to the sterner objectives that Saddam Hussein must go, that Iraq's military establishment and the threat to the region must be dismantled or eliminated, et cetera, then whatever incentives Saddam Hussein may presently have to acquiesce in the international community's present demands and to leave Kuwait will shrink toward zero."

The Senators even turned to "International Affairs Consultants" who were eager to suggest that a Gulf War would be a disaster. Consultant Christine M. Helms argued that the United States would be stepping into quicksand by destabilizing the desert countries. "American-led forces could well win a military victory, but the Bush administration could suffer severe political defeat." Helms said. "Resulting economic, political, and military problems may then become intractable, costly, and extend far beyond Kuwait and Iraq, to the Arab, Islamic and Third Worlds, and indeed, even into Southern Europe."

Middle-East historian and specialist on Iraq, Dr. Phebe Marr worried that the United States might alienate Jordanians.

Senators joined in, not only with their own gloom, but also with the explicit threat that they might try to block any military action if the public didn't support it. "Initiating a wide-scale offensive could result in the deaths of thousands of American soldiers. That course of action also risks destroying the fragile international alliance that is united against Iraqi aggression," warned Sen. Carl Levin. "One final point," the Michigan Democrat said. "The President is properly seeking U.N. authority before he uses military force to drive Iraq from Kuwait. But he surely should seek congressional authority before initiating any offensive action as well. In the absence of congressional authority the President will lack the consensus that is essential to sustain public opinion and support of his actions."

Glenn sounded an ominous note. "Just saying that Kuwait was attacked or that hostages have been mistreated will not be of much solace if flag-draped coffins line up in the hangars of Dover, Delaware."

Sen. Ted Kennedy held nothing back. "Our current policy of sanctions is working, and it should be given adequate time to work," the Massachusetts Democrat said. "If ever there was a case for giving peace a chance, this is it. This is one search for peace that does not involve appeasement of aggression, and we should do all we can in Congress to stop this war before it starts."

The problem was that by making such declarations — that the Congress would do everything in its power to stop the President from using force—Kennedy may have very well brought the nation closer to war. It was widely known that Saddam Hussein's prime source of intelligence was television, particularly the C-SPAN and CNN networks. To Hussein and his advisors, the hearings were a display of a nation divided, and thus paralyzed. What force could the President's threat of an imminent invasion have when the Iraqis thought it would never happen? It is like pointing a gun at a thief, while declaring that it isn't loaded.

That the hearings were problematic in this way was admitted by some of the Senators, but the issue was summarily dismissed. "A number of people have asked the question, what would be the impact of these hearings upon Saddam Hussein," ventured Sen. William Cohen. "After all he is apparently a devotee of CNN. And he gets his news and apparently sends foreign policy signals through that medium. There is a danger, of course, that these hearings will provide him with an opportunity to, perhaps, even lengthen his stay in Kuwait, that he will view debate as dissention. And dissention as a political defeat for President Bush."

The Maine Republican ultimately did not think it was that big a problem: "I think it is far better that the President know whether Congress and the American people are going to support his actions before the shooting starts, than discover that he may command the military but lose his countrymen after the battle begins."

True, the President needed to know whether the Congress was behind him, but lawmakers had every opportunity to tell Bush how they felt in confidential briefings and meetings the President held repeatedly with Congressmen. So too, legislators had access to all the information they needed in the confidential meetings, and were free to ask all the tough questions they wanted. But as we have seen, congressional hearings are rarely about getting at the truth. The play's the thing. And as we have also seen, these plays have consequences. Lawmakers get the publicity or political cover they are looking for and get to ignore the costs that the shows have created. The Alar scare, for example, had costs, to consumers and producers of apples. The Senate's show in late November of 1990 had costs too.

A variety of high-ranking military and administration officials say that the congressional sideshow may have pushed the nation onto the path to war, by encouraging Saddam to be intransigent. If the Congress is going to try and stop the war in the first place, and if a battery of retired generals say the battle couldn't be won anyway, why should Hussein have felt chastised? The hearings not only likely changed Hussein's calculations, they also made the

allies doubt the resolve of the United States and question whether
President Bush would be able to fulfill the commitments that he was
making on behalf of the nation. This was further solace to Hussein.

Yet for all their nattering about public opinion, the Senators were
out of step with the citizenry. Overwhelmingly the public supported
the force buildup, and approved of the use of that force. How did
the legislators stay out of the mainstream of public opinion, given
how slavishly most adhere to the latest polls? Fundamentally because the hearings did not require them to make any choices. They
were just asking questions, after all. A few, like Kennedy, made their
positions known, but most took refuge in ambiguity. Perhaps they
would support the President and perhaps not. But first, some more
tough questions.

This posture allows legislators to avoid accountability, as do all
of their other non-legislative activities. If lawmakers do not actually
vote—if they do not make their positions known—how are citizens
to assess their views and behavior? And if they do not vote, there
is no resolution to the question at hand. As the hearings dragged on
it was up in the air how Congress would react to hostilities. It was
not until the question was forced into an up or down vote to support
the use of force or not, that Congress got into line with the convic-
tions of the nation.

The debate and the vote on the use of force in the Gulf has been
widely heralded as one of the modern Congress' finest moments.
Cheap political postures were largely set aside and an air of purpose
settled on the Hill more serious than any that had been seen for
decades. The praise is justified. And we should take a lesson from
the situation that ennobled the same lot that had been casually
distorting the nation's foreign policy only a little over a month
earlier. Voting brings accountability. And accountability forces
Congress to do the right thing.

Again and again we have seen how Congressmen avoid taking
clear stands on issues, and how they leave it to others to make the
tough choices. It is not, we now see, that Congress is incapable of
rising to the challenge, just that legislators have made it too easy
for themselves to slip out of being challenged in the first place.

On a few occasions, such as the resolution over the use of force in the Gulf, it is possible for Congress to address foreign policy issues in an accountable way — voting. But for the most part the world of realpolitik changes, and thus demands action, too quickly to be treated through legislation. This is why the Constitution leaves little role for the Congress in foreign policy, leaving most day-to-day questions of the United States abroad to an energized executive. Because the President is the one ordering the action he is accountable for the decisions he makes. But unless Congress takes legislative action—which more often than not in foreign affairs it cannot —it cannot be held similarly accountable.

535 Secretaries of State

Though Congress fundamentally lacks accountability when it acts in foreign affairs, lawmakers have become eager for a more activist role in foreign policy. After the combined debacles of Vietnam, which got under way in earnest when a pliant Congress gave President Lyndon Johnson a blank check with the Tonkin Gulf Resolution, and Watergate, which discredited the executive, Members made a grab for power. The most symbolic expression of this new desire was the War Powers Act, enacted over President Richard Nixon's opposition, which essentially grants the legislative branch a veto over the President's exercise of military authority. Of such dubious constitutionality is the act that even its main supporters have not wanted to see it invoked against a President for fear that it would be summarily thrown out by the Supreme Court. For that reason, key congressional powers allowed the Bush administration to ignore the demands of the War Powers Act throughout the Persian Gulf crisis.

A case can be made that congressional involvement in foreign affairs has been beneficial over the last decade. Journalist David Brock argues persuasively that the efforts of key conservative lawmakers in both parties have been crucial in making a recalcitrant State Department bureaucracy do the right things.[1] Congressional leaders played pivotal roles in Afghanistan, Angola, and Cambodia, ensuring that the United States supported anti-communist forces.

The Congress was well ahead of President Bush and Secretary of State Baker in recognizing that then-Soviet President Mikhail Gorbachev's time had passed: When Bush was still treating Boris Yeltsin like a step-child and condoning Soviet crack-downs in its rebellious republics, Congress was embracing Yeltsin and egging on the Baltic separatists. Congress was also tougher on Communist China than the Bush administration in the aftermath of the Tiananmen Square massacre, with resolutions condemning the bloodletting and by blocking, time and again, Bush's efforts to extend Most Favored Nation trade status to China with no strings attached. And after the Gulf war, when Saddam Hussein hung on to power and began to slaughter the Kurds, it was not until a cry went up on Capitol Hill that the administration moved in to protect them.

Whatever the benefits of congressional involvement, however, the real problem with Congress' foreign policy pursuits has to do more with *how* they go about it than what they actually do. It has been the thesis of this book that Congress works best when it legislates. Open-air votes on clear policy choices force lawmakers to evaluate and defend their actions. Accountability, then, is the most fundamental reform that can be imposed on Capitol Hill. If lawmakers make foolish policy choices, but do it with the voters' full knowledge and acquiescence, then the fault lies with voters rather than legislators. But most congressional action in foreign affairs is outside of legislative channels, and not uncoincidentally leaves them largely unaccountable. This is not true of the executive branch. When an American policy fails abroad, the President takes the heat. But Congress gets off scot free, and therein lies the opportunity for untold mischief.

One of the new sources of mischief is the Hughes-Ryan Amendment of 1974. This amendment gave Congress a strong hand in covert operations by requiring that no covert action be taken without a Presidential finding that it was "important to the national security of the United States." The crucial provision demanded that the foreign affairs and foreign relations committees in Congress be informed of any such actions in a timely fashion. What this means in practice is that every single Member on the relevant committees is capable of single-handedly vetoing any covert operation he doesn't like. A secret operation becomes useless if it is no longer secret; thus all that a legislator has to do to end a covert action is leak its details. In practice, moreover, all a lawmaker has to do is *threaten* to leak, and the operation will likely be shut down. Sen. Joseph Biden for one has bragged about how he stopped at least two cloak-and-dagger operations by threatening to divulge their details.[2]

Then-House Speaker Jim Wright did more than threaten. Not content with merely trying to thwart President Reagan's policy toward Nicaragua on the House and Senate floors, the Texas Democrat apparently spilled the beans about CIA assistance to non-military democratic forces in Nicaragua at a press conference. In furtherance of his own Latin America policy, Wright also met with officials of the communist government of Nicaragua in 1987 and 1988, giving them advice on how to counter Reagan administration actions and build support in Congress. At best such actions render U.S. foreign policy incoherent and thus ineffective. At worst, they border on treason.

This was the situation in the mid-1980s, with planeloads of legislators and aides shuttling between Washington and Central America, each pursuing his own idea of what U.S. policy, regardless of whether it was consistent with the policies of the administration, or even those of the other congressional continent-hoppers. Rep. Obey, for example, used his control of foreign aid earmarks secretly to pressure Central American countries to appease the Sandinistas. Thus did an Obey aide, Mark Murray, warn Honduran President Azcona in 1987 that if he did not take an anti-Contra stand, his foreign aid would be cut off. Similar pressure was put on other Central American leaders to support regional peace plans that accommodated the Nicaraguan communists.[3]

The Iraq-gate investigation, discussed in Chapter Five, with its focus on the need for an independent counsel, speaks volumes about the effect congressional involvement has on U.S. foreign policy. For starters, the whole tilt toward Iraq, pursued so myopically by the Reagan and Bush administrations, might have never taken place were it not for the Iran-Contra affair. As James Ring Adams points out, Congress' prosecution of officials who had dealings with Iran, discredited and drove out any voices in the administration who had favored a relationship with Iran over one with Iraq. Is it any surprise, then, that it was those who favored a relationship with Iraq who dominated the administration's Persian Gulf policy? One result of the criminalization of policy disputes has been to distort the diplomatic and policy-making process through occasional purges of entire administration factions.[4]

Pork Barrel Hill

For all these new congressional foreign policy responsibilities, most legislators continue to think of foreign affairs as just another vehicle for constituent service. Nowhere are these parochial interests on clearer display than in Congress' approach to foreign aid. Money for countries and causes abroad has never enjoyed much support in the United States. Such support as does exist, moreover, tends to come from special interests, either immigrant ethnic groups with concerns about the countries and relatives they left behind, or industries with products to sell to the foreign grantees. Ideally, foreign aid should serve two purposes: first, for purely humanitarian ends, such as helping victims of famine or natural disaster; second, to reward countries who are friendly to the United States and the democratic capitalist ideals America stands for.

Were the President given the flexibility to hand out foreign aid dollars as he saw fit, both of those ends might be accomplished. In negotiations with foreign governments, the administration could raise the prospect of aid dollars as a deal-sweetener; in crises, the President could respond quickly with U.S. disaster relief. But the way Washington practices foreign aid today leaves little room for the President to use aid creatively because the Congress has locked into place almost every dollar that is spent abroad, using "earmarks" that say how and where foreign aid must be delivered.

Indeed, today over 95 percent of the dollars in foreign aid bills come with congressional ropes attached. The largest of those earmarks—those reserving the lion's share of aid for Israel and Egypt in a venerable formula that gives the former more than the latter— reflect the concerns of the most vocal of domestic constituencies concerned with foreign affairs, Jews and Arabs. And many other earmarks reflect the preferences of key lawmakers who are either members of particular ethnic groups or who have loyal ethnic supporters and contributors. Former Rep. Steven Solarz, for example, got PAC donations from Taiwanese-American and Indian-American groups largely because of his position as Chairman of the Asian Affairs Subcommittee.

In addition to all this there is the out-and-out pork angle. Even when aid is being given strategically, as was the case with commodity credits to Iraq, the aid is given in a form that helps American interest groups, such as farmers or defense contractors. Ordinarily the money foreign countries receive from the United States can only be used to buy American goods shipped by American carriers. For most Congressmen, then, foreign aid becomes yet another U.S. jobs program.

This is the case even when Congress is acting quickly in response to international developments. When Poland and Hungary broke free from communist domination, Capitol Hill was actually ahead of President Bush in calling for aid to the new and struggling democracies. But still they couldn't help first think about pork for their own constituents. Far more food could have been shipped to Poland, for example, if the goods did not have to be transported on unionized U.S. cargo ships, which charge far more than vessels under different flags. But when Rep. Marcy Kaptur proposed an amendment to the 1989 Poland aid bill that would have done just that for half the food designated for Poland, the maritime industry and the AFL-CIO (which includes dock workers) screamed. And then they got even by proposing that if Poland didn't have to ship its grain with U.S. carriers, it also shouldn't be forced to buy American grain in the first place, which also happens to be more expensive than food bought on the world market. They thus had port-state lawmakers propose amendments to allow Poland to use the aid to buy off-shore grain. Then it was the turn of legislators from farm states to scream.

The upshot was that shipping state, pro-labor state, and farm-state Members all got together out of their mutual interests in sinking both amendments. In the end Poland had to buy U.S. grain and cart it on U.S. ships. Warsaw received its aid, but it would have been of much more help had our Congressmen had as much interest in promoting democracy as they had in doling out shares of the pie to their constituents.

Some foreign aid pork is even more shamelessly direct. In the House-Senate conference on the 1990 foreign aid appropriations bill, Sen. J. Bennett Johnston inserted a provision to bring money home to Louisiana State University. The amendment required the federal Agency for International Development to give $1.2 million each year of the appropriation to the university's Leadership Center for the Americas, a program to train Latin American politicians. The head House conferee, Rep. David Obey was trying to cut back on pork in the bill and chastised the Senator for pushing the amendment. According to *Congressional Quarterly*, Obey asked Johnston "If I'm not going to do it for my own state, why should I do it for yours?" Johnston shot back that Obey was ridiculous for trying to be "pure." The best defense Johnston could offer for his proposal was to say "I'm not for good government. I'm for pretty good government." Apparently that was good enough for Capitol Hill. Rep. Obey eventually relented and Sen. Johnston got the money for his local university.

That same bill restricted the Export-Import Bank from financing military sales to most countries. But there was one exception. Inserted by conferees at the behest of Sen. Christopher Dodd, the provision allowed the Bank to offer such loans for arms to Greece and Turkey. These happened to be the same countries that were in the market for more than 200 helicopters. And who best to provide them than the Sikorsky helicopter company, whose parent United Technologies just happens to be based in Dodd's home state.

As pointed out in Chapter Five, a raft of Congressmen glibly wrote to the Department of Agriculture to bolster economic ties with Iraq, putting their districts' needs before any American foreign policy agenda. Well into 1990—just months before the invasion of Kuwait—Sen. Orrin Hatch, a Utah Republican, continued to try to build support for the truck deal.[5]

As the evidence of the scope and depth of the Iraqi-BNL bank fraud grew, the administration decided to cut off the $500 million in U.S. government-guaranteed agricultural credits that had pre-viously been approved for the Iraqis but which had not yet been delivered. A number of legislators wrote to the Department of Agriculture, which had launched an investigation into whether the credit guarantees had been used illegally to put together arms transactions, to inquire about the investigation, and express discontent with the suspension of the credit guarantees. These included Jack Brooks and his Texas colleague, Democratic Rep. Mike Andrews.

The Republican Senators from Mississippi, Thad Cochran and Trent Lott, also put pressure on the USDA in a letter dated April 26, 1990, three months before the invasion of Kuwait:

"We urge you to take whatever steps are necessary to expedite the review of the Iraq GSM credit guarantee program, with the objective of correcting any operational deficiencies and extending the second half of the credit guarantees."

Sen. J. Bennett Johnston wrote to the USDA that the investigation had gone far enough, and had already satisfied him that there was no wrongdoing. The Louisiana Democrat wrote Agriculture on June 7, 1990, to argue that nothing "suggests that rice shipped under GSM-102 was misused (as barter to purchase war supplies and materiel, for example) or that there was an organized, deliberate effort to misuse the program."

Perhaps the toughest letter was also one of the latest. Rep. Jimmy Hayes wrote to Undersecretary of Agriculture Richard T. Crowder six weeks before Iraq invaded Kuwait, on behalf of the rice growers in his Louisiana district. "The withholding of credit guarantees of over $500 million would cause a severe setback for many people in Louisiana's 7th District," the Democrat wrote, telling Agriculture "to complete this investigation expeditiously, and if no impropriety is found, to restore funding for the full Iraq GSM-102 request."

"Should improprieties be found," Hayes warned, "I would like to know what you would intend to provide as an alternative market for our rice farmers. I would strongly oppose our rice farmers bearing the financial burden of U.S. foreign policy alone."

The grain sales and the truck venture all would have helped vocal constituents, and apparently that is all it takes to establish the legitimacy of a program. Congressmen who were worried whether the programs were susceptible to abuse had ample information available to them. Sen. Jesse Helms and his staff had actually been looking into Saddam's regime in Iraq, and based on what they had found, Helms refused to join the rest of the North Carolina congressional delegation in a letter urging approval of loans to Iraq. When Helms withheld his signature, his colleagues might have asked him why, and might have taken a look at the evidence against Hussein that the Senator had compiled. But they did not. Constituent service is what matters; for most Congressmen, issues of state take a distant (if even extant) second place.

Like foreign aid, Members of Congress view the defense budget as a Christmas tree, to be loaded down with ornaments favoring local industries and economies. Air Force bases in Europe are required to run their power plants on American-mined coal even though the use of such a dirty fuel has angered host governments. Why? Because the Chairman and Ranking Member of the House Defense Appropriations Subcommittee, Democrat John Murtha and Republican Joseph McDade, are both from the coal-producing state of Pennsylvania. Military bases abroad are required to "Buy American" in everything from cars and trucks to anchor and mooring chains.

Also up for grabs in defense bills are juicy research contracts for local universities and hospitals, construction projects at local bases, and equipment for home state National Guard units. Rep. McDade raided the Air Force budget for a $10 million grant for Marywood College, a Catholic women's school. Inasmuch as Marywood devotes itself to the training of teachers and social workers, it was not immediately apparent what kind of research the college would be able to provide to the Air Force. A spokesman for the school helpfully suggested it might try to develop family relations programs for servicemen.

Sen. Robert Byrd made it clear to the Navy that he expected it to spend money in his land-locked state. "What more can be done to accelerate the construction of West Virginia Navy and Naval Reserve facilities in response to language included, at my request, in the report accompanying the 1986 military construction appropriation bill?" Byrd had demanded of then-Navy Secretary John Lehman, Jr. According to the *National Journal*, Byrd finally got his way when he shoved a $13.2 million grant into the 1992 defense appropriation earmarked to renovate the Allegheny Ballistics Laboratory, which makes parts for Navy missiles.

Knowing that Congressmen are suckers for pork, the military plays along, parlaying the parochial interests of legislators to build coalitions for large-scale defense projects. When the Reagan administration's Navy Secretary Lehman embarked on his goal to create a 600-ship Navy for the United States, including two new carrier groups, one of his first actions was to circulate a memo on Capitol Hill outlining how the construction subcontracts would be spread out around the 50 states. Every Member was promised dollars for his constituents. Once paid off, legislators lost interest in any debate. "There was no substantive discussion of whether to build those carriers," says Stanley Heginbotham, now Vice President of the Social Science Research Council but at the time chief foreign policy specialist at the Congressional Research Service. "We at CRS geared up for nothing to talk about the merits of the extra ships," says Heginbotham. "The decisions were made on completely other grounds—they could only see the jobs that were going to be created."

Indeed, the relationship between the military and Congress is actually far more cozy than might be imagined. The Defense Business Operations Fund (DBOF) is a good example of how the Department of Defense can get what it wants from Congress simply by spreading some home-state cash around. Created in October 1991, the DBOF is charged with streamlining the provision of everything from Band-Aids to uniforms to all the services. Each branch of the military has its own funds with which to purchase supplies from the DBOF. To get an idea of scale, if the DBOF were a private company it would be the fifth largest corporation in the world.

Operating as a monopoly provider of services to the military, the Pentagon's DBOF has quickly racked up a profit. By April 1992 the DBOF had built up a surplus of $6 billion. This gives the Department of Defense a pile of unmarked cash with which it can fund unappropriated projects. At first blush this might look like just the kind of slush fund Congress would holler about, complaining that the military was using the DBOF as an accounting gimmick by which to free money for its own purposes. But when Rep. Andy Ireland, a Florida Republican, tried to abolish the DBOF in the summer of 1992, Members rallied around in its defense. They did not want to lose a ready source of funds for their private pork. Rep. Murtha, the Defense Appropriations Subcommittee Chairman, used $1.9 billion from the DBOF to have three Navy destroyers built. His reasoning for the ship purchases—not included in any authorization or appropriations bill — had nothing to do with defense policy. When Rep. Ireland demanded that Murtha explain the purchase, the latter merely cited the benefit to Philadelphia ship-builders. Without the money, said Murtha, 11,000 workers would be "on the street in the morning." So long as they are manufactured in the home district, Congressman have no problem with $500 toilet seats. As Stanley Heginbotham says, "Congress is eminently seduceable."

The end of the Cold War has put a strain on the Pentagon's affair with Capitol Hill, because for all their posturing about the Reagan build-up they hate to see spending cut. And if cuts do have to be made, no legislator wants the slice coming from his district. Reductions in the size of the military have meant that many bases are superfluous. Yet bases bring money into a district, and so legislators defend them aggressively. Thus does Congress urge the Department of Defense to close even vital bases abroad at the same time it tries to protect even those most marginal ones at home.

Similarly, Congress has fought to save every weapons system that Defense Secretary Dick Cheney proposed cutting at the end of the Cold War. The Midgetman mobile missile, the V-22 Osprey tilt-rotor plane, and the Grumman F-14 fighter have all been saved by congressional sponsors. Rep. Thomas J. Downey, a liberal Democrat whose New York district is the home of Grumman, gave a typical defense for the F-14: "The significant job loss, the financial burdens placed on Grumman, and the rippling effect on smaller businesses threaten the future of the island." Notice again the absence of a tactical or strategic argument.

It is obvious that congressional pork does less than nothing for America's defense or its interests abroad. But, even when Members are pursuing noble goals, their diplomacy tends to do much more harm than good. Again the reason lies in the mechanics. By its nature Congress is a fragmented institution. Earlier chapters have discussed how ambitious members can distort domestic policy (e.g., hyping bogus health scares). In foreign policy, such distortions can be dangerous. Foreign governments often don't know how to negotiate with the United States, or with whom. Individual diplomacy by Congressmen weakens the United States by garbling the nation's voice abroad.

This is not to say the President should have a free hand in making foreign policy, just that the nation would be better off if Congress stuck to making its will known through legislation. Not only does legislation force accountability, it also resolves conflict and debate, providing an answer to the question. It is no accident that Congress' finest moment in the Gulf crisis came about when the body voted on whether to authorize the use of force. The debate was open; legislators who might have tried to throw wrenches into the military action were forced to listen to their constituents; and in the end the country had a clear indication of just who was and who was not behind the President. Nor is it an accident that this is precisely the kind of moment Congress spent the previous months trying to avoid.

8

THE REELECTION MACHINE

I have to be—you heard of a whore? I'm a whore. I am a political whore. And I'm going to play it to the hilt... Shaking hands and kissing everybody. I mean I'm here to get elected.

I'll be going to a lot of funeral homes. Just walk in and —if I faintly remember who these people are—just walk in and shed a little tear and sign my name and take off.

—Former Rep. Joe Kolter explaining his election strategy to his staff.[1]

Going into her 1992 primary, Former Rep. Mary Rose Oakar found herself in a good deal of trouble. First there were the 213 rubber checks that ranked the Ohio Democrat as one of the top 22 abusers of the House Bank. Then she had to withdraw from an investigation of drug sales and money-laundering at the House Post Office because she herself faced charges (later refuted) of sponsoring ghost employees. Facing serious competition for the first time in years, Oakar didn't address the scandals she was implicated in. Instead, she ran television ads heralding the constituent services she has provided her district. In one, Cleveland residents were paraded across the screen to tell about how Oakar helped them when they were in need. At the end of the spot the crowd is gathered around Oakar while a voice announces that she deserves to be returned to office as a payback for all these good works.

The reliance on constituent service apparently did the trick — in a crowded primary field, Mary Rose Oakar squeaked past her nearest opponent with a plurality of 39 percent. It was evident from her commercials that Oakar thought casework was her strongest card. Noted congressional scholar Morris Fiorina estimates that 5 to 10 percent of an incumbent's vote-total can be attributed to gratitude for constituent services.[2] Though she was later defeated in the general election, it is clear that casework is what saved Oakar.

So popular is the practice of doing favors for constituents, that lawmakers use it as an excuse for almost everything. When Sen. John McCain of Arizona was accused of using his influence with federal regulators on behalf of constituent (and campaign contributor) Charles Keating, he wrapped himself in the armor of Social Security. "I have done this kind of thing many, many times," said McCain, the only Republican member of the Keating Five. What he did for Keating was no different than "helping the little lady who didn't get her Social Security."[3]

Actually, McCain—who was ultimately cleared of any wrong-doing—was telling the truth. Helping constituents has become the primary reelection strategy, involving everything from clearing a path with federal, state, or local regulators to firing up the pilot light in the kitchen when it goes out. Today's legislator has evolved from statesman to ombudsman. Although other members of the Keating Five were found to have violated even the very flexible standards of Senate ethics, the real scandal vis-a-vis congressional favors for campaign contributors and supporters is not what is not permitted but what is.

As errand boy for his district, the average legislator builds up a base of nonpartisan goodwill that puts him out of range of most any challenger. Now, Charles Keating's campaign contributions obviously did buy him some special attention, but McCain was probably speaking for almost all Members when he said he would have gone to bat for Keating even had the banker not given him mounds of

money. Such constituent service is even more important to reelection than campaign cash. And, inasmuch as Keating was a large
employer in McCain's state, helping him amounted to helping
hundreds or even thousands of voters.

When the guffaws got too loud McCain did finally switch from
the Little-Old-Lady's-Social-Security-Check to the Mistakes-
Were-Made tack. But the other half of Arizona's Senate delegation,
Democrat Dennis DeConcini, never did. DeConcini was perceived
as the ringleader in the Keating affair: The key meeting between
Senators and regulators who were investigating Keating was held
in DeConcini's office, and he persisted in accusing the regulators
of trying to put Keating out of business. Unlike McCain (who had
backed off regulators when they told him Keating might be engaged
in criminal fraud), DeConcini could not get away with a simple
apology. So he turned to constituent service with a vengeance.

Consequently, as the Keating scandal ripened in 1989,
DeConcini's State Director, Mike Crusa, said his boss's record of
constituent service would "stand him in good stead." If voters
punished the lawmaker for intervening on Keating's behalf, Crusa
argued, then lawmakers would in the future shy away from constituent service. In other words, the message was: If voters want
someone around to take care of glitches in their disability payments
or to find lost Medicaid forms, they'd better treat DeConcini with
kid gloves:

> I hope [the Keating affair] does not have a negative
> impact on what I think is the most valuable resource or role
> that an elected official plays, and that's working in constit-
> uent services. Constituent services is what elected officials
> are all about, whether it's VA checks, whether it's the fact
> you can't get your Social Security on time, or your city
> needs help with federal funding allocations for a needed
> highway. That's what elected officials are supposed to be
> for — to mitigate problems with the federal government,
> with regulators, quite frankly. Regulators have discretion.
> I hope that this doesn't [reduce constituent service] and I
> don't think it will, because legitimate constituent services

—like Dennis was doing in this particular case—shouldn't
be affected by this kind of thing.[4]

The Senator's message to his state was loud and clear: You too
may want a favor some day. Thus has constituent service become a
cure-all for incumbents; even when it gets them into trouble, it
offers the way out.

Death of the Competitive District

It wasn't always this way. Until the 1930s few citizens had much
direct contact with Washington, and even fewer needed help coping
with the feds. What changed all this was the New Deal; with the
creation of Social Security, after all, came the little old lady with
the missing Social Security check. With each new federal program
created in the years since voters have been given both new carrots
and new sticks encouraging them to appeal to their Congressmen.
The carrots are the grants federal agencies hand out; the sticks are
regulations wielded clumsily on innocent voters by a creaking
bureaucratic machine. Congressmen have neatly positioned themselves as the only ones able to stay the blows, even while clearing
the way to the grant trough.

What makes it all so beautiful is how it plays on popular sentiment. No one likes a bureaucrat. Drivers don't return to their local
Division of Motor Vehicles because of customer satisfaction, after
all, so there is no incentive to make the experience a pleasurable
one. "We don't care, because we don't have to," goes the joke. Even
bureaucracies staffed with the kindest and most accommodating
workers tend to be infuriating. Every decision must run through
labyrinthine channels, each to be navigated in triplicate.

For Members of Congress, by contrast, customer satisfaction is
everything. Legislators have become political entrepreneurs, and
they have found their most lucrative market niche in providing fix-it
services to those whose encounters with the bureaucracy have been
unpleasant, which means just about everyone.

Constituent service started picking up in the 1950s, when the
burgeoning bureaucracy began to produce "clients." As the federal

government blossomed like so much kudzu, more and more lawmakers found their constituents complaining about their treatment
by Washington. By the 1960s a trend had emerged, one recognized
by the more savvy tenants of Capitol Hill: Legislators who engaged
in aggressive constituent service earned the gratitude of voters and
were far more likely to get reelected than those who didn't. By the
1970s that trend had become a racket. More than anything else—
more than PAC money to incumbents, more than the disproportion-
ate amount of advertising that money buys—this institutionaliza-
tion of constituent service has killed competition in congressional
races.

Political scientists David Mayhew and Morris Fiorina recognized
this critical relationship between constituent service and incumbency early on. Mayhew pointed out that by the early 1970s, not
only were incumbents winning reelection more often, they were
winning by larger and larger margins. Ever rarer were the so-called
marginal districts, where the winner in an election gained less than
55 percent of the vote. If the winner's victory is narrow, he is more
likely to be vulnerable to a challenge the next time around. Conversely, if the winning percentage is high (60 percent or more) even
widespread voter dissatisfaction probably won't be enough to de-
throne an incumbent in the next election. High electoral margins
insulate lawmakers from the vicissitudes of politics.[5]

Mayhew offered several explanations for why marginal districts
were disappearing, mainly that franked mail and pork-barrel politics helped incumbents boost their popularity. But Fiorina recognized that it is constituent service that makes the difference. As we
saw in Chapters One and Three, lawmakers avoid taking politically
sensitive stands. Indeed, the lawless Congress avoids making decisions at all, delegating tough choices to the federal agencies. Yet,
while votes can be politically dangerous, finding Social Security
checks is not. Fiorina explains the relative risks involved:

> For every voter a Congressman pleases by a policy stand
> he will displease someone else. The consequence is a
> marginal district. But if we have incumbents who de-em-
> phasize controversial policy positions and instead place
> heavy emphasis on nonpartisan, non-programmatic con-

stituency service (for which demand grows as government
expands), the resulting blurring of political friends and
enemies is sufficient to shift the district out of the marginal
camp. We do not need to postulate a Congressman who is
more interested in reelection today than previously. All we
need postulate is a Congressman sufficiently interested in
reelection that he would rather be elected as an errand boy
than not be elected at all.[6]

The shift in staff assignments confirms the trend. In the 1950s the
vast majority of Members of Congress had only one district office,
an office that was likely to be open only when the Member was
home, or no district office at all. But as legislators started to realize
that reelection could be all but assured by solving constituents'
problems, they started franchising district offices faster than
McDonald's. By 1987, two-thirds of new Members of the House
set up two or more full-time district offices. More than 40 percent
had at least three district shops.[7]

Manning these constituent service shops is a small army of
caseworkers. The argument for creating new staff jobs was that
Congress needs to match the analytic skills and resources of the
executive branch. The President has a large White House staff, the
argument goes, not to mention all the workers in cabinet departments and federal agencies. The separation of powers would be
undermined if the President were to wield the kind of power that
comes from having a monopoly on legislative and programmatic
analysis. The extra congressional staff, then, helps legislators keep
up, maintaining a sort of balance of analytic power, or so the
argument goes.

Staffing practice is another matter altogether. The thousands of
new congressional staffers have not been put to work at legislative
analysis; they have been hired as constituent-service caseworkers.
As the number of staff has increased, so has the proportion of the
staff assigned to district offices. In 1972, an eighth of Senate staff
and less than a quarter of House workers were based in the home
state. By 1990 more than a third of Senate staff worked in district
offices, as did more than 40 percent of those on the House side. In

the last 20 years, Congress has added at least 3,000 new constituent-service jobs to the Capitol Hill payroll.[9]

The real number of caseworkers may be much higher. If anything, focussing only on the number of district office staffers underestimates the percentage of workers a lawmaker assigns to constituent service. Much of the time of Washington-based congressional staff also is spent dealing with voters' problems. It is no exaggeration then to say that well over half, and perhaps as much as two-thirds, of congressional staff is engaged primarily or exclusively in constituent service.

Each of these staffers amounts to a full-time campaign worker, whose salary is remitted by the taxpayers. No wonder incumbents have an edge.

For Incumbents Only

The bipartisan cynicism with which this power is used to get reelected is on display in two handbooks for Members of Congress prepared by the Congressional Management Foundation (CMF) and endorsed by both Speaker of the House Thomas Foley and House Minority Leader Robert Michel. The first of the two books, *Setting Course: A Congressional Management Guide*, is addressed to new Members. In addition to general advice (such as, that the Member-elect should get to know his new colleagues), the manual gives crucial specifics. For example, how to get envelopes printed with the Members' signatures where stamps should be so the franking machine can be used from day one: "New House Members must submit three copies of their signatures to the House Office Supply Service. Those signatures allow the stationery service to print envelopes with the Member's frank. If Members want to 'hit the ground running' on their mail, they must have the envelopes ready."[10] For new Members, the guide is considered a bible.

Not only do the manual's authors set out the nuts and bolts of how to get things done on the Hill, they offer suggestions about what the new Member ought to do once the offices are in place and ready to go. The meat is found under the heading "Creating a First-Term Plan," which has two subheadings, "Choosing Legislative Goals" and "Choosing Constituent Service Goals." The advice on choosing a legislative strategy is fairly straightforward: the Member-elect should go with the issues that either he or his constituents care about, which his committee assignments allow him to pursue, and which will get him some play in the newspapers and on television.

But the more-detailed information is reserved for choosing a constituent-service strategy. First, the new Member is advised to do basic market research to identify the needs of his clients. He should figure out just what kinds of services his constituents need.

> For example, a Florida Member with heavy concentrations of senior citizens in her district might structure the casework staff to respond to their particular requests (e.g. Social Security benefits).... Similarly, a New York City Member might focus on techniques to address housing problems and a Colorado Member might offer assistance on water supply needs. The point here is to analyze your district's service requirements and organize to fulfill them.[11]

As any business-school textbook will tell you, however, identifying a market niche is only half of a market strategy. The entrepreneur knows not only what his clients need and want, but who his competition is.

The *Congressional Management Guide* advises Members how to keep others from cutting in on their constituent-service turf, or at least how to choose a niche without competitors vying for the public credit legislators so desire:

> Who else is presently serving your constituents in this area? Are state legislators, county government agencies, voluntary organizations, or other entities already addressing the community's needs in an area in which you would like to be proactive? If other entities are already involved in such casework, will it be difficult for you to receive proper credit for your successful efforts and those of your staff?[12]

Displayed here is all the cynicism of the constituent-service scam. The Member of Congress who is the least bit interested in the well-being of his constituents would be happy to learn that their needs were being met by other levels of government or by charitable organizations. In this case the concern would be not to duplicate efforts but to look for areas to be of help where no helpers are now working.

The problem for new arrivals to Washington is that these other areas probably lack the electoral payoff that finding Social Security checks has. The real concern, as the manual points out, is not that felicitous efforts will be duplicated and thus wasted, but that some-body other than the lawmaker might get the "proper credit" for the effort. A wasted effort, then, is not one that addresses a problem that has already been solved, but an effort for which one doesn't receive credit.

This is not to say that Members of Congress do not take satisfac-tion from helping their constituents. Helping constituents is one activity for which they (with exceptions such as the Keating Five) get no grief. For any policy position he takes, a legislator alienates some potential voters and sets himself up for criticism by those who disagree with him. Not so with casework. It is non-controversial, indeed, almost philanthropic. The irony is that the prime reelection vehicle appears selfless. Lawmakers get to pass out favors like Boss Tweed, and feel like Mother Teresa for doing so.

So developed is the effort that lawmakers do not wait for business to come to them, they go out and beat the pavement for new clients. "Members love creating constituent-service work for themselves— much of it not legitimate," said the late Rep. Ned Patterson, a Democrat from New York.[13] The difficulty is that voters may hesitate to call their legislator with a problem except as a last resort. And that just will not do for the legislator who wants to ride casework to ever-higher margins of reelection victory. Once again, the *Congressional Management Guide* is appallingly exact in its advice. "A constituency-oriented Member," it says, "might conduct outreach mailings to generate additional casework.... This might also require adding caseworkers, or recruiting volunteers, and training them to help resolve the additional casework generated by the targeted mailings."[14]

So popular did this guide prove that the CMF followed it with a sequel devoted exclusively to constituent-service operations. *Frontline Management: A Guide for Congressional District/State Offices* has a host of suggestions on how Members can maximize the mileage they get out of casework. And just in case there are any Members left who doubt that constituent service is the key to incumbency, the authors include the results of a survey in which senior congressional staff were asked the most important factor in solidifying legislators' political support. They overwhelmingly endorsed constituent service: 56 percent said it the most important. By contrast, the Member's legislative record was considered the key factor by only 11 percent.[15]

The helpful hints offered by the casework manual tell us much about how Congress now operates. The first suggestion is that the Member go home to his district as frequently as possible; the most effective casework is that which is solicited by the Member himself and thus appears to have been handled by him as well. Once upon a time legislators would go home only during recesses, but now Members travel to their district nearly every weekend. About a third of them spend 30 to 40 weekends in their districts; nearly 40 percent go home for more than 40 weekends a year![16] On the surface this may seem like a good idea. How better, after all, to keep legislators in touch with their voters. This assumes, however, that Members are home to find out their constituents' views on the issues of the day. But that is what polls are for. Instead, legislators are in the district to drum up casework and get their faces in front of the voters.

In fact, lawmakers enjoy a number of perks that make travelling home for casework possible. Members used to be limited in the number of round-trip tickets to and from Washington that they could put on the federal tab. But as legislators discovered the electoral advantages of zipping home every weekend to promote their constituent services those limits were raised. In 1978 the travel budget was finally freed of any restrictions as travel, mail, office supplies, and other such expenses were consolidated into one office budget which each Member may use as he sees fit. Most Members see fit to fully fund their casework campaign stops. And not least of the perks that flow from taxpayer-funded travel are frequent-flyer miles that are used for personal trips.

The constant travel is facilitated by even more perks. For example, lawmakers enjoy free parking at Washington's National Airport in a lot that is not only reserved, but which is the closest parking to the terminal, a great convenience when you're parking at the airport for four days of every week. The weekends are four days long for Members of Congress because the legislative schedule has been adapted to fit their casework needs. Except for the end of the year crunch, when lawmakers try to fit the legislative duties they ignored all year into a few weeks before campaigns or holidays, the congressional work-week runs Tuesday through Thursday. It was not, for instance, until July of 1992, that Senate Majority Leader George Mitchell announced with great fanfare that the Senate would henceforth work five days a week! Two extended vacations and plans to end work for the year on October 2 left only about nine weeks under the Senate's new arduous schedule, however.

The CMF's casework guide also offers some helpful hints about how to increase business on these visits home. Members are encouraged to install toll-free long-distance numbers so out-of-town constituents can call for help without charge. And three or four district offices are really not enough: The guide suggests lawmakers deploy "mobile offices," like constituent-service bookmobiles, to "allow caseworkers to reach constituents who don't live or work near any of the Member's district/state offices."[17] The vans serve the added function of mobile billboards, as most have the officeholder's name emblazoned in huge letters on the side.

High on the manual's list, of course, is the use of mass mailings. Much is said about how the franked newsletters with which Members bombard their districts work as an incumbency advantage: They allow Members to keep their names and faces in front of an electorate that votes in large part on the basis of name recognition. But this analysis misses one of the main purposes for the mailings, which is to advertise constituent services. Few newsletters go out that do not encourage the recipients to come to the lawmaker with their problems. The ads are usually put where the client can't help but see them, right next to the address on the front of the folded mailing. Rep. Jim Moran's newsletters, for example, are emblazoned with the Virginia Democrat's name and the slogan, "We Are Here to Help You," right above the address for his "Constituent Services" office. When Delegate Walter Fauntroy left the House it was not because the District of Columbia Democrat lost his seat but because he decided to run for Mayor of the District of Columbia; his casework would have kept him in Congress forever had he so desired. His newsletters, in fact, were a paradigm of casework advertisement, as illustrated by the back cover of a letter mailed in January 1990:

> CONGRESSMAN FAUNTROY WANTS TO HELP. Our offices are available to serve you. Just give us a call or write to our office and our well-trained staff will be glad to help you with matters such as:
>
> Locating late or missing Social Security checks*Cutting red tape in immigration cases*Problems regarding Veterans Hospitals*Obtaining timely information about government programs*Unraveling regulations affecting small businesses*Clearing up problems with the Internal Revenue Service*Relaying your views and questions about issues to the Congressman*Obtaining copies of legislation or other government documents*Help with prisoner-related problems*Assistance in getting nominations to the various military academys (sic).
>
> These are only a few examples of the kinds of matters that we can assist you with. Please call us between 9:00 am and 5:00 pm, Monday through Friday, about any government-related matter affecting you or your family.

Nor do congressional staffers limit themselves to political services. It's not a huge leap from finding a lost Social Security check to scraping up a plumber on the weekend for a home-bound senior citizen or doing homework for a constituent's child. As with the Keating Five, the eagerness to help can sometimes get Members in trouble. Sen. Larry Pressler was accused, in the spring of 1990, of using his Senate office for political purposes. The South Dakota Republican's staff had typed and mailed a letter to a South Dakota newspaper on behalf of an elderly woman who had been unable to type the letter herself because of her arthritis. The letter expressed opinions about a political campaign, and so the Democratic Senatorial Campaign Committee asked the Senate Ethics Committee to investigate whether Pressler had violated Senate rules by using his staff for electioneering.

The irony is that election politics is precisely what such services are all about. The problem is that there is no logic to "ethics" rules on Capitol Hill (or if there is a logic, it is only that a Member of Congress should be able to do whatever is most productive of reelection). Thousands of taxpayer-funded caseworkers advertise and deliver the constituent services of legislators to eager home-state clients, all the while being sure to cut out the competition in grabbing for credit. But type a letter for a constituent that includes a political sentiment and the ethics dogs are unleashed.

Not that Sen. Pressler ever got in any real trouble. In best Keating Five fashion, the Senator's staff invoked the "little old lady with a problem" defense. "If it is a mistake to respond to a constituent's request to assist someone with arthritis in typing a letter," said the Senator's top aide, Kevin Schieffer, "that is exactly what we did." In other words, remind voters that they too might someday need a favor.

"Any Member who has any trouble puts everything else aside and makes constituent service his only job," says former Rep. Vin Weber, a Minnesota Republican. Nor was this limited to the Keating Five. Constituent service is rolled out when Members feel the heat on other issues, which is why those who bounced the most checks at the House Bank have been those most keen to provide services this election cycle.

Because casework is so productive of votes, lawmakers are equal-opportunity suppliers of constituent service. Supplicants do not have to be campaign contributors, or members of the legislator's political party, or even registered voters. Casework is fastidiously nonpartisan. Sen. Pressler's staff likely would have just as happily typed a political letter for an arthritic Democrat. Casework is nonpartisan because its purpose is to render partisan politics unimportant in elections. In the wake of Watergate, for example, dozens of liberal Democrats were elected in heavily Republican districts. Once the revolutionary fervor of 1974 had died down, these new Members recognized that they would not be able to hang on if future contests revolved around their voting records. And so those elected on a platform of reform dropped their snouts in the constituency-service trough. They've been there ever since.

Sometimes the anxiousness to please gets the better of lawmakers' judgment. Since the early 1980s a New Orleans woman named Sally Fox has been writing the FBI, the President, newspapers, and television networks, asking them to investigate the "criminal insanity" of comedian Bob Hope. Fox complained that Hope was interfering with her thought patterns because she began to see him in her mind when she closed her eyes. When the FBI would not open an investigation, Fox became convinced that Ronald Reagan's friendship with the comedian was at the root of a vast conspiracy to cover up Hope's mind crimes. She then sent letters propounding this theory, and got her only favorable response from—you guessed it — her Representative, who happened to be Democrat Lindy Boggs. On May 2, 1990, Boggs wrote Fox to let her know that she was on the case:

> This will acknowledge receipt and thank you for your recent correspondence concerning Bob Hope.
>
> You will be pleased to know that I have already contacted appropriate officials on your behalf.
>
> Naturally, I will be in touch with you again as soon as I hear from them. In the meantime, please know of my continuing interest in this matter.
>
> My kindest regards.

Rep. Boggs was as good as her word. She got in touch with the appropriate officials—inspectors at the FBI's Congressional Affairs Office. Within the month John E. Collingwood, the Inspector-in-Charge, had written to Boggs to let her know that the Bureau would not be taking any action on Fox's complaints. The May 25 letter was coy to the point of being deadpan: "These matters... fail to reveal a violation of federal law within this Bureau's investigative jurisdiction."

But it didn't stop there. Boggs helpfully forwarded the FBI's letter to Miss Fox along with an explanation:

> I am enclosing a response received from the Federal Bureau of Investigation in reply to my inquiry.
>
> Naturally, I do regret that the information provided is not more encouraging.
>
> In the meantime, do know that it was a pleasure to be of assistance to you and I was glad to have contacted the Bureau on your behalf.[18]

Lawmakers, it seems, make no effort to distinguish between those legitimately in need of relief from bureaucratic meddling, and those whose requests are frivolous, or even crazy. Not that this is without a certain logic. After all, crazy people vote too.

The FBI angle is likewise interesting. The Bureau did not mind responding to Rep. Boggs, because that's exactly what its Congressional Affairs Office is for. Like most federal agencies, the FBI has a full-time staff devoted to responding to congressional inquiries. Few inquiries are about policy questions that would allow the staff to draft more careful or effective legislation. Almost all approaches from a Member's staff are in pursuit of favors for constituents. According to Kevin Wilkinson, a spokesman for the FBI Congressional Affairs Office, 95 percent of the shop's interaction with Congress is about constituent matters. The story is the same at the Congressional Affairs offices of other departments. The Labor Department's Legislative Relations Office says that 80 percent of the requests they receive are for constituent service; at the Department of Education the rate is 70 percent.

If there is anything more important than constituent service, it's getting credit for it. Channeling federal grants is a good example. As we might expect, the CMF's casework manual offers some sound advice here. "Remember that the constituent is your client," it reads. "Therefore, it's important that they hear from you if an award is about to be made. This not only reinforces your relationship with the constituent, but reminds him of the instrumental role your office played in obtaining the grant—a point you would like them to remember when reporters call."

The most amusing (and cynical) suggestion in the guide is that congressional offices should have letters ready claiming credit even for grants that the Member had nothing to do with. "For awards you're not expecting, make sure you have a standardized procedure to follow so you can still be quick in getting the word out," the guide says. "A grant announcement form with blanks to be filled in means that anyone [in the congressional office] can take the information if you're not available at the time.... A nice touch is to follow up with a congratulatory letter to the recipient."[19] And how does the Member know about a grant to his constituent? A helpful package put together by the (taxpayer-financed) Congressional Research Service (CRS) gives the answer. Entitled "Grants Work in a Congressional Office" (the cover of which warns that the report is for *"CONGRESSIONAL OFFICE USE ONLY"*), the report explains that "the usual announcement procedure in cases of allocated Federal funds is for the agency making the award to notify the Senate office first, then the House office, and finally the recipient." This inside information allows Members to make a killing on the credit-claiming market.

The CRS notes that Members have a variety of resources at their disposal to ensure they get credit. For one thing, there is the *Federal Funding Report* provided by the House Information Systems, a weekly publication containing current information on all domestic grants. Then there is the General Services Administration's (GSA) *Catalog of Federal Domestic Assistance*, which contains exhaustive information on every grant available through more than 50 federal agencies and departments. That information can be retrieved on-line by Capitol Hill computers through the Federal Assistance Program Retrieval System database. But the grantmasters on the Hill leave nothing to chance and so take this a step further. The House Information Systems office digests the voluminous details provided by the GSA and condenses them into two useful databases available only to House offices. The first is called PREA, which stands for the PRE-AWARD database, where lists of available grants can be found; the other is POST, which stands for the POST-AWARD database, which provides details on all grants handed out over the last year.

Patching Tires or Sweeping Tacks

The most distressing aspect of these arrangements is how they pervert incentives for Members. If lawmakers confined themselves to helping constituents out when they had a legitimate gripe against the government, that would be one thing. But not only are most Members of Congress part of the problem in the first place, they have an incentive to encourage the bureaucracy to injure voters just so they will be made into constituency-service clients. They have become like the owner of a gas station who throws nails on the road in front of his business and then cleans up when motorists must have their flat tires repaired. The drivers, who don't know the full story, do not blame the gas station attendant for their punctured tires. Instead they are grateful he was there to fix their tires so quickly and conveniently.

The majority of those in Congress are not as overt as this gas station owner. Then again, they don't have to be. They are more like the gas station owner who sees that a box of nails has been spilled on the road in front of his station. He didn't put them there, and he could easily sweep the street, but he has no incentive to do so. In fact, the business the nails produce provides an incentive to do just the opposite. And so, while drivers get their tires fixed, the real problem goes unattended. In other words, while Members of Congress are fixated on casework, they are, of necessity, not paying attention to the larger governmental problems that generated the cases in the first place.

There might be more hope that Congress would reform this system were it not for the way the constituent-service scam has affected legislators' character over the last 30 years. When Morris Fiorina identified the casework racket in the 1970s, he expected it to fall apart at some point because people capable enough to become lawmakers "might not be willing to spend their careers as errand boys."[20] But Fiorina has since changed his mind, and has written off his earlier view as hopeless optimism. Now, he says, the type of people drawn to Capitol Hill are those who don't mind being glorified go-fers.[21]

"Glorified" is the operative word here. Although perks rile the public, and legislators know this, they still court public revolt by perpetuating special privileges. On one level it makes no sense. Why, when so much of their activity is aimed at reducing the risk of offending voters, do Members of Congress wallow in perks bound to annoy these same constituents? Perhaps because, as they have become mere errand boys, lawmakers have sought to lend themselves gravitas through the trappings of office. Privilege gives lawmakers the sense of worth and importance that they have not been able to earn through their meager legislative accomplishments. Perks are essential to the congressional cult of personality through which Members are treated—as John Jackley puts it in his book *Hill Rat*—as Gods Who Walk. Lawmakers may be mere errand boys, but they are the only go-fers on earth who never have to pick up their own dry cleaning, walk their own dogs, or drive around looking for a parking space.

Whenever the perks of office become an issue, congressional apologists complain that the public is being silly, that ending perks would not put a dent in the deficit. When really pressed, lawmakers defend themselves by pointing to the perquisites enjoyed by the administration. To begin with, these two arguments are inconsistent: If cutting Hill perks won't balance the budget (and it won't), then neither will cutting the benefits of the executive branch. Beyond that, the argument misses the point because citizens do not think of the President the same way they think of legislators. As President Jimmy Carter found out, a President who downplays the accoutrements of his office comes across as ridiculous. People get the uncomfortable feeling that the nation is seedy and down at the heels. Those in Congress, by contrast, are representatives of the people, and as such should embody the democratic ideals of the nation rather than its power and stature. The self-glorification Members maintain through their perks flies in the face of that democratic idea.

The public dislikes congressional perks, not because of what they cost, but because they are the trappings of an Imperial Congress.

This is the lesson of the check-kiting scandal at the House Bank. The public has been chastised again and again for finding Representatives' proclivity for bouncing checks offensive. The bank was not really a bank, we are told. No public money was lost, we are reassured. But those in Congress just don't get it. Voters do not care whether some trivial amount of money was or was not lost at the House Bank. They care that Members got to write checks without worrying whether they could cover them, something no other citizen can do. Voters care that legislators have set themselves up as a privileged class. And the more the public finds out about Washington's ruling class, the angrier they get.

Nevertheless, in a paradox so often noted by pundits that it has become a cliche, voters manage to like their own particular Member while holding the institution and the rest of its inmates in contempt. The televised talking heads of Washington's political gab shows love this paradox because it lets them chuckle over how clueless the average schmoe is. But the voters are not to blame: The cognitive dissonance of hating Congress and loving one's own Member is precisely the goal of the constituent-service racket. It doesn't matter how big a mess Washington is in, as long as their Member is there as the handy fix-it man. Consequently, in liking their own representatives while disdaining the rest, voters are not behaving irrationally at all. They are simply responding in a sensible way to the incentives of a rigged and fraudulent system.

The Money (non-)Problem

So what can we do? For starters, we should not get distracted by that perennial red herring, campaign-finance reform. Whenever the question of incumbency is raised in Washington, it is pointed out that incumbents on average raise and spend two to three times as much as challengers. To rein in incumbency, the argument goes, we need to put limits on campaign spending, perhaps even initiate public financing of congressional elections so Members are not corrupted by the pursuit of money.

The problem here is that the enormous inequalities in campaign spending have come about not because of a lack of spending restrictions. They owe themselves to a previous round of reform. In the 1974 election, the last before the Watergate-era reforms that put limits on certain types of campaign fundraising, the average amount spent by House incumbents was $56,539, compared with $40,015 for challengers. Since then, the gap in spending has grown steadily. In 1990 the average challenger spent little more than a fourth of the $399,310 thrown around by the average incumbent.[22] Is there any reason to believe that a new set of finance rules drafted and approved by incumbents would be any fairer to challengers?

Indeed, campaign finance becomes a chicken-or-the-egg dilemma: Does money produce incumbency, or incumbency, money? Without doubt, an incumbent's chances are related to how much more money he spends than does the challenger. In House races where a Democratic incumbent won with 60 percent or more of the vote in 1990, the incumbent spent on average more than five times the amount spent by the Republican challenger. Spending was much closer in races where the margin of victory for officeholders was under 20 points; there, challengers spent somewhat less than half of the incumbents' total. In those rare instances where officeholders were chucked out (only 15 incumbents vying for reelection lost in 1990), the average challenger spent well over half that spent by his opponent.[23]

But money does not make incumbents. Rather, it is the other way around. In fact, it is the challenger's spending rather than the incumbent's that has most to do with creating a competitive race. Incumbents spend more money because they have more money to spend; they have more money to spend because Political Action Committees (PACs) tend to give more to the candidate they believe will win. And PACs know that the constituent-service racket, and all the perks that make it so effective—franked mailings, free travel, and hordes of casework staff—all but ensure that incumbents will get reelected. This puts officeholders in a position to shake down PACs for all they are worth. The money incumbents get, then, is not the fuel of their reelection machines, it is instead a product of the absurdly high rate of reelection enjoyed by congressional incumbents. The money does, in turn, add to incumbents' success rates, but most likely only marginally. Without PAC money congressional reelection rates might not be as high: Maybe only 95 percent rather than the 98.3 percent it hit in 1988.

Brooks Jackson's book on big money in congressional politics, *Honest Graft*, is full of stories about incumbents shaking down PACs and other contributors. The National Association of Home Builders (NAHB) became a target of the congressional protection racket in 1984, because it was giving more than half of its money to Republicans, including a challenger to Rep. Joseph Minish, a 22-year House veteran from New Jersey. When Democrat Rep. Minish needed money for his campaign, the Democrats' chief fundraiser, California Rep. Tony Coelho wrote a letter to the NAHB demanding that it give Minish the maximum amount allowed, $5,000. The letter was signed by a list of Democrats sure to instill fear in a lobbyist's heart: Speaker of the House Tip O'Neill, Majority Leader Jim Wright, Ways and Means Committee Chairman Dan Rostenkowski, and Banking Committee Chairman Fernand St. Germain. "The NAHB has a good relationship with Democrats in the House, and we would like to see that relationship continue and grow," wrote Coelho. "Your action in this race causes us to be concerned that the relationship will be damaged."[24]

Coelho's achievement was to figure out a way to get the money from business groups, whose interests would more likely be with Republicans. The answer was to enforce a protection racket. "[We] are going to retain control of the House for the remainder of this century," he told well over a hundred business groups. "...We have the advantage. We're the incumbents. They have to beat us."[25] Incumbents don't win because they have the big money; they have the big money because the PACs know they are going to win.

Even being a relative or a friend of an incumbent is enough to be able to tap into the PAC protection racket. Bennett Johnston, a Democrat running as an environmentalist for a San Francisco-area congressional seat, received $172,000 in the first quarter of 1992 —four times the money gathered by any of his primary opponents. Nearly $65,000 of that came from PACs, and strangely, it would seem for a pro-green candidate, much of that from energy lobbies, including oil, coal, uranium, and natural gas PACs. It is not so strange though when one realizes that Johnston's father is Sen. J. Bennett Johnston, the Louisiana Democrat who chairs the Energy and Natural Resources Committee and the Appropriations Subcommittee on Energy and Water Development. The younger Johnston also received thousands of dollars from the campaign chests of his father's congressional colleagues.[26] Nonetheless, in a clear example how money is not the decisive factor in congressional elections, Johnston came in last in the four-candidate House primary.

Shutting Down the Favor Factory

Given that incumbents are unlikely to write rules that will do themselves serious damage, real reforms are generally those that Members of Congress hate. And more than anything else, legislators hate the idea of term limits.

On no issue are the opinions of lawmakers at greater odds with the views of the electorate than on this subject. Three-quarters or more of Americans see no reason anyone should stay on Capitol Hill for more than 10 or 12 years. Three-quarters of the legislators could not disagree more. The most popular argument made by congressional opponents to term limits is that it would throw out the good with the bad, that talented and dedicated legislators would be lost when their Hill time was up. This line of reasoning assumes, of course, that there will not be an equal number of talented and dedicated citizens eager to take their places. And, even if that assumption were true, the loss of experience would not come close to outweighing the gains. Take away the possibility of staying in the job forever and legislators would soon tire of playing the role of errand boy.

The solution to the constituent-service racket may ultimately be the same as the answer to the problem of legislative delegation: Force Congress to legislate and nothing more. By removing Capitol Hill's tools of ethics assassination the President would then be able to ignore Congress' non-legislative demands. The administration might begin by ignoring congressional letters written on behalf of the Sally Foxes of the world.

As an interim step, we could shine some cleansing sunlight on the constituent-service process by requiring government agencies to keep public records of requests from Congress. Better yet, make Congress report on itself. Knowing that their letters and the substance of their phone calls would be made public would quickly curb the worst abuses of congressional favor-seeking.

Finally, part of the solution rests with us, the voters, who are in a position to reject constituent service. We can let our Representatives and Senators know that we expect them to legislate, not run errands; we can tell them we are not impressed or amused by their publicity-stunt hearings. And, when the power goes out on the weekend, we can call the electrician ourselves rather than ringing our friendly neighborhood lawmaker.

9

REFORM

The Congress shall have power... To make all laws which shall be necessary and proper for carrying into execution the foregoing powers and all other powers vested by this constitution in the Government of the United States....

Constitution of the United States
Article I, Section 8

To make all laws. When the Founding Fathers divided our government among three distinct branches, the role they intended for Congress was clear: Congress was to legislate. It is no coincidence, then, that problems in Congress are in direct proportion to how far the legislature has moved from its assigned task. Congressmen today prefer to do just about anything *but* legislate. What pass for laws are either vague exhortations empowering bureaucrats and special interests to fill in the details (the ADA and the Clean Air Act) or self-parodying pork (traffic crossings in Chambersburg, Pennsylvania). We have seen what Congress does instead, and the

---

The reform agenda in this chapter flows not only from the analysis of this book, but also from the policy recommendations developed in writings and working groups of The Heritage Foundation's U.S. Congress Assessment Project, led by David M. Mason.

results: enthronement of special interests, enervation of the executive, confusion abroad, debasing of political debate, and policy
gridlock. Congress prefers this system because by abandoning
legislation, Congressmen escape accountability. Fixing Congress
thus requires a return to legislation and the accountability it brings.

Accountability, of course, is essential for citizens to fulfil their
responsibilities in a government of, by, and for the people. So long
as lawmakers' activities are evident to the public, voters bear
responsibility for any resulting faults. Congressional apologists like
to pretend that this is in fact what we have: Because Members
regularly face the voters and are repeatedly returned to office, they
argue, the voters must approve. Reform isn't needed because citizens have it in their power to throw the bums out, as the 1992
turnover in Congress demonstrates. But as John Fund and James
Coyne point out in their recent book advocating limits on congressional terms, "Almost all the turnover in 1992 is due to three simple
(and simply outrageous) reasons: redistricting, the House Bank
scandal, and this year's once-in-a-lifetime campaign fund 'retire-
ment bonus.' How often can voters count on such a political
windfall."[1]

To know whether to throw the bums out, the electorate has to
know what the bums have been up to. And as we have seen again
and again, the bums are very good at hiding what they have done.
Through procedural sleight of hand, Congressmen make it appear
they are doing one thing when they are doing another. Backwards
legislating has created an administrative state, shifting the responsibility for making laws onto the shoulders of bureaucrats and
setting Congressmen up as monopoly providers of fix-it services
for those injured or inconvenienced by the regulators' laws. Capitol
Hill hearings allow legislators to confront, interrogate, and accuse
without themselves having to take a stand on the issues. Spending
is structured so that only those hollering "gimme" are heard. Congressional staff run a shadow government, often unaccountable to
even their bosses, not to mention the voters, from whom they are
twice removed. And anyone who challenges the system is run out
of town by a special prosecutor.

In all these ways, Washington's Ruling Class has perfected the art of grabbing credit while avoiding blame. This—not voter satisfaction—explains why Congressmen are returned to Capitol Hill with such regularity. It also explains why even the hint of scandal is electoral nitroglycerin: Voters know the system is broken, and they will take whatever clues they can find. Check-kiting was not the cause of the legislative morass, but the public assumes, not unreasonably, that those who abused the House Bank may be part of the problem in other respects as well.

Lawmakers know how to write clear and specific laws when they need to—that is, when there is credit to be grabbed. Appropriations bills, stuffed with pork ripe for the picking, have become treatises of infinite legal detail specifying exactly who gets what. But the broadest-reaching legislation, addressing issues such as civil rights and the environment, is either contradictory or, more often, bewilderingly vague. Congress has been reduced to legislating noble sentiments, leaving unelected, unaccountable bureaucrats to hammer those sentiments into the legal specifics that everyone but Congress has to live with. This makes Congress unaccountable as well. Indeed, the more onerous regulations are, the more constituents turn to their representatives for relief. We become supplicants at the foot of Capitol Hill, and in gratitude for whatever balm is applied to our wounds, we reelect the very legislators who allowed the bureaucrats to injure us in the first place.

It's not hard to see why this is bad for America. The rule of law means nothing if the law is different in every place and circumstance, or so vague that you cannot know beforehand what constitutes a violation. It is not much more difficult to see why abandoning legislation is bad for Congress: unaccountability ultimately unravels authority. What is gained in detail and warm feelings is lost in the ability to act decisively on major issues. Details displace larger decisions, issues remain unsettled, interests are at odds, and no one wins in the resulting gang warfare. Legislating forces our representatives to make choices, to take stands, to resolve issues.

Making legislators responsible for the size and shape of the federal government (and making voters aware of that responsibility) not only will reform Congress, it will transform Congress. The

only way to make Congressmen accountable in this way is to
demand that they return to true legislation. This requires eliminating
all the non-legislative powers with which lawmakers have armed
themselves. Congress may have delegated most of its legislative
duties, but Congressmen still want to be in charge. They use
legislative vetoes to trump agency decisions that run contrary to
lawmakers' druthers. They fabricate ethics violations to ruin officials who challenge Congress by writing regulations the denizens
of Capitol Hill do not like. They cut the budgets of agency offices
that do not toe the congressional line. They make special-interest
allies part of the rule-making process through regulation negotiations. Take away these and other powers that allow Congressmen
to direct the making of regulations and lawmakers will think twice
about delegating their legislative authority.

Reforms that would restore Congress' legislative powers would
also help the executive branch do its job better. This is not to argue
in favor of replacing an imperial Congress with an imperial presidency. If Congress knows it is actually giving up its powers when
it delegates, the President may very well end up with less power as
the legislature turns to writing real laws. Ending its non-legislative
activities, then, would increase rather than reduce Congress' power
and authority.

As pointed out in Chapter Three, restoring the constitutional
distinction between legislating and executing the laws is also a
recipe for ending policy gridlock: real legislation produces final
decisions rather than initiating extended regulatory squabbles. And
final decisions will make Congress (and the President) accountable.

To be sure, effecting these reforms is just as important as deciding
what reforms to effect. For the most part the necessary reforms are
structural: constitutional or other changes external to Congress.
This means that public pressure, through the ballot box and otherwise, is critical. It also means that reform is possible; incumbent
Congressmen don't hold all the keys. The President can help by
organizing his administration to counterbalance legislative over-
reaching, and leading a public battle for congressional reform.
Accountability can also be promoted through internal, procedural
reforms to make the legislative process more fair and transparent.

Once Congress is accountable, the burden will be on us, the voters, to decide whether we approve of the laws being made. And if we don't, we'll know who to send packing.

Earlier chapters touched on a number of structural and procedural reforms that will put the law-writing quill back into the hands of Congressmen. These suggestions, designed to make legislators legislate, draw upon the lessons and examples contained in this book to present a comprehensive agenda for reforming Capitol Hill.

Limit Terms. Legislators like pork because it helps them get reelected. They are interested in administrative details because long tenure promotes narrow specialization. The constituent service racket allows lawmakers to ignore big problems by fixing small ones. In becoming ombudsmen, glorified errand boys, incumbents build up enough good will for most to survive even a watershed year like 1992. By ending congressional careerism, term limits will encourage attention to larger legislative issues. By changing the understanding of the legislator's role, term limits are probably the most effective single reform that can be imposed on Congress. And imposed it will have to be: While great majorities of the American people support term limits, lawmakers oppose them in even larger proportions.

With a career Congress, voters face a dilemma: They do not like paying taxes to Washington and getting them back in the form of pork and entitlements, but as long as the system is rigged, it makes sense to vote for the incumbent to maximize your own take. Congressmen face a similar dilemma: Take the easy road to reelection or face the often difficult choices of balancing local and national interests. Take away the career mindset and both representatives and voters can make choices based on philosophy and the merits of each case.

Ideally, legislators in a democracy are not professionals, but, as Olympic athletes of yore, skilled amateurs. They must be somewhat detached from governing and far more a part of the communities they represent. They must feel a stake in returning, not only to where they once lived, but to what they once did for a living. Even if term limits result only in a cadre of politicians rotating amongst state, local, and federal offices, limiting tenure in Washington would help maintain links between legislators and the communities they represent.

Career incumbents claim that the amateurs sent to Congress as part-timers would have the wool pulled over their eyes by the Washington establishment. That might happen occasionally, though probably not as often as the insiders would have you believe. In fact, one of the biggest benefits of non-professional legislators is that they would be unlikely to join with the bureaucrats and special interests in blowing smoke at the voters.

Given the historic congressional turnover of 1992, some ask whether term limits are moot: Haven't we already thrown the bums out? Despite the turnover, two-thirds of the House and an even higher percentage of Senators are returning. Twenty -, 30-, and even 40-year incumbents remain in key positions where they can frustrate reform and tame the reformers. More important, unless incentives change, new Members will be lured, some slowly and some more quickly, into the paths that have produced today's problems. Even before they take office, the new representatives elected on a reform platform will be admonished to study the constituent service handbook. Under the current corrupt system those who do so are likely to stay while those who devote their energies to ultimately more important topics run a far higher risk of not being reelected. Thus, the time servers endure, and all too many of the idealists leave. Certainly a few skilled and visionary leaders will be sent home with the rest under term limits, but that is a tiny price compared to the benefits of government by citizen-legislators rather than a ruling class of overrated errand boys.

Limit Sessions. Term limits may not be enough. The number of days spent in Washington is as damaging as the number of years. Alan Ehrenhalt diagnosed the problem in *The United States of Ambition*[2]: As legislating becomes a full time job, citizen-legislators, who must tend to other careers, are driven out of public life by professional politicians, for whom office-holding is a career. Better representation, and better representatives, will result if Congressmen return for some time each year to their own communities and occupations, not as caseworkers or campaigners but as colleagues of their constituents.

It might be objected that Congress gets too little done as it is, that legislators should earn their keep. It was not until July of 1992, after a year and a half of three-day work weeks (interrupted by some long vacations), that the 102nd Congress went on a five-day schedule. Owing to the urgent press of business, congressional leaders explained, they would work full time for nine whole weeks before going home to campaign. Congress should replace three-day weeks with a five-day schedule, and compress their year-round sessions into six months of honest work. A definite end to sessions will also communicate to Congressmen that they are representatives rather than managers of the permanent bureaucracy.

Cut Staff. There is a staff infection on Capitol Hill, a shadow government of unelected, unaccountable pseudo-legislators. As a panacea for congressional ills, staff cuts rank just behind term limits. Reducing the size of the staff would have productive effects in just about every area: reducing incumbent electoral advantages; trimming the length and complexity of legislation (and encouraging legislators to read it); cutting the volume of midnight deals in conference sessions and committee reports; limiting improper interference with regulatory and other executive branch functions. With fewer aides, lawmakers would have to do more legislative work themselves. They might even go so far as to read bills before voting on them.

To make a real difference the cuts need to be large. In the November presidential elections, Bill Clinton proposed a 25 percent cut in congressional staff, and George Bush offered to slash a third of Capitol Hill's workforce, with an equal percentage of his own aides. But even those numbers are probably not enough. House Republicans have proposed a 50 percent cut in committee staff: a palatable proposal for them since they are dramatically short-changed in committee staff allocations anyway. The problem with the GOP proposal is that committee aides represent only 10 percent of all congressional employees. Cutting the House numbers in half would reduce the overall congressional payroll a paltry 3 percent.

Besides, committee staffers actually help with legislation part of the time. Serious reform requires across-the-board cuts, including personal staff, to force Congress to reassess how it operates and change its behavior. Staff should be cut by at least 25 percent immediately and eventually by 50 percent. Anything less won't be enough to change the way Congressmen conduct casework or micromanage executive agencies.

Limiting terms, limiting the length of Congress' yearly sessions and limiting the number (and the tenure as well) of staffers are all parts of a package. Any one of the three can be implemented with success, but for the legislature to be wrested from the ruling class and returned to the hands of the citizenry, all three must be in effect.

Limit Spending and Balance the Budget. A constitutional amendment is the only way to bring discipline to congressional spending. The 1974 Budget Act, which governs congressional budget decisions, has proven to be a machine to increase spending rather than a tool to control it. The Budget Act consists primarily of internal congressional rules, rather than statutes, so the few restrictions that do exist can be violated at will. Most notably, the annual Congressional Budget Resolution is not a law (and thus cannot be vetoed or signed by the President), making the budget process Congress' most outrageous non-legislative exercise. The result is that spending decisions are made on a case-by-case basis, only the advocates are heard, and too many cows end up on the commons.

Setting a spending level first, and then dividing up the pie would solve this problem. A constitutional amendment would force Congress to do just that. It is by no means impossible to design a system which either automatically limits spending or forces Congress to make difficult decisions. In fact, two different versions of Gramm-Rudman (which altered the 1974 Budget Act) were quite effective; but when the limits began to pinch, Congress just changed the rules. The most flawed of those changes, made in the 1990 budget deal, reinforced the "current services baseline" system of automatic spending increases: No votes are required. Indeed, any limitation in the growth of these bureaucratic wish lists is advertised as a spending "cut."

Most of the arguments against a balanced budget amendment just don't wash. We are told, for instance, that the ratification and phase-in period simply postpones action to balance the budget. This argument might have some merit if Congress were making progress in that direction, but aside from Gramm-Rudman nothing has worked even to limit deficit growth in the last twenty years. Others predict dire consequences when Congress is forced to choose between huge tax increases and draconian spending cuts. This is a congressional version of the "Washington Monument ploy": politically popular programs are the first offered for cuts.

Voters do not object to a choice between spending cuts and tax increases. It is Congressmen, who would have to make such decisions and then be held responsible, who find the alternatives daunting. That 49 states have workable balanced budget provisions renders laughable the arguments that this just cannot be done at the federal level. From time to time, those state requirements have forced unpleasant choices, but nowhere has it proved impossible to live with such budget discipline.

To make a balanced budget amendment honest, however, there must be no automatic tax increase provision—an idea the House Democratic Leadership proposed when the amendment came up for a vote in the spring of 1992. Automatic taxes would make a mockery of any spending limit. Given the choice between voting to cut spending (and taking the heat) and failing to act, thereby triggering an "automatic" tax increase which each legislator can disavow individually, Congress will go for the tax increase every time. We have already seen the results of similar automatic non-votes, under House Rule XLIX, to increase the debt ceiling.

Given the congressional proclivity for higher spending, a balanced budget amendment needs a tax provision that cuts in the opposite direction, making it harder to raise taxes. Wisconsin Republican Sen. Bob Kasten and Texas Republican Rep. Tom DeLay, for instance, have proposed a balanced budget amendment which includes a requirement that any tax increase be approved by a 60 percent majority. Raising the barrier for increasing taxes will make it more difficult to assemble a coalition of spending advocates to provide political cover for new tax schemes.

Like the 60 percent tax requirement, other procedures to enforce a balanced budget amendment should require votes and real legislation rather than automatic devices, which encourage legislative stalemate. If a failsafe mechanism is necessary, it should be in the President's hands, which would provide a strong inducement for Congress to legislate rather than abdicate.

Enhance the President's Role in Setting the Budget. Today the President submits a budget to Congress and has no more to say about overall taxing and spending levels. Making the Concurrent Budget Resolution, which sets those targets, subject to Presidential approval or veto would probably result in lower overall spending and taxation levels. The President's national constituency lends itself more to those broad concerns than to interest in individual programs. Further, setting spending targets by statute would make it far more difficult for Congress to circumvent the limits. Doing so would require a change in the law, signalling the public the budget was about to be busted, and giving the President an opportunity to veto the increases. Coupled with a statutory budget resolution, the President's authority to withhold ("impound") spending in excess of established limits should be restored. These reforms could follow or precede a balanced budget amendment.

Allow a Line-Item Veto. A Presidential line-item veto would help limit spending, though it is far less helpful in this regard than a balanced budget amendment. (Unfortunately Presidents are little more willing than Congress to take the heat for necessary but unpleasant spending cuts.) More importantly, an item veto would allow the President to limit unreasonable congressional encroachments on executive authority, and would enable him to excise pork and other crooked deals concocted by committee chairmen, or even staffers, against the will of the congressional majority. This would greatly limit the degree to which conference committees, for instance, could be abused to approve unpopular provisions in unaccountable secrecy.

While the Founding Fathers did not write an item veto into the Constitution, obviously they did not contemplate the huge and complex omnibus bills that have become so common today. Neither does an item veto equal unlimited executive power. Knowing that their bills were subject to challenge, piece-by-piece, lawmakers would no longer paste bewilderingly large bills together with pork. Instead they would perfect simpler, clearer statutes that could not be pried apart with such a veto. Again, state experience is instructive. Governors in 43 states have item vetoes, which are exercised without irreparable harm to the balance of power between the executive and the legislature.

Make Congress Obey the Laws. Congress exempts itself, actually or effectively, from most civil rights, worker safety, and environmental laws. So too with good government measures. The Freedom of Information Act, and key provisions of the Ethics in Government Act, apply only to the executive branch, not Congress. Even when lawmakers agree, under pressure, to cover themselves, they strip the laws of all meaning by arranging for cozy enforcement by their own staff.

The attitude of being above the law corrupts the legislative process at its heart. Incumbents claim that Congress must be exempt from the law so as not to fall under the control of the executive or judicial branches. This makes no more sense than arguing that Congress should not be allowed to pass legislation affecting judges or cabinet members, lest those officials become subservient to the legislature. Separation of powers means that Congress makes the laws, not that it is *exempt* from them. Indeed, that doctrine dictates that Congress keep its hands off the administration and adjudication of laws. More narrowly, Congressmen cite the constitutional protection against being questioned elsewhere for speech or debate in Congress, but speeches are rarely the issue.

In most cases there is no constitutional issue in applying the law to Congress. True, we don't want an FBI or IRS conspiracy to coerce legislators with threats of investigation, but it is difficult to see what constitutional damage would be wrought by, for instance, OSHA inspectors visiting congressional offices. Republican Rep. John

Boehner of Ohio invited just such an inspection of his office on a voluntary basis in the summer of 1992, uncovering numerous violations of worker safety standards. In fact, most of the OSHA "violations" were clearly insignificant, proving Rep. Boehner's point that making Congress subject to the laws it approves would provoke more attention to the problems a well-intentioned law may present. More importantly, making Congress live under the laws it passes would drive home a point that too many legislators have forgotten: they are not rulers but servants.

If Congress believes an investigation is politically motivated or otherwise improper, it has plenty of tools to fight back. Legislators and their employees are required to present any subpoenas delivered to them to the full House or Senate. If some constitutional principle is at stake, Congress can object and interpose its institutional prerogatives at that point rather than declaring before the fact that Congressmen are above the law. The minority of Hill workers who have legislative responsibilities may be a special case, for which there is a ready model: the treatment of political appointees in the executive branch. Those appointees are covered by all the laws applying to other employees, but they can nonetheless be fired, with no practical appeal, for policy reasons or violations of confidence.

Congress should adopt a blanket congressional coverage statute, and House and Senate rules should require all legislation to cover Congress unless there is a specific, recorded vote to the contrary. If Congress insists on maintaining its own enforcement offices (as some executive branch agencies are allowed to do), then it should use enforcement standards identical to those used in other government agencies, to provide an objective standard for measuring congressional compliance. Court appeals must be allowed, and most especially, Congressmen should not be permitted to escape jury trials. With a jury, Congress is not subject to another branch of government, but to citizens. Businesses fear unpredictable verdicts in lawsuits as much as the specific requirements of regulatory legislation. It would be productive for Congress, no less than the rest of us, to contemplate the same possibility when crafting vague laws.

Apply Freedom of Information. If there is a single law that most needs be applied to Congress it is the Freedom of Information Act. Congress gets away with many abuses simply because no one can find out about them: the cozy relationships that comprise the Barnumocracy, the petty acts of retribution that keep bureaucrats in thrall of Capitol Hill. If Congressmen and their staffs were required to keep adequate records and to make them available to the public, many congressional abuses would go away overnight, and questionable behavior would be subject to the informed judgment of voters. Again, the light of accountability is the key to reform.

End the Constituent Service Racket. Casework, helping constituents solve problems with the government, is Congress' number-one occupation. Stopping it will do wonders to restore a legislative focus to Congress. If constituents are continually being shafted, Congress should fix the systemic problems rather than patching up faulty operations one problem at a time. As it is, Congress turns legislative power over to bureaucrats, then stands ready to apply bandages when the regulations pinch. We're supposed to express gratitude by voting for them. This process removes any incentive for Congress to limit the size of government or to fix the problems that cause voters so many headaches. In fact, bad government gets Congressmen reelected. Large reductions in staff, especially in personal staffs, are probably the only way to achieve this goal.

For those inevitable cases where paperwork is lost, or constituents confused, an ombudsman system, either within agencies or as an arm of Congress, would be far preferable to the current arrangement. Short of stopping, Congress could come clean about casework. All manner of scandalous political favors are covered by the little-old-lady-with-the-lost-check ploy. Congressmen should be required to report all correspondence with, and phone calls to, executive agencies periodically in the *Congressional Record*. If it is all just honest casework, Congressmen should be proud. If they're not, we can only assume they have something to hide. If Congress won't take this step itself, then the President should order executive agencies to log and report congressional contacts as public matters.

Establish Fair and Open Procedures. One reason Congress has difficulty acting on important issues is that its committees, dominated by special interests, are allowed to bottle up popular legislation. When bills do reach the House floor, controversial amendments are often blocked. As we saw in Chapter One, through a variety of ruses, Members are able to stake out positions on both sides of an issue, voting one way while doing the opposite, or even not voting at all on controversial issues. In this process, too, accountability is lost. House and Senate rules should be revised to produce a more orderly, fair, and open process. This can start with setting the legislative agenda.

Frustration over important legislation getting bogged down has led some to recommend giving new scheduling powers to a few House and Senate leaders. This would only open the door to new abuses. A better system would give every lawmaker a voice, and stake, in setting an agenda. This could be accomplished with a brief debate on legislation when it is introduced, a system followed in early Congresses. Simple bills were approved, silly ones disposed of, and complex ones sent to a committee. (The Senate retains vestiges of this procedure: If a Senator objects to referral of a bill to committee it is placed on the calendar immediately.)

Reviving this procedure would allow Congress to decide on an agenda openly and enforce it. In referring a bill, Members could instruct committees to complete action within a given time or indicate in a general way how a bill should be amended. The clutter of congressional calendars would be reduced, and frivolous proposals cut down, as sponsors would be loath to endure their colleagues' taunts for introducing pointless legislation. The complexity of bills would probably be reduced since simpler measures would be more likely to be approved. If debating every bill seems like too much, Congress might allow the procedure to be invoked selectively by the leadership of either party or by a significant number of Members.

The House Rules Committee, which sets ground rules for debating bills on the House floor, too frequently bends procedures in favor of the Democrat majority, especially by blocking politically contentious amendments. While some variation in rules may be necessary, a few standard procedures should be developed to cover most bills. Changes in those standard rules should require a super-majority (60 percent or more) vote. Absent an agenda reform such as the one described above, significant minorities within the House should be given a greater voice in what legislation is considered. Currently, action can be forced on legislation if a majority of the House (normally 218 Members) signs a "discharge petition." Because the petition is kept secret, however, voters have a hard time keeping score: Representatives can claim to support legislation while refusing to do what is necessary to get it enacted. Discharge petitions should be made public, and the threshold for forcing action should be lowered. There is no reason why the House should not consider legislation supported by, say, a third of its Members.

Senate rules, which already give more protections to minorities, need fewer revisions. In fact, changes to make Senate procedure more centrally controlled, as in the House, should be avoided.

Finally, congressional rules should be revised to make votes more meaningful. The House practice of approving legislation or amendments without votes ("deeming") should be prohibited. Conference committees, which are supposed to work out differences between House and Senate versions of bills, should not be allowed to practice stealth legislation by deleting provisions both bodies have agreed to or adding new material neither had approved.

Cut Committees. Much mischief in pork and micromanagement is conducted by committees independent of the knowledge or will of the majority of Members. Several previous reforms have limited committee and subcommittee numbers, but like weeds, they require periodic clearing. The rearrangement of committee jurisdiction is relatively unimportant as long as the numbers are significantly reduced, by half or more. The resulting broader jurisdictions would promote a more integrated approach to lawmaking. Congressmen would sit on a handful of panels, rather than as many as 23, as is the case with one Senator today. Among other salutary effects, this would increase the attention Congressmen give to each committee position, and therefore reduce the role staff plays.

Members who are concerned about the concentration of power in the hands of fewer chairmen should impose term limits on those chairmen as suggested by Oklahoma Democratic Rep. Dave McCurdy. While McCurdy's proposal is in the form of a change in House rules, it is the Republican and Democratic caucuses in each body that designate chairmen and ranking members. There is no reason why those party organizations should not move on their own to limit the tenure of committee chairmen, or even of all committee members. Over the course of six years or so even the most ambitious chairman should be able to advance a legislative agenda. Allowing Members to remain chairmen, or senior committee members, for long periods simply allows the natural process of forging common links with bureaucrats and interest groups to overtake the detachment necessary to the legislative role.

Limit terms, sessions, staff, committees, chairmen, spending and pork; apply all laws to Congress, open up congressional procedure and junk the casework scam. This is an ambitious program, but one that will work, one that can be achieved through continuing public pressure. The point of these reforms is not to attack Congress but to rejuvenate it, and, by restoring accountability, to rejuvenate American government with it. The reforms point in one direction: bringing Congress back to its assigned task, legislation. Only by stopping many current activities can this succeed. Congressmen will argue that the activities we want them to cease are necessary to control the huge federal bureaucracy, and in this they are probably right. Surely, however, it is not a matter of asking Congress to give up control and leave bureaucrats roaming at will but to give Members incentives to limit the powers they delegate to that bureaucracy. Thus doing, they will at once reclaim their legislative responsibilities and political dignity.

Make Congress legislate. That is its job. A Congress that makes law through fair and open legislative procedure is a Congress that can be held accountable for its actions. A Congress accountable to the voters is a Congress that, by definition, will do the right thing. A Congress that legislates will be a Congress no longer in need of reform.

ENDNOTES

Chapter 1: Sleight of Hand

1. Morris P. Fiorina, *Congress: Keystone of the Washington Establishment* (New Haven: Yale University Press, 1989), p. 49.

2. Thomas Schelling, *Choice and Consequence* (Cambridge, Mass.: Harvard University Press, 1984), p. 226.

3. Walter J. Oleszek, "Legislative Procedures and Congressional Policymaking: A Bicameral Perspective" in *Congressional Politics* by Christopher Deering, ed. (Pacific Grove, Calif.: Brooks/Cole Pub. Co., 1989), pp. 176-196.

4. Steven S. Smith, *Call to Order, Floor Politics in the House and Senate* (Washington, D.C.: Brookings Institution, 1989) pp. 15-48 (particularly pp. 24-28); Stanley Bach and Steven S. Smith, *Managing Uncertainty in the House of Representatives: Adaptation and Innovation in Special Rules* (Washington, D.C.: Brookings Institution, 1988), pp. 12-15.

5. *Congressional Record*, July 17, 1970, p. H25796.

6. Bach and Smith, *op. cit.*, p. 18.

Chapter 2: The Bullies' Pulpit

1. Michael Fumento, "The Politics of Cancer Testing," *American Spectator*, August 1990, pp. 18-23.

2. Joseph Rosen, "Much Ado About Alar," *Issues in Science and Technology*, Fall 1990.

3. Justin D. Simon, "Make Congress Play by the Rules," Criminal Justice, Spring 1989.

4. Mary Collins, "News of the Congress BY the Congress," *Washington Journalism Review*, June 1990, pp. 30-34.

5. Timothy Cook, *Making Laws and Making News: Media Strategies in the U.S. House of Representatives* (Washington, D.C.: Brookings Institution, 1989, pp. 62-68 and 192-198.

6. Hedrick Smith, *The Power Game*, (New York: Random House, 1988) pp. 122-132.

7. David Truman, *The Governmental Process* (New York: Alfred Knopf, 1971).

8. Gabriel Escobar, *Washington Post*, "Experts Strip Car to Drive Home a Point," April 1, 1992, p. D1.

9. Arthur Maas, *Muddy Waters—The Army Corps of Engineers and the Nation's Rivers* (Cambridge, Mass.: Harvard University Press, 1951).

10. Christopher Bosso, *Pesticides and Politics* (Pittsburgh: University of Pittsburgh Press, 1987).

11. Norman Ornstein and Thomas Mann, *Vital Statistics on Congress* (Washington, D.C.: American Enterprise Institute, 1992), p. 114.

12. Hugh Heclo, "Issue Networks and the Executive Establishment," in Anthony King, ed., *The New American Political System* (Washington, D.C.: American Enterprise Institute, 1978), p. 88.

13. Mancur Olson, *The Logic of Collective Action: Public Goods and the Theory of Groups* (Cambridge, Mass.: Harvard University Press, 1965).

14. Thomas Gais, Mark Peterson, & Jack Walker, "Interest Groups, Iron Triangles, and Representative Institutions in American National Government," *British Journal of Political Science*, Volume 14, pp. 161-185.

15. Kay Lehman Schlozman and John T. Tierney, *Organized Interests and American Democracy* (New York: Harper & Row, 1986), pp. 302-310.

16. *Environmental Defense Fund Annual Report 1991-92*, p. 10.

17. Eric Felten, "Money from Water Suits can follow a Winding Course," *Insight* Magazine, February 18, 1991, pp. 18-20.

18. Senate Report No. 102-197, pp. 177-78.

Chapter 3: Legislating Backwards

1. Charlotte Allen, "Disabling Business," *Insight* Magazine, March 29, 1992, p. 26.

2. Jonathan Adler, "Clean Fuels, Dirty Air," in *Environmental Politics: Public Costs, Private Rewards*, eds. Greve and Smith, (New York: Praeger Publishers, 1992), pp. 24-30.

3. Adler, *op. cit.*, pp. 21-24, 31-37.

4. Letter to William K. Reilly, from Daschle, Dole, *et al.*, dated July 31, 1991.

5. Marc Landy, *et al.*, *The EPA: Asking the Wrong Questions* (New York: Oxford University Press, 1990).

6. Christopher H. Foreman, Jr., *Signals from the Hill: Congressional Oversight and the Challenge of Social Regulation* (New Haven: Yale University Press, 1988), pp. 55-62.

7. Peter Woll, *American Bureaucracy* (New York: W.W. Norton & Co., Inc., 1963), pp. 110-13.

8. *Panama Refining Company v. Ryan*, 293 U.S. 388 (1935) and *Schechter Poultry Corp. v. United States* 295 U.S. 495 (1935).

9. *Yakus v. United States*, quoted in Woll, *op. cit.*, pp. 116-18.

10. Woll, *op. cit.*, p. 119.

11. Theodore J. Lowi, *The End of Liberalism* (New York: W.W. Norton & Co, 1979), p. 106.

12. Lowi, *op. cit.*, p. 117.

13. Lowi, *op. cit.*, p. 118. Also, Steven Kelman, "Regulation by the Numbers—A Report on the Consumer Product Safety Commission," *The Public Interest*, Summer 1974, pp. 83-102.

14. Richard E. Cohen, "It Sounds Great, but What's It Mean?", *National Journal*, Sept. 16,1989, p. 2276.

15. *Federal Register*, Vol. 56, No. 144. July 26, 1991, pp. 35744-45.

16. John Irving and Timothy Stephenson, "ADA Update: EEOC Regulations Governing Employment Practices," The National Legal Center, White Paper, Volume 4, No. 1, January 1992, p. 3.

17. 462 U.S. 919 (1983).

18. Antonin Scalia, concurring opinion, *Blanchard v. Bergeron*, 109 S.Ct. 939 (1989).

19. *Chevron v. Natural Resources Defense Council*, 467 U.S. 837 (1984).

20. Intermodal Surface Transportation Efficiency Act of 1991, Conference Report, Nov. 27, 1991, House Report No. 102-404, p. 102.

21. Jeffrey H. Birnbaum, "White House Competitiveness Council Provokes Sharp Anger Among Democrats in Congress," *The Wall Street Journal*, July 8, 1991, p. A8.

22. Henry Waxman, "Quayle Group Meddles With Our Safeguards," *Los Angeles Times*, December 23, 1991.

23. *Bowsher v. Synar* (478 US 714, 92 L Ed 2d 583, 106 S Ct 3181).

Chapter 4: Staff Infection

1. John Lancaster, "Payback Time for Parks Poke at 'Perks,'" *Washington Post*, November 20, 1990, p. A21.

2. Norman Ornstein and Thomas Mann, *Vital Statistics on Congress* (Washington, D.C.: American Enterprise Institute, 1992), p. 151.

3. John Jackley, *Hill Rat* (Washington, D.C.: Regnery Gateway, 1992), p. 12.

4. Ornstein and Mann, *op. cit.*, p. 126.

5. Richard Cohen, "The Hill People," *National Journal*, May 16, 1987, pp. 1170-72.

6. Burt Solomon, "Staff at Work," *National Journal*, May 16, 1987, pp 1174-76.

7. *Ornstein and Mann, op. cit.*, p. 128.

8. Mark Bisnow, "Memo to Congress: Fire Half Your Staff," *Washington Post*, January 17, 1988.

9. Ted Gup, "Life in the Tax Lane: Staff Gets trips, Too," *Washington Post*, June 7, 1982, p. A1.

10. John Yang, "Honoraria, Bounty of Special Interest Groups, Trickle Down to Some Congressional Staffers," *Wall Street Journal*, May 26, 1989.

11. Jay Finegan, "Whodunit," *Inc.* Magazine, July 1989, pp. 81-85.

12. Public Law 101-507, November 5, 1990.

13. See U.S. Senate Document #102-20, Part 1, "Report of Temporary Special Independent Counsel," pp 11-18. David Brock, "The Real Anita Hill," *The American Spectator*, March 1992, pp. 18-30. George Archibald and Michael Hedges, "Staffers Paid Well to 'Dig up Dirt,'" *Washington Times*, October 15, 1991.

Chapter 5: The Grandiose Inquisitors

1. Personal interviews with Jack Blum and Jonathan Winer. August 1991. Also see, Eric Felten, "The Beltway's Two-Party Scandal," *Insight* Magazine, September 9, 1991, pp. 28-31.

2. Edward McFadden, "There's No Accounting for Congress," *The American Spectator*, July 1992, pp. 24-28.

3. Glenn R. Simpson, "Congress' Own Iraq Connection," *Roll Call*, July 6, 1992, p. 12.

4. Letter from Attorney General William P. Barr to Rep. Jack Brooks, August 10, 1992.

Chapter 6: Other People's Money

1. Quoted by Teresa Riordan, "Monumental Boobs," *Worth* Magazine, August-September 1992, p. 75.

2. Garrett Hardin, "The Tragedy of the Commons," *Science*, Vol. 162 (No. 3859), December 13, 1968, pp. 1243-48.

3.   House Report 102-404, "Intermodal Surface Transportation Efficiency Act of 1991," p. 114.

4.   Robert Crease "Yesterday's Pork Projects" *Science*, November 1, 1991.

5.   Senator Daniel Patrick Moynihan "Reflections at Fifteen" *New York State and the Federal Fisc: XV*, Fiscal year 1990.

6.   As Robert Nozick suggests, "Is there really someone who, searching for a group of wise and sensitive persons to regulate him for his own good, would choose that group of people who constitute the membership of both houses of Congress?" *Anarchy, State and Utopia* (New York: Basic Books, 1974), p. 14.

7.   Woodrow Wilson, *Congressional Government*, 1885 (Baltimore: Johns Hopkins University Press, 1981), p. 50-51.

8.   House Report 102-404, p. 196.

9.   *Ibid.*, pp. 156-158.

10.   *Garcia v. San Antonio Transit Authority,* 469 U.S. 528.

11.   "Federal Regulation of State and Local Governments," d raft report prepared for the Advisory Commission on Intergovernmental Relations, Washington, D.C., April 1992, pp. IV-4-IV-7.

12.   *Ibid,* pp. IV-13-IV-15.

Chapter 7: Not-so-Innocents Abroad

1.   David Brock, "Mr. Symms Goes to Jamba," *Policy Review,* Winter 1992, pp. 32-39.

2.   Brit Hume, "Mighty Mouth," *The New Republic*, September 1, 1986, p. 20.

3.   David Brock, "The Prince Metternichs of Congress," *The American Spectator*, February 1990, pp. 22-27.

4.   James Ring Adams, "The BNL Scandal," *The American Spectator*, August 1992, pp. 18-24.

5.   Glenn R. Simpson, "Congress' Own Iraq Connection," *Roll Call*, July 6, 1992, p. 12.

Chapter 8: The Reelection Machine

1. Quoted in *The Pittsburgh Press*, March 8, 1992, pg. A1.

2. Morris Fiorina, *Congress: Keystone of the Washington Establishment* (New Haven: Yale University Press, 1989).

3. Richard L. Berke, "Helping Constituents or Themselves," *The New York Times*, November 5, 1989, p. 24.

4. Personal interview. Also, Eric Felten, "DeConcini Banks On Voter Loyalty," *Insight* Magazine, December 18, 1989, pp. 20-21.

5. David R. Mayhew, "Congressional Elections: The Case of the Vanishing Marginals," *Polity* 6 (1974), pp. 295-317.

6. Fiorina, *op. cit.*, pp. 35-36.

7. Ira Chaleff, *et al. Setting Course: A Congressional Management Guide* (Washington: American University, 1988), p. 93.

8. Norman Ornstein and Thomas Mann, *Vital Statistics on Congress* (Washington,D.C.: American Enterprise Institute, 1992), p. 126.

9. *Ibid.*, pp. 126-129.

10. Chaleff, *et al., op. cit.*, p. 22.

11. *Ibid.*, p. 122.

12. *Ibid.*

13. "Constituent Disservice," *The Wall Street Journal*, April 18, 1991, p. A16.

14. Chaleff, *et al., op. cit.*, p. 122.

15. Richard H. Shapiro, *Frontline Management* (Washington: Congressional Management Foundation, 1989), p. 94.

16. *Ibid.*, p. 7.

17. *Ibid.*, p. 97.

18. "The Bob Hope Special You Can't Turn Off," *Harper's* Magazine, December 1991, pp. 28-32.

19. Shapiro, *op. cit.*, p. 218.

20. Fiorina, *op. cit.*, p. 80.

21. Personal Interview, March 1992.

22. Ornstein and Mann, *op. cit.*, table 3-1, pp. 74-75.

23. Ornstein and Mann, *op. cit.*, table 3-5, pp. 80-81.

24. Brooks Jackson, *Honest Graft*, revised edition (Washington, D.C.: Farragut Publishing Company, 1990), p. 79.

25. *Ibid.*, p. 80.

26. Tim Curran and Glenn R. Simpson, "Johnston & Johnston: Sen. Dad a Big Helper," *Roll Call* , April 27, 1992, p. 1.

Chapter 9: Reform

1. James K. Coyne and John H. Fund, *Cleaning House: America's Campaign for Term Limits* (Washington, D.C.: Regnery Gateway, 1992), p. 117.

2. Alan Ehrenhalt, *The United States of Ambition: Politicians, Power, and the Pursuit of Office* (New York: Times Books, 1991).

INDEX

H

Hardin, Garrett, 148
Harkin, Tom, 21, 22, 37, 38, 76
Harriman, Pamela, 123
Harter, Philip, 82, 89
Hatch, Orrin, 11, 19, 176
Hayes, Jimmy, 177
Health and Human Services, Department of (HHS), 152
Heclo, Hugh, 56
Heginbotham, Stanley, 179, 180
Helms, Jesse, 16-18, 136, 178
Hill and Knowlton, 43
Hill, Anita, 20, 107-113
Hoerchner, Susan, 109
House Bank, 125, 136, 183, 195, 201, 208, 209
House Post Office, 14, 125, 183
House Rule XLIX, 29, 30, 215
Housing and Urban Development, Department of (HUD), 99, 100, 103, 104-107, 113, 115-118
Hubbard, Allan B., 84-87
Hungary, 175
Hussein, Saddam, 43, 119, 128, 129, 134, 135, 137, 165-170, 172, 178
Hyde, Henry, 11, 12, 27-29, 129-132

I

Interior, Department of the, 15, 17, 85, 93
Intermodal Surface Transportation Efficiency Act, 3-5, 82, 151, 157
Iran, 119, 128, 135, 136, 173, 174
Iraq, 43, 119, 128-131, 133-137, 139, 165-168, 173-178
Iraq-gate, 119, 128, 133, 135, 139, 173
Iraqi-BNL bank fraud, 176
Ireland, Andy, 180

Iron triangle, 55-57, 147

J

Jackley, John, 95, 200
Jackson, Brooks, 203
Jeffords, James, M. 70, 71
Johnson, Lyndon B., 116, 171
Johnston, Bennett, 203-204
Johnston, J. Bennett, 165, 176, 177, 203, 204
Jones, David C., 167
Judiciary Committee, House, 11, 26, 128-129, 132, 133
Judiciary Committee, Senate, 11, 46, 107, 109-112, 128

K

Kaptur, Marcy, 175
Kasten, Bob, 215
Keating Five, 20, 124, 184, 191, 194, 195
Keating, Charles, 184
Keating, Frank, 104
Kelly, Kevin, 103-107
Kemp, Jack, 103-106
Kennedy, Edward M., 76, 85, 109-111, 168, 170
Kerry, John, 119-124, 144
Kessler, David, 47, 48
Kolter, Joe, 183
Kuwait, 43, 44, 48, 128, 129, 134, 165-169, 176, 177

L

LaFalce, John, 103
Lantos, Tom, 35, 43, 44, 61, 115-117
Laster, Gail, 108, 109
Lead industry, 39-42, 48, 51, 58

Leahy, Patrick, 111, 128
Legislative Reorganization Act, 25
Lehman, Jr., John, 179
Levin, Carl, 168
Levitas, Elliott, 84
Lieberman, Joseph, 36, 40, 42
Line-item veto, 31, 216
Lobbyists, 51, 54, 57-61, 63-66, 73-75,
    81, 85, 88, 101, 107, 110, 117,
    149, 203
Lott, Trent, 177
Lowi, Theodore, 74, 75

M

Maas, Arthur, 55
Madison, James, 19, 20, 31
Magnuson, Warren, 93
Malbin, Michael, 95
Mapplethorpe, Robert, 16
Martin, Lynn, 15
Mason, Kent, 102, 103
Mass mailings, Congressional
    (Franking), 10, 13-15, 193
Mayhew, David, 187
McCain, John, 184, 185
McCurdy, Dave, 222
McDade, Joseph, 151, 152, 178
McGrory, Mary, 121
McNeil, Robin, 145
McNeil/Lehrer Newshour, 145
Medicaid, 159, 185
Medicare Catastrophic Coverage Act, 150
Meese, Edwin, 84
Metzenbaum, Howard, 44-46, 108-110,
    112
Michel, Robert, 102, 189
Mikulski, Barbara, 103, 106
Miller, George, 85
Mine Safety and Health Administration,
    68

Minish, Joseph, 203
Mitchell, George, 7, 193
Monticciolo, Joseph, 115-118
Moran, Jim, 194
Moyers, Bill, 145
Murtha, John, 178, 180

N

Nader, Ralph, 51, 54, 59, 74, 85
National Aeronautics and Space Adminis-
    tration (NASA), 142, 153
National Conference of State
    Legislatures, 159
National Endowment for the Arts (NEA),
    10, 15-18, 142
National Endowment for the Humanities
    (NEH), 142
National Governors Association, 159
National Highway Traffic Safety Admin-
    istration, 68
National Institute of Occupational Safety
    and Health (NIOSH), 70, 71
National Institutes of Health (NIH), 41
National Park Service, 94, 151
National Public Radio (NPR), 112
National Science Foundation, 142
Natural Resources Defense Council
    (NRDC), 36-38
Needleman, Herbert, 40-42
New Deal, 68, 71-73, 186
New Left, 57, 73
Nicaragua, 135, 173
Nickles, Don, 17
Nixon, Richard, 116, 171
Noriega, Manuel, 119-122
North, Oliver, 135
Nunn, Sam, 165, 166

O

O'Neill, Thomas P. "Tip", 25, 26, 203
Oakar, Mary Rose, 183, 184
Obey, David, 15, 173, 176
Occupational Safety and Health Act, 20
Occupational Safety and Health Administration (OSHA), 68-71, 217, 218
Office of Management and Budget (OMB), 85, 96, 97, 158, 161
Oleszek, Walter, 24
Olson, Theodore, 84
Omnibus Crime Control Act, 3, 11, 18, 26-28

P

Paxon, Bill, 150
Payne, James, 146, 147
Pell, Claiborne, 120
People for the American Way (PAW), 109
Perot, H. Ross, 102
Persian Gulf, 43, 128, 130, 131, 165-167, 170-172, 174, 181
Pierce, Samuel, 106
Planned Parenthood, 147
Poland, 175
Political Action Committees (PACs), 202, 203
Powell, Colin, 166
Pressler, Larry, 194, 195
Proxmire, William, 100
Public Broadcasting System (PBS), 141-145
Public Citizen, 54, 85
Public Interest Research Groups (PIRG), 59

Q

Quayle, Dan, 85, 86

R

Rayburn, Sam, 24
Reagan, Ronald, 47, 115, 135, 158, 160, 162, 173, 179, 180, 196
Regulation negotiation (reg neg), 63-67, 82, 89
Rehabilitation Act, 20, 158
Reid, Harry, 39, 41, 42, 51
Reilly, William K., 67
Resolution Trust Corporation (RTC), 45, 46, 159, 160
Rodino, Peter, 84
Roosevelt, Franklin, 68, 72
Rose, Charlie, 128, 130-133, 135, 136
Rostenkowski, Dan, 101, 203
Roukema, Marge, 116
Rules Committee, House, 5, 24-28, 32, 220

S

S&L scandal, 44, 45, 160
Sandinistas, 173
Sasser, James, 141, 151
Scalia, Antonin, 81
Schelling, Thomas, 23
Schlesinger, James, 167
Schumer, Charles, 53
Seidman, Ricki, 109, 110
Serrano, Andres, 16
Shays, Christopher, 117, 118
Sierra Club, 59, 147
Sikorski, Gerry, 36, 85
Silbergeld, Ellen, 41, 42
Skeen, Joseph, 15

Slattery, Jim, 154, 155
Smith, Hedrick, 50
Social Security, 160, 184-187, 190, 191, 194
Solarz, Steven, 175
Souter, David, 137
Specter, Arlen, 44
Streep, Meryl, 36-38
Superfund Law, 71, 84
Supreme Court, 16, 45, 72, 79, 81, 82, 89, 97, 107-110, 137, 158, 171
Symington, Fife, 44-46

T

Tax Reform Act, 102, 103
Television Studios, House/Senate 49
Thomas, Clarence, 20, 45, 46, 107-113, 137
Thurmond, Strom, 11, 12
Tiananmen Square massacre, 172
Tonkin Gulf Resolution, 171
Totenberg, Nina, 112, 113, 131
Tower, John G., 100
Transportation, Department of, 83, 153
Treasury, Department of the, 160
Tribe, Laurence, 112
Truman, David, 51, 54

V

Veterans Affairs, Department of, 161

W

Walsh, Lawrence, 136
War Powers Act, 171
Washington Post, 53, 86, 94, 121
Watergate, 96, 119, 171, 195, 202

Watt, James, 116, 117
Waxman, Henry, 47, 48, 85, 86, 88
Weber, Vin, 63, 195
Weiss, Ted, 85
Whitten, Jamie, 55, 56, 155
Will, George, 143, 145
Wilson, Pete, 14
Wilson, Woodrow, 156
Woll, Peter, 73
Wright, Jim, 173, 203
Wyden, Ron, 52, 53

Y

Yates, Sidney, 16-18
Yeltsin, Boris, 172
Yeutter, Clayton, 129